RETHINKING OUR PRIORITIES

Books by DR. J. SIDLOW BAXTER

AWAKE MY HEART
A devotional Bible study for every day in the year.

DOES GOD STILL GUIDE?
An answer to this important question in our time.

EXPLORE THE BOOK
A basic, progressive, interpretative course of Bible study, six volumes in one, from Genesis to Revelation.

GOD SO LOVED
An exposition of John 3:16, the best-known text in the Bible.

GOING DEEPER
A series of devotional studies in knowing, loving, and serving our Lord Jesus Christ.

HIS DEEPER WORK IN US
A further enquiry into New Testament teaching on the subject of Christian Holiness.

HIS PART AND OURS
Enriching exposition and devotional studies in the reciprocal union of Christ and His people.

MARK THESE MEN
Arresting studies of little understood aspects of Bible characters with special relevance for our times.

RETHINKING OUR PRIORITIES
A heart-to-heart talk with the church: its pastor and people.

STRATEGIC GRASP OF THE BIBLE
The marvelous design and structure of the Scriptures, with a discussion of the dispensational characteristics of biblical revelation.

STUDIES IN PROBLEM TEXTS
The problem texts of the Bible in patient and painstaking investigation.

CHRISTIAN HOLINESS: RESTUDIED AND RESTATED
Three works on the scriptural teaching on personal holiness, combined in one volume: *A New Call to Holiness, His Deeper Work in Us, Our High Calling*. These three are also available individually.

RETHINKING OUR PRIORITIES
The Church: Its Pastor and People

Heart-to-heart talks with ministers, music directors, leaders, and workers in our evangelical churches.

by
J. SIDLOW BAXTER

ZONDERVAN PUBLISHING HOUSE OF THE ZONDERVAN CORPORATION
GRAND RAPIDS, MICHIGAN 49506

RETHINKING OUR PRIORITIES
© 1974 by The Zondervan Corporation

Library of Congress Catalog Card Number 73-22698

Fourth printing 1978
ISBN 0-310-20691-X

All rights reserved. No part of this publication may be reproduced, stored in a retrieval system, or transmitted in any form or by any means, electronic, mechanical, photocopy, recording or otherwise, without the prior permission of the copyright owner.

Printed in the United States of America

Contents

A "Letter of Introduction"

A Reminiscence

PART ONE: OUR BIBLE

    A Needed Return 13

    The Basic Divide 25

    Some Big Issues 37

    The King's Seal 49

    Critical Tactics 61

    Where Are We Now? 73

PART TWO: PENTECOST

    The Present Hour 101

    The Local Church 111

    The Pulpit Today 123

    Personal Witness 133

    Inner Experience 143

PART THREE: PUBLIC WORSHIP

    Reverence, Please! 155

    Concerning Hymns 167

    Sunday Evenings 181

    Newfangled Perils 201

    Another Peril Today 223

    Preach the Word! 237

there are dependent on me. They all have to be fed, armed, and strategically directed from this tent. If I were to run away from this and join them, the campaign would collapse.' Similarly, we pastors would merely lose ourselves in the crowd if we were forever running off to industrial plants for individual evangelism there. *Our* special business (oh, that we were all true to it!) is to feed, teach, equip, and inspire our church members so that *they* go everywhere as effective witnesses for Christ." But my friend always came back to this, that we needed "reformed" *pastors*.

After our meal we lingered a few minutes near Princes Street, where he resumed his demand for reformed *pastors*. I leaned against one of the tall street lamps, and noticed in the wire litter basket attached to it a leatherbound book. Slowly pulling it out, I read the gilt-lettered title: THE REFORMED PASTOR. Scarcely believing my eyes, I opened it to the inside title page bearing the author's name — the wonderful old Puritan, RICHARD BAXTER! There was I, Sidlow *Baxter*, being lectured that I needed to be a "reformed pastor," and in that wire basket was *The Reformed Pastor* by my famous namesake! When I showed the book to my friend, he almost stared his eyes out. Then, quickly recovering, he exclaimed, "There, now, didn't I tell you so? This is a divine sign to prove it!"

How Baxter's *The Reformed Pastor* came to be there remains a mystery, but it has been a treasured companion ever since. I have read and reread it, and I am surer than ever now that a first big need of organized Protestant Christianity today is *reformed pastors*. I want to tell you why. But who am *I* to be telling many of *you* who are far more gifted and qualified? My reasons are three. (1) These addresses are printed at the prompting of ministers who heard them, (2) they flow from an anguish of concern over the present plight of Protestant Christendom, (3) they emerge after twenty-five years in the settled ministry. Do I not know that to a certain type of minister such pages as these can be wonderfully irritating? Well, what I have said stands, and I mean every word of it. My prayer is that others may see things the same way, and do something about it.

J. S. B.

A Reminiscence

Back in the nineteen-forties, during my ministry in Edinburgh, Scotland, a curious little incident occurred which I venture to relate as an introduction to my theme. An attractive looking couple and their young son started attending services in our sanctuary, always listening with keen interest. Later I came to know them well and learned that they were converts to the evangelical faith through British-Israel teaching. I rejoiced in their conversion but did not hesitate to advise them against overcredulity toward British-Israelism.

Eventually disillusionment with British-Israelism came, and with it, alas, a shaking of their whole faith. Then I lost sight of them. An important job had opened up in the photographic advertising department of a large engineering firm in London, England. About a year later the husband contacted me. He was back in Edinburgh for a time. We met for a meal and a chat in a Princes Street restaurant. Through his experience with crowds of men in that London engineering plant, he was obsessed with the idea that the Christian *ministry* needed "reforming." "You *pastors* need reforming," he kept insisting. "If you were with that crowd of men where *I* work you would know how badly out of touch with life you pastors are today. You are smugly aloof from present-day industrialized human struggle. You *pastors* are the main cause of the religious breakdown. Leave your sheltered sanctuaries. Get into the factories."

I pointed out certain problems. In many cases managements were against so-called "religious" invasions of the workshops. Also, getting in did not guarantee a hearing. And if evangelicals were given the privilege, why not Roman priests or Jehovah's Witnesses? However, my friend was convinced that if we *pastors* got "reformed" all difficulties could be surmounted.

At that time General Montgomery was doing exploits in North Africa. The Germans were on the run. I said, "Suppose you were to walk into the general's tent and protest, 'Sir, what are you doing here, wearing that fine uniform and sitting at that desk while all those other fellows are out there fighting amid the heat and dust of the desert?' What would Montgomery reply? 'Intruder, you don't know what you are talking about. All those grand fellows out

A "Letter of Introduction"

Dear Pastor, Music leader, Officeholder, Church member: Never did I let a book slip through the press to the public with more diffidence. It is not easy to write things which may severely displease. There is in each of us an inborn self-protectiveness which prefers the "safety of our own skin"; and some of you may think that I should be "skinned alive" for things written in part three of this book, i.e., my critique of public worship in the evangelical churches of America. Those of you who are my brethren in the ministry may find provocative jolts, also, in part one; but I am brave enough to hope you *will!*

Maybe those of you who are *not* ministers or song leaders or public servants of the churches may think there is not much for you in parts one and two, but in reality there *is*, for I want you to eavesdrop on what is said to our ministers. Who knows? Perhaps as a result you may want to give a copy of the book to *your* minister!

I am comforted to think that all of you who know me or my books will know that I am not a disgruntled old grumbler "agin everybody." I love my brethren in the ministry and my fellow evangelicals too well for that. But I am concerned deeply to see some wrongs put right for the sake of the cause which is supremely dear to all of us. Perhaps I should add that these pages are spoken lectures now in print, not a set treatise. I hope that an incidental repetition here and there may be kindly excused on that account. Also, the form of presentation is not meant for scholars (I do not have enough erudition for that), but for Christian ministers in general, and, indeed, for all who have Christian concerns at heart.

In some things wherein you may differ from me it could be that I myself (strange thought!) am wrong; but naturally I hope you will agree that in the main what I say is both true and needful. Underneath all else is my fervent desire that these chapters may effectively express *His* mind and purpose whose we are and whom we seek to serve. May God Himself guide your thinking, if and as you read. Heaven's crown of "lovingkindness" be ever yours.

J. Sidlow Baxter

Part One

OUR BIBLE

These challenges in Part One are addressed to ministers whose thinking has not become so blurred by the theological dialecticism of Barthianism and Brunnerism and the Neoliberalism that they can no longer assess and accept evidence in the *really* dialectical sense of true logic. To deny the very possibility of a direct revelation of God to man in history and experience is an *a priori* irrationality which renders truly dialectical argument about the Bible farcical. To deny temporal creation and blur the basic distinction between Creator and creation is to give us a phenomenal universe without a beginning, and a God who is not really free, which is to deny the uniform teaching of the Bible and of Christ Himself. No literature in all history has been so antipathetically investigated and searched for contradictions as have the Jewish and Christian Scriptures. There is scarcely a page, now, which has not been racked by a desupernaturalizing critical scholarship. Yet here is the biggest of all big significances: *not any one part of the Bible has been actually disproved.* It is time we listened realistically to it again, and especially to Him who said, *"I AM THE TRUTH."*

J.S.B.

Nothing can be rightly known if God be not known. . . . Your study of physics and other sciences is not worth a rush if it be not God that you seek after in them. To see and admire, to reverence and adore, to love and delight in God as exhibited in His works, this is the true and only philosophy; the contrary is mere foolery, and is so called again and again by God Himself. . . . If you perceive not, in your study of the creatures, that God is all, and in all, and that "of Him and through Him and to Him are all things," you may think, that you "know something," but you know nothing as you ought to know.

Richard Baxter
Puritan: 1615-1691

OUR BIBLE: A NEEDED RETURN

Everywhere nowadays one hears Christian people saying, "The big need is for religious revival." One might almost say that the remark has become fashionable. Yet everything depends on the content which is put into that word "revival." Do we want a revival of *religion*? There is much religion in Christendom which is Christian in name but not in nature. Do we want a revival of that? Look around our major Protestant denominations. See the kind of Christianity which characterizes them in general. Do we want a revival of that? Or look through the evangelical churches. In how many, what skin-and-bone fare from the pulpit! What sentimental lip worship in the pew! What nursery-type spirituality in the members! And in many of those churches which pride themselves on being most "fundamental," what brittle hardness! What cactus spikiness of disposition! What bristly suspicion! What fierce no-compromise in belief going with brazen compromise in behavior! Do we want a revival of that?

The blunt truth is that today a considerable percentage of "Christianity" is not really Christian — because it is not Christlike. It still gathers round the age-old sacrament, but in quality of life it is far from the New Testament. It retains the outward forms but has lost the original force. It has redundance of sermonizers who can always say something, but few prophets who really have *something to say*. The half-truth of the pulpit and the half-faith of the pew mix in a half-hearted profession without any spiritual glow. C. H. Spurgeon once said of a popular preacher in southern England, "He preaches something which is somehow like the Gospel." Much that goes by the name Christian today is "something somehow like." Are we wanting a swollen flood of that? Nay, it needs sweeping away by a new tidal insurge of the life-giving reality. The revival we need is a deep-going, wide-spreading revival of true, full, New Testament Christianity. The whole life, thought, fellowship and witness of our Protestant churches needs a divine renewing. Yes, that is the need; and as an urgent first step to this we are needing *a reformation among ministers*.

The blackest tragedy which ever befell Protestant Christianity came when our leaders and seminaries two or three generations ago were gulled by those siren voices from Germany, the schools of the "New Biblical Learning." With dazzling novelty and brilliant show of ability the "higher critics" paraded their "assured results" as the ultimate in biblical scholarship. With new approach and new scientific method they were now able so to rationalize the supernatural in Scripture that at last our Bible would be acceptable to educated human reason. They abundantly succeeded. Over large areas today the Bible has been made so acceptable to human reason that there is no further reason to accept it, for it is no longer the supernatural Word of God. The "higher criticism" of those radical schools, issuing successively in the "New Theology," "modernism," "liberalism," "neo-orthodoxy," "Bultmannism," "neoliberalism" has succeeded beyond dream. In the space of a century it has turned Protestant Christianity into a graveyard — a graveyard of former glad certainties and soul-saving verities, of expired beliefs and perished hopes, of lost faith and vanished assurance, of buried ideals and murdered morals.

No, that is no gloomy overstatement. There are millions of people who suppose that the present moral collapse is mainly due to two world wars; but those two world wars, rather than being the cause of the breakdown, were an ugly expression of it, giving it further blatancy. Some of our most penetrating thinkers today are persuaded that the age of Christianity is now petering out, that Christian names and forms are merely lingering on into a different era, somewhat as pagan residua lingered on into the new Christian era two thousand years ago. Who can deny that today Christian sanctions are less and less determining human behavior and social patterns, while non-Christian concepts are more and more shaping our culture? Or who can inspect the mounting crime, divorce, gambling, drink, and drug statistics, not to mention others, without being frightened for tomorrow unless there is some big change? And who can witness the ominous union of violent wickedness with scientific invention today without sensing that an unprecedented danger point has been reached?

Look at the salient features of our collectivized life today. Was there ever a period of more deadening *materialism?* Whatever we may be dialectically, in practice are we not the most materialistic generation ever? American outlook is more than ever colored by dollar worship. "How big are you?" more than ever means "How much have you?" That is a deadly threat to spiritual survival. In Britain the Welfare State mothers you from cradle to grave, covering your birth expenses, education, jobless intervals, sick periods, accidents, old-age amenities, and even your funeral costs. Why bother looking to God? We used to be told it was no use preaching the gospel to men with empty stomachs. It is now found that men with guaranteed full stomachs do not even bother to listen. British trade-unionism owed its beginnings to definitely Christian impulses, but it has developed a hard-as-nails materialism which devotes itself exclusively and excessively to physical wants. What is it doing to British character? Britishers who go back to their homeland after twenty years or more find strange alteration. Not all the great old inherited British qualities are worn out, but the old British laughter, verve, toughness, godliness seem missing. There is a lackadaisical "Why bother?" attitude in general, with a spiritual darkness deep as that in the unevangelized jungles of Africa. Mammon worship and state-godism are equally deadly in their threat to Christianity.

This materialism expresses itself today in brazen *secularism*. Here, in America, there is a dam-burst of Sunday desecration. Television, radio, newspapers all boldly announce Sunday sports, games, races, political meetings, and what not? More and more stores are open, and are competing to publicize their Sunday trading. Among the churchgoing percentage thousands have now cut down the Lord's day to a half: it ends just as definitely at noon as the American summer officially ends on Labor Day. Roman Catholic and Jewish influences have contributed to this spoliation of our Christian sabbath, and possibly in a lesser way the Seventh Day Adventist confusion of the issue; but the big cause of the rebellion is obviously a widespread *secular mentality*.

I challenged the manager of a large food store on the matter of Sunday opening. He seemed a bit surprised, and said, "I could give you the names of seventeen local ministers whose wives do their week's shopping here on Sunday afternoons." Does that explain the guilty dumbness of our pulpits concerning Sunday desecration? Of course, Sunday abuse is only one aspect. The wave of secularism rolls wide in the large elimination of Scripture reading from American schools, the objections to school prayers, and to the naming of God in civic functions, and in many other ways.

Despite outward religious trappings America was never so secular as today, nor was Britain ever more so, even in that all-time, "low" just before the Methodist Revival. Europeans and Orientals who formerly viewed the American way of life with admiration now do not want it. Faith in money instead of faith in God has engendered a hard-headed materialism, an educational secularism, and a Hollywood profanity which have won America the name "Modern Babel." Orientals and Europeans who visit America often react with shock at the secular grossness and loudness of what they had considered a "Christian nation." Such is America now — the hope and the *scandal* of the free nations.

Does this seem a gloomy rigmarole? Very well, I will cut it short; but remember that I have not mentioned our lax compromise with evils which our fathers denounced: the overall national habit of living continually in debt — of buying cars, televisions, washing machines, gadgets, all on borrowed money; the widespread domestic quarreling and breakup of homes, largely caused through the deadly debt habit and the prevailing moral compromises; the unblushing pandering of public amusements to the animal passions; and the perversion of freedom into insurrection against all disciplines. Let Dr. Mary Alice Tenney's trenchant little book *Living in Two Worlds* clinch it all for us:

> We are victims of a vicious definition of freedom. For some time freedom has meant only self-expression. The rights of the self to the exclusion of God's sovereign rights over us have been extolled in education, philosophy, religion and literature. Freedom has come finally to mean abandonment of all discipline. . . . Rather than wear strait jackets we choose to wear no clothes at all. We reject every authority but the self. Any law made by another, even by God, must make an appeal to the self, if it is to be accepted.

There are those who will point us to the notable resurgence of churchgoing in the U.S.A. during the past fifty years. Only too gladly do we acknowledge it and thank God for it. We would not omit that from the total picture, nor splash pessimism where there should be glad gratitude. Yet the sad accompaniment of those fifty years is that the pulpits of our well-known Protestant denominations were largely unprepared, through limping faith in the divine inspiration of the Bible, to guide the wonderful inflocking into what could have become the mightiest spiritual visitation in American history. It is not pessimism but simple realism when Dr. Tenney adds, "For half a century the secularized church has sought for numbers, not Christians. And the present resurgence back toward the church will leave it just as powerless if converts are not made disciples. Some go so far as to declare that the only hope for the future of Christianity lies in a return to discipline."

Brethren, I am not one of those who find morbid pleasure in always dwelling on gloomy aspects. My nature tends the opposite way. I much prefer seeing rainbows to counting thunderclouds. But, unless I strangely misread the pointers, the present situation is *critical*. That which makes the moral cave-in more disturbing is the synchronizing climax of scientific discovery and invention: such deadly triggers near such trembly fingers amid such nervous tensions! Things move on a scale of immensity and at a pitch of intensity and with a baffling complexity such as have never been known before. Perhaps the most *sickening* feature about the moral landslide is that it came with such suddenness, mixed in with global wars, and is already pretty well coextensive with Christendom.

What has caused it? Brethren, my own reply is unhesitating. Beneath all the mix-up of more obvious secondary aggravations, the basic explanation is *departure from the Bible* — from the authority of its claims, and from the practice of its teachings. The Bible is the basis of everything Protestant. It was, and has remained until recently, the bedrock foundation of our Protestant nations. Our ethics and morals, our individual, domestic, social, educational, and commercial behavior-patterns have derived both sanction and incentive from it. So long as the Bible was deemed to be verily the Word of God, there was final authority. Its precious gospel and dynamic doctrines were the acknowledged sure way of individual and social regeneration, and of national well-being. The effect of this was seen, despite many setbacks, in the wonderful progress, expansion, prosperity, leadership, and higher moral levels of the Protestant nations.

That reverence for the Bible, alas, has been largely dissipated. Even the ghastly havoc inflicted by the Nazi fanatic Hitler pales beside that subtler, deeper, deadlier soul-havoc inflicted throughout Protestant Christendom by those Continental higher critical schools which, in the name of the "New Biblical Learning," have desupernaturalized the Bible, thereby destroying its authority for millions. It has been the devil's master stroke to do this from *inside* the Church by so-called Christian scholars. Hitler's technique of weakening countries from within by his "fifth columnists" was an outward mimic of this satanic strategy. Down from university chairs, through seminary faculties, theology professors, divinity students, ministers, pulpits, pews, out to the highways and byways of human life and thought, in one country after another, the faith-betraying "New Theology" and liberalist teachings have spread, until the whole of Christendom is thoroughly infiltrated.

The inevitable has happened. This derogation of the Bible has undermined the ethical culture of our Protestant world, thus precipitating this most fateful moral landslide since pre-Reformation times. The authoritative standard having been discredited, everything now becomes more or less relative. What is "sin"? — a mere phantom of religious credulity. What is "right"? What is "wrong"? All the answers outside the Bible are subjective; there is no objective moral "law."

We have the popular theory of *evolution*. We have struggled up from the beasts. We differ only in degree. We cannot help the lingering ape in us. Man is to be praised, not blamed. The idea of blame is a misunderstanding. Quite so; and what a sublime help to human morals *that* is! Instead of testing "organic evolution" by a closer ascertainment of what Genesis teaches, we have allowed a self-sure brand of speculative zoologists to set the public sneering at the God-given account through Moses and endorsed by our divine Lord, while to this day Protestant leaders and ministers are telling people that those early chapters of Genesis are mythical. Yet the more honestly the available data are investigated the *less* do they support organic evolution. Many of the startling "discoveries" earlier announced by paleontologists or comparative anatomists are now exposed as extravaganzas; and the supposedly human fossils of vast age are probably not those of Adamic human beings at all, but those of a pre-Adamite order, similar to us in physical structure though not identical with man. Organic evolution has never been more than a plausible theory. Today it is a largely discredited theory. Yet it is still palmed off in our institutions of learning as the certified finding of "science." Its fearful effect on morals is everywhere in evidence.

So, also, we have our *new psychology*. All the Nazi and Communist leaders have been evolutionists and new-psychology products; broods of liars and lusters. In our democratic countries the new psychology murders chastity and begets sexual promiscuity. Not long ago a well-educated young woman asked for counsel after one of our meetings. Brilliant in the field of psychology, she had been elected to a team of specialists sent by the American government for certain work overseas. She later became truly converted to Christ. What a mental revolution — from godless psychology to an inspired Bible with its moral absolutes! Can I ever forget her agonies of memories? Under the usual teaching about self-expression, she had given way to sexual relationships with all but one of her psychology professors as well as with students. Now she could never go to a husband in the undefiled purity which she had purposed in precollege days.

"Self-expression"! What modern psychology teaching usually means by that deceptive phrase is *animal* expression, the expression of only the fleshier urges in human nature, as though they were the *only* drives native to our humanhood. Is there nothing in the human "self" which *protests* against our yielding to the animal? Are not intellect, conscience, and an intuitive moral "sense" part of our total nature? Is not the urge to *control* bodily appetites an inherent reality? Many of us ministers can tell about the pitiful backwash from this twentieth-century "self-expression" code — young women, scarcely out of innocent childhood, virginity gone, vulgarized, played about with, pregnant, or mothers of illegitimate children! — or young men who have betrayed all that was noble in their upbringing, and have mixed bodies for lust, and know themselves now to be unworthy of a pure woman's love. There are older victims, too, who come to us disillusioned and with futile remorse. They have found, as all other such do, that eventually sexual indulgence on the promiscuous animal basis, and without marital love, becomes stale and unsatisfying, even ugly and repulsive. There is heartbreak over a purity forever lost and a sacredness irremediably profaned. There is a longing for the response of true *love,* instead of sexy paramours whose urge is no more than gratification; but it is too late. The sweetness of that which is most of all sacred between loving, wedlocked human hearts is forever lost. Oh, the desolate hearts and blasted paradises of your proud, new, non-biblical psychology!

But I forbear; the various aspects of the present moral deterioration are legion. What I have said is no more than a lead-up to an urgent challenge. Brethren, the call to all of us Protestant ministers is **threefold:**

(1) **To renew our faith in the Bible as the written Word of God, and as the means whereby the Holy Spirit regenerates men.** This determines all else; which is my reason for devoting this first group of addresses to the *Bible.*

(2) **To renew our experience of the Holy Spirit as the Sanctifier and Enduer of those who minister the Word.** That is why my second group of five addresses is concentrated on the meaning of Pentecost.

(3) **To renew waiting on God, with searching of heart, by pastor and people, until drought and dearth give place to "latter**

rains" and "fulness of blessing." That is why my third group of addresses concerns spiritual revival.

It is our attitude toward the *Bible* of which I am thinking just here. Brethren, I cannot tell you my ache of heart when I meet on my travels Protestant ministers who (to quote some of them) "don't believe in this nonsense about being 'converted' or 'saved' or 'born again.'" Their glib sarcasm plainly advertises that they themselves are spiritually dead, strangers to God, and blind leaders of the blind. The harm they do, who shall calculate? Appeals like ours can scarcely reach such as they. There are others, however, not a few, who away back somewhere had a real experience of conversion and a true call of God to the ministry, but who, alas, during seminary days or through later influences have lost their first faith and have slid into merely humanistic ideas of the Bible. Most of them are not happy in their ministry. They never thought it would become what it now is. They know that they are not preaching the message by which they themselves were brought to Christ. Their minds are not comfortable, though they try to disguise this to themselves. How I wish that these talks might have meaning for some of *them!* Of course, those of them who have developed the fashionable liberalist scorn for evangelicals can only be irritated. Well, I would have them know that even those remarks which most ruffle them are made with brotherly respect; and I shall thank God even though I cause annoyance, if it can provoke reconsideration.

Brethren, it must be a fearful thing for one who has posed as a Christian minister to find at last, when he stands before God the Son, that he has *not* preached the salvation which was procured for men at the cost of Calvary! It must be an unspeakable torture to discover that through his conceit of scholarship so many who listened have passed into eternity unsaved! If the cleavage between the evangelical faith and the several schools of liberalism were only a matter of dissonant theories, the whole matter would be comparatively trivial; but, if the New Testament is true, the eternal destiny of souls is involved! I believe that the liberalist view of the Bible is not only intellectually wrong but spiritually *ruinous* — ruinous to that faith in Christ which eternally saves. How then can we help speaking with stirred feeling? The coldness of logic is out of place here! I can never forget a great meeting in London, England, during the nineteen-twenties, when one of the speakers, a scholarly-looking visitor from China, sobbed from the platform, "Oh, friends, my mind is distraught. I was the first college professor to introduce the rationalistic higher critical novelties to the student bodies in China! I know now how mistakenly bewitched I was, and have recanted; but already I see the first damages, yet seem powerless either to halt the damage or to abate the strange infatuation with these faith-shattering new critical attitudes."

Fellow ministers, church leaders, and members, deep in my heart I am sure that the first step toward any considerable revival of Christian godliness among our countrymen is to restore the Bible to its rightful place in the nation; and I am equally sure that the initiating move in that direction must be made by us Christian ministers. I plead extra attention to our Lord's witness to the Old Testament, which comes up in these addresses. How can any of us unfeignedly call Jesus "Lord" yet presume superiorily to contradict His clear, deliberate, repeated, binding endorsement of the whole Old Testament as the uniquely and plenarily inspired Word of God? We must surely meet Him one day, and give answer. Shall we *then* dare tell Him He was wrong? Can He who said, "I am the truth," and "Before Abraham was, I am," and "Moses wrote of Me," be wrong when in unmistakable syllables He accepts the Mosaic authorship of the Pentateuch and the genuineness of the prophets (including Daniel) in their traditional settings and datings? Is it not an *awful* presumption for a Christian minister to "know better" than the incarnate Son of God?

It occurs to me to mention, also, that in chatting with ministers who hold the documentary theory of the Pentateuch, the mythical content of early Genesis, the late-dating of Old Testament documents, and the presence of "historiographical" errors in Scripture, I am frequently surprised at the one-sidedness of their reading. None whom I have met seem familiar with great conservative treatises on those subjects (as, for instance, James Orr's *The Problem of the Old Testament*, and Bishop A. H. Finn's masterly work, *The Unity of the Pentateuch*, not to mention others); and some of them seem surprisingly out of touch with the testimony of our archeologists and decipherers. Only recently an out-of-date young "modern" told me that Second Chronicles 33:11 obviously blundered in saying that "the king of *Assyria* ... took Manasseh ... with fetters ... to *Babylon*." The capital of Assyria was not Babylon, but Ninevah. No king of *Assyria* would carry Manasseh to *Babylon* said the young modern. Yet some decades ago it was unearthed that one of Assyria's kings made his residence in Babylon because of restiveness there; and *that* king was the one who carried Manasseh prisoner!

I must apologize for bringing in that young minister's slovenly slur, but it represents plenty of similarly cheap irreverence toward the Old Testament. Such ministers may well tremble at our Lord's warning: "Many will say to me in that day, Lord, Lord, did we not prophesy in thy name? Then will I profess unto them, I never knew you; depart from me."

Yes, I know that this kind of speaking plays on sensitive chords; but why not? I would fain use every appeal in urging a return of our pulpits to the Bible as the inerrant Word of God. I prophesy that without such a return the present moral downgrade will go from bad to worse. Without such a return, the World Council of Churches will prove a forlorn hope, top-heavy, base-faulty, and elaborately futile. There can be no safe building without a sure foundation, and no real union without a fixed center. A supernaturally inspired and divinely authoritative Bible is the only safe foundation and sure center; for unless we can be sure about the Bible we cannot be sure about the *Christ* of the Bible. As Richard Baxter would say, "Wanted: Reformed Pastors!" And the first-required reformation is to get right again on *the Book*. Until we get right there we never get properly right *anywhere*. God bring us back there with contrition that we have been so unfaithful; with prayer that yet again new light may break from the immortal pages to match the present hour. God bring us back there with tears and entreaties that the Holy Spirit who inbreathes the precious pages may endue us as prophets of the Word, powerfully recalling our misdirected leaders and people from the broken cisterns of mere man-wisdom to the "Fountain of living waters" and to the "good old paths" wherein is peace!

OUR BIBLE: THE BASIC DIVIDE

Take heed to yourselves, because you [ministers] are exposed to greater temptations than other men. If you will be the leaders against the prince of darkness, he will spare you no further than God restraineth him. As he hateth Christ more than any of us because he is the General of the field . . . so doth he hate the leaders under Him more than the common soldiers: he knows what a rout he may make among them if the leaders fall before their eyes. He hath long tried that way of fighting, neither against great nor small comparatively, but of smiting the shepherds that he may scatter the flock; and so great hath been his success this way that he will follow it as far as he is able. Take heed, therefore, brethren.

Richard Baxter

OUR BIBLE: THE BASIC DIVIDE

Brethren, after twenty-five years in the settled pastorate, followed by eighteen years of itinerant ministry, I am more persuaded than ever that the life-and-death issue for Reformation Christianity is *the inspiration and authority of the Bible*. Although time and reflection have strengthened this conviction, it is no new emphasis. Vividly do I recall contending for it more than thirty years ago in ministerial circles when it was superciliously resented by brethren who preened themselves on being theologically "modern" — some of whom now speak differently after seeing the withering effect of liberalism in our British churches. My heart still gives an extra beat when I recall some of those encounters. In fact, it could be useful to mention one or two as bearing on what I shall say later.

At one point there was such concern at the number of ministers who were defecting from our Baptist ranks to link up with the Church of Scotland that a "Commission of Enquiry" was appointed by the Scottish Baptist Union to investigate and report. The "Report," a twenty-four page pamphlet, was masterly in statement but pathetic in misdiagnosis and dud remedies. According to it, there were four sets of reasons for the defections: (1) "Spiritual and Theological," i.e., the new emphasis of the times on the ecumenical at the expense of the denominational; (2) "Ecclesiastical," i.e., reaction against our Baptist polity of local church independency; (3) "Personal," i.e., clash of strong personalities, or of pulpit and pew; (4) "Financial," i.e., strain due to inadequate sustenance in a union too small to offer much prospect of promotion. Not a thing did the "Report" say about the *root* cause of which the above were merely secondary expressions. Underneath all four, the really determining cause was a *broken or shaken faith in the true inspiration of the Bible*. The commissioners advertised the telltale outer symptoms but gave no diagnosis of the causative disease.

In an earlier day our Baptist forefathers would *never* have yielded to those four sorts of seductions. Why? Because to them the Bible was uniquely and finally the Word of God, and they believed that their theological doctrine and ecclesiastical polity squared more truly with it than did those of other bodies. Even sore financial straits did not cause them to hive off for more lucrative employ with better-off communions. They were willing to bear penury for their convictions because to them the Bible was the supernaturally indited Word of God. But at the time of which I now speak, some forty or more years ago, the confusing impact of the "new biblical scholarship" was everywhere evident. There were ministers in our Baptist churches mesmerized by the exciting new attitudes to the Old Testament, and the *kenosis* idea of a Christ demoted to the level of human fallibility. Some brethren known to me doubted or denied the virgin birth and bodily resurrection of our Lord, questioned the atoning reality of the Cross, sneered at the idea of being "born again," and derided the hope of our Lord's visible return. It was pronouncedly obvious that if you are shaky about the Bible you are shaky everywhere. I mention no names. We did not do so even then. Nay, if we dared complain in denominational quarters we were "heresy hunters"!

Yet our Commission of Enquiry Report naïvely wondered at "the apparent ease" with which ministers could transfer to another denomination. How *could* they (it wondered) so easily discard our Baptist system of independency and our ritual of baptism by immersion? It would have been comic if it were not so tragic. A minister could doubt or deny our traditional Baptist belief in the supernatural inspiration of the Bible; he could doubt and set others doubting basic doctrines of our historic faith; yet so long as he got on well with Baptist officialdom and baptized by immersion, he could remain a Baptist minister. On the other hand, though he were as evangelically sound and as traditionally Baptist as Spurgeon, if he did not baptize by immersion he must be dismissed! Even a simpleton could see that a point was thus reached where a mere rite was *ipso facto* elevated above vital doctrine. I myself am Baptist by thoughtful conviction; therefore I too hold that the only true water baptism as per the New Testament is the baptism of believers only and only by immersion. Yet however meaningful believer's baptism may be in its proper context of soundly evangelical doctrine, it is empty *apart* from that. To expect ministers to stay Baptist just for our form of administration ritually and ecclesiastically when they had already let go the inerrant authority of the Bible was inanity.

What was the upshot? I never saw our Baptists so stirred as they were at the Annual Assembly when that "Report" and its

OUR BIBLE: THE BASIC DIVIDE 27

"recommendations" were voted on. The session was jammed with delegates. Our people showed that in the main we Scottish Baptists were still wanting "the good old paths" and not the veneered infidelity of the "new biblical scholarship." They realized that most of the commissioners' proposals were subtle but radical encroachments on our cherished Baptist beliefs and liberties. In the Assembly, however, proceedings were so manipulated that if the voters went against the commissioners' "recommendations" they were obliged to vote on an "amendment" to the effect that the Report "be not further discussed." In vain two of us besought the delegates not to be thus edged into gagging themselves. They voted overwhelmingly against the objectionable "recommendations" and then dazedly discovered that they were precluded by their own vote from dragging out the hidden Judas who was betraying us with a kiss, the so-called "New Theology" of the liberals. Thus with a hectic showdown the vexatious "Commission of Enquiry" became "splendidly null." I remember some of the letters which came to me afterwards from delegates who now saw with new clearness that the really decisive issue was *the inspiration and authority of the Bible.*

I am reminded, too, of a ministerial conference in Edinburgh. It was going to be epochal. The religious deterioration in Britain had become such (said the invitation) that we ministers simply must get together and do something. "Revival and Evangelism" was the theme. As minister of our largest Baptist church I felt it my duty to attend. Naturally, the Church of Scotland brethren were the greater number, including some of their finest men, Dr. George S. Gunn, Professor James S. Stewart, Rev. William C. MacDonald, not to name others. The introducer of the subject said the time had come when we must organize carefully trained groups to go out systematically to the homes in our cities (which won my "amen"); and they must let the people know that Christianity is no longer something they have to *believe,* but something they have to *do* (at which I groaned). I decided to sit through in silence, and would have done so had not our chairman later pressed me to speak. I thought it pertinent to note that our theme, "Revival and Evangelism," linked two concepts which should be carefully distinguished. "Revival" is the sovereign act of God. "Evangelism" is an activity of the *Church.* The first step to revival is *prayer.* I asked the brethren which nights their congregational waitings on God were held, but I was downed by a vigorous brother who with verbal mallet blows assured me that you cannot judge the *private* prayer-life of church members by the *public* prayer meeting (which comment we all slyly knew was wrong!).

But it was my comment on "evangelism" which brought a squall, namely, that we could never have unity of *action* until we had unity of *conviction,* especially about the Bible. "Much as I esteem you, brother ministers, how could I conscientiously unite with some of you in evangelistic effort, when *I* tell the people to trust the whole Bible as the inspired written revelation of God, while some of *you* represent it rather as a human record of man's religious evolution, containing myths, errors, and doubtful parts? Professor Stewart, in characteristically charitable vein, said he felt sure that all the local Church of Scotland men were sound enough on the Bible, only to be followed by one of them who said, "Frankly, I don't think it matters two hoots *what* theory of the Bible you hold!" In a concluding assessment, Dr. George S. Gunn, always a judicious thinker, said, "Gentlemen, I believe there is far more in this than perhaps we have been thinking. I remember how, when I was in university here, efforts were made to unite the two Christian groups, the S.C.M. and the Edinburgh University Christian Union, but always, in the end, those efforts broke down because of different attitudes to *the inspiration of the Bible.*" Yes, that is always the basic divide!

About the same time we had a ministers' dinner and conference in Richmond, Surrey. It brought together a quite representative assortment: Anglicans, Methodists, Baptists, Congregationalists — some of them conservative, but more of them otherwise, and a couple of them Anglo-Catholics. I hope we get on better in heaven that we did in that little tete-a-tete! There were two speakers, I being second. My line was, that if Protestant Christianity was to recapture its lost initiative there must be a return to the Bible as the Word of God in the truly evangelical sense. Then came a long period of open discussion. Although my heart was heavy over the spiritual decline in Britain I will not deny that I naughtily enjoyed that day's skirmish. It was my first hand-to-hand thicket-fighting with Modernist arguments, and I was surprised how quickly they crumpled. But the most striking exposure that day was that all in a matter of minutes the deepest divider among those men was not denominational; it was the gulf between those to whom the Bible was *the inspired Word of God* and those to whom it was *less.* I, a stubborn Baptist, had more in common with an Anglo-Catholic who accepted the Bible as in truth the divine Word than with a fellow-Baptist of the modernist sort; and a Church of England clergyman who really believed his Bible had more in common with a Salvation Army major than with another Anglican cleric who desupernaturalized it. This has always been so: attitude to the Bible is the vital uniter — and the basic *divider*.

During that hour a Congregationalist professor of theology rose and said, "To me, Baxter's idea is preposterous, that we must all believe the same about the Bible. Why, the very genius of Protestant religion is its diversity of belief. Even Paul championed this freedom and called it the 'liberty of the gospel.'" My reply was: "Professor, you say that the genius of Protestant Christianity is its 'diversity' of belief. Yes, Protestant freedom has always been healthily characterized by incidental diversity in the *interpretation* of the Bible, but until the rise of the radical higher critical schools Protestantism was *never* divided as to the *inspiration* of the Bible. *That* is the crippling division today. As for Paul's word about the 'liberty' of the gospel, where does it occur? — in Galatians 2:4, 'False brethren unawares brought in, who came in privily to spy out our liberty which we have in Christ Jesus. . . . ' That liberty was liberty to preach and practice the gospel, not to *under mine* it! And to those who would then have tampered with it (see text) Paul 'gave place. . . , *no, not for an hour.*'"

Brethren, from then until now observation has confirmed my persuasion that for Protestant Christianity the Bible is the basic question. It was because the Reformers broke through encrusted Roman Catholic perversions and went right back to the authentic sources of our Christian faith in Holy Writ that there came the never-to-be-forgotten triumph of the Reformation. Always, therefore, we have made our *appeal* to the Book. We have found our *message* in the Book. We have derived our *authority* from the Book. The veracity and validity and vitality of our Protestant faith are inseparably bound up with the authority of the Book. Protestantism stands or falls with the Book. We are seeing that, today, more poignantly than ever, in what is now happening!

The fatal blight on modern Protestantism is *not* its plurality of denominations (and the World Council of Churches is wasting our time belaboring that dreary blunder), but the chaotic attitude of the main Protestant officialdoms and of far too many Protestant ministers toward the Bible. If the foundation is faulty the edifice is tottery. That is why Protestantism today cuts a sorry figure. I do not speak thus in any pettiness of controversy, any more than a doctor would argue for the mere sake of a verbal victory over a dying man's disease. Nor am I a scaremonger; but it seems to me that organized Protestant Christianity is so inwardly weakened today, after a deadly eight decades of rationalistic Bible criticism, that a wide collapse might happen under excessive pressure. Are we, indeed, seeing signs of that already? This, at any rate, is true: our Protestant pulpit loses its hold on men in exact degree as faith in the supernaturalness of the Bible is broken down among them.

With rueful memories let me refer to Britain again. Most of the evangelists who were in their prime about the time of the First World War have now passed on; but to their last days they all testified that the decade following that First World War was the most responsive they ever knew. Hundreds of thousands of men — fathers, husbands, brothers, sweethearts — had been slain. The minds of the countless bereaved, and of people generally, were turned to the beyond. The soul of the nation was stricken. There was a heartsob after a disobeyed God and a neglected Savior. Thousands were brought to Christ.

But after the *Second* World War, a generation later, did the same thing happen? No; the very opposite. There was cynical apathy. Instead of stricken conscience and dire sense of spiritual need there was a marked breakaway from the churches. Why? Well, there were various contributory factors, but the main reason was that for another quarter-century our people had been having their faith in Scripture destroyed by liberalist pulpits, books, magazines, until now, in general, they were *incapacitated* to make the Godward response of that earlier generation.

It seems the vogue in the U.S.A. just now, even in magazines more or less evangelical, to disparage the early "Fundamentalists"; but Americans will never know all they owe to those clear-brained men who saw the crisis over the Bible for what it really was and had the courage to "come out and be separate." Christianity would have been in far worse plight today in the U.S.A. but for those brave separatists. They not only came out; they fought the intellectual battle for the Bible. They built their own new churches and colleges. They wrote books, launched magazines, invaded the radio and, later, the television. They brought the issue over the Bible to the American public at large and made it a living, throbbing concern. We must never judge those first Fundamentalists by some of the bossy little bigots (I have *no one* particularly in mind) who followed them.

Over in Britain, alas, it was different. There were protests, but there was no coming out, no preferring to die rather than compromise. The British evangelicals were wiser (we said) than "those drastic American fundamentalists." They protested but stayed in. They parleyed into gradual paralysis. Liberals took the best seats in denominational administration. The evangelical cause lost its voice and soon could scarcely breathe inside the main Protestant headquarters; until today there are whole areas in Britain (I know some of them well) where evangelical witness is nonexistent, while the spiritual slump throughout the nation is a heartbreak to the godly remnant.

Brethren, I hold that the desupernaturalizing theories about the Bible which have been spawned and spumed by successive schools of "modernism" have been so truly refuted by evangelical scholarship and archaeological testimony that it is pathetic to see how some theology professors and ministers cling sycophantically to the magic bits of floating wreckage, lest by standing firmly on "the impregnable rock of Holy Scripture" they should be considered old-fashioned! But the point I make here is that every weakening of faith in the Bible is a weakening of our whole Protestant witness. I do not bind any man to a particular theory of inspiration, but I do say that any theory which makes it less than the authentic Word of God throughout is *un-Protestant*.

That leads to this: there can be no evangelistic grip and no real spiritual power where the Bible is degraded to lower levels like those of the neo-orthodox and the liberals. Every Protestant denomination which is untrue to the traditional Protestant view of the Bible is *spiritually weak*. Look around and see. Every local Protestant church which is shaky about the Bible is *spiritually weak*. Look around and see. Every minister who has doubts about our precious old foundation-book is to that extent spiritually weak — as you and I know well enough. Practically all the indefiniteness of indefinite preachers arises from indefiniteness about the Bible.

Fellow-ministers whom I now address, do some of you belong to what we evangelicals call "the *other* school"? With tolerant courtesy you have borne with me thus far, though many of my remarks may have been like irritating smoke to the nostrils. I thank you, and hope that an extra word to you in particular may not seem *too* amiss.

I do not here debate with you the rival *pros* and *cons* of our different attitudes to the Bible. It is a purely pragmatic question which leaps to my lips. Does your liberalist handling of the Bible make its *promises* more precious and trustable to you? or does it provoke doubts whether they *are* divine promises? Does your liberalist view of the Bible make its precepts and doctrines and warnings divine absolutes to you? or does it reduce them to merely human approximations?

Does your liberalist Bible make you more powerful in the pulpit? more earnest in winning perishing sinners to the Savior? or do you no longer believe that they *are* perishing or that there is a Gehenna in the beyond? Do you still revel in the New Testament doctrine of the Lamb, the Paraclete, the Body, the Bride, election, inwrought sanctification, the inward "witness of the Spirit," the hope of the Lord's return, the millennial Christocracy, the everlasting glories of the "new heaven and new earth"? or have you now learned to despise these as the effete ideas of an worn-out mode of belief? Poor, starved, shrunken "liberal"! How much you miss! You have *no* real theology — for if the Bible is not directly inspired, even its didactic teachings are not strictly theology, but only human philosophy. You are hugging a skeleton; and, if you only knew it, when we evangelicals hear you preach we can often hear the rattle of the bones!

I ask you to give up your liberalist ideas, and return to a full-fledged faith in the Bible. Yes, there are *some* problems in verbal inspiration, as in any other theory of inspiration, for when we have said our last word the Bible will remain a mystery. The union of the human and the divine in it are as mysterious as is their union in Christ. Mystery, however, never disproves reality. Some of the biggest mysteries are the greatest realities, as, for instance, the eternality and triunity of God.

Yes, I ask you to discard your liberalist beliefs or disbeliefs. You *can.* The faulty rationalizings of years can be jettisoned in minutes when the mind is convinced and humbled. I have seen it happen. Not long ago, after a long discussion, I knelt in prayer with a seminary professor, my intellectual superior in every way; and there in my hearing, honoring me with his confidence, before God he renounced with tears his liberalist scheme of teaching. Some years ago in New Jersey it was my responsibility to address three successive afternoon conferences of ministers. There were about fifteen hundred of us present each time. My subject throughout was *Jesus Christ: Kenosis or Pleroma?* Over one hundred and forty of those men afterward confided that their neo-orthodox or liberalist vagaries had brought them only depletion, restlessness, and pulpit starvation.

Brethren, the mightiest recovery which could come to our wilting Protestant cause around the world today would be that our well-known Protestant denominations should publicly reavow faith in the true inspiration of the Bible, and that all Protestant pulpits should once again ring with a prophetic "Thus saith Jehovah." I urge that all of us ministers who still believe the Bible in the less critical but equally intellectual way of our Protestant forefathers should spend far more time in teaching our people the solid arguments for its divine origin, at the same time exposing the flimsiness of the desupernaturalizing expedients. All brain and effort thus expended would be gilt-edged investment. As never before, let us champion the truly Protestant esteem of the Bible. Much depends on our open and vocal loyalty. The struggle is urgent. The issues are immense. Far more than some of us suspect, maybe, all around us in their thousands there are thinking, wondering, groping human minds longing to hear not what man thinks but *what God says*. It is ours unabashedly to tell them, and therein will lie the intrinsic strength and glory of our ministry.

OUR BIBLE: SOME BIG ISSUES

It is a fearful thing to be an unsanctified preacher. Doth it not make you tremble when you open the Bible, lest you should there read the sentence of your own condemnation? . . . I would advise [you] preach over Origen's Sermon on Psalm 50:16, 17. "What hast *thou* to do to declare My statutes, or that *thou* shouldst take My covenant in *thy* mouth, seeing thou hatest instruction, and castest *My Words* behind thee?"

Richard Baxter

OUR BIBLE: SOME BIG ISSUES

With your consent, dear brethren, may I here return to the theme already introduced, namely, the basic importance of the Bible? I do not wish to belabor the matter unduly, but so convinced am I of its *decisiveness* for our Protestant ministry that I am minded to specify a few of the vital issues involved.

Theology properly begins with the one simple yet vast postulate that "God is." Thereupon, the first question in theology is, "Has God spoken?" Until recent days Protestant Christianity has always answered that question with united voice, "Yes, God has spoken; He has spoken uniquely through the divinely inspired Scriptures, and supremely in His incarnate Son, our Lord Jesus."

As you well know, however, during the past century certain influential schools of biblical criticism in Protestant Christendom have played havoc with the traditional view of the Bible, and in effect have turned the historic assertion, "God has spoken," into the dubious query, "*Has* God spoken?"

This, of course, immediately impinges upon the inspiration of the Bible, and reopens that issue which, above all others, either validates or invalidates our Protestant stand; for we justify our very existence, as well as claim our mandate, by appeal to the Bible. For the thousandth time we say it: if that foundation is insecure, our whole superstructure on it is wobbly, including (let us not forget) our democratic form of govenment and the social ethics of those countries which, at least in name, are still Christian. Do we not all know that the "new psychology" of today, with its ethical vulgarity, its doctrine of moral relativity, and its license to animal self-expression is a by-product of broken-down faith in the Bible?

Nay, more, if we have reason to doubt the Bible, then we know nothing at all with certainty about origin or destiny, about the beyond or the future, about the supernatural or the divine, about the real meaning of "good" and "evil"; we have only human science and philosophy, which means that one theory may be as good as another.

But, more specifically, let me submit several *special* reasons why an authentically inspired Bible is nothing less than vital to Protestant survival.

Obviously, to begin with, a divinely inspired Bible is vital to *genuine divine revelation.* The neo-orthodox schools representatively headed by Karl Barth and Emil Brunner have warned us again in recent decades that we must not confuse "inspiration" with "revelation," and they have strongly inveighed against that much-castigated "absurdity" of evangelicals, the *verbal* inspiration of the Bible. But, to those of us who like to feel solid rock beneath our feet, such airy ambiguities as those of neo-orthodoxy concerning revelation *without* inerrant inspiration are utterly unconvincing.

We ourselves are just as alive as anyone to the difference between revelation and inspiration — revelation being the truth itself which is revealed or recorded, and inspiration the *means* whereby it is communicated or transmitted in written form. Yet surely, as any unprejudiced reflection will endorse, we cannot be sure that revelation really *is* revelation apart from supernaturally attested *inspiration.*

Neo-orthodox scholars have insisted that revelation is known only by "divine encounter." To my own thinking, this has been the brilliant blunder of murdering the objective in magnifying the subjective, of blinking away the evidential for the sake of supposedly liberating the spiritual. Be that as it may, nothing will ever gainsay this: we can never be sure of genuine divine revelation apart from authentic *inspiration* — a supernatural inspiration, that is, which carries its own clear credentials.

Nor can we admit *degrees* of inspiration which supposedly make some parts of the Bible more authoritative than others. There can be, and there are, degrees of *revelation,* for biblical revelation is progressive; but there *cannot* be degrees of divine *inspiration.* A person either is or is not divinely inspired. We may admit degrees of moral and spiritual *value* in different parts of Scripture, as, for instance, certain Old Testament records in comparison with the higher doctrines of the New Testament; but that does not affect the inspiration of the whole. In the case of historical records, inspiration safeguards the accuracy of what is related or reported. It need not mean any more than that, but it cannot mean less. In each part, as well as in total, the Bible either is or is not inspired. There can be no degrees. Second Timothy 3:16 says, "*All* scripture is given by inspiration of God. . . ." Even if we prefer to read that text as in some later versions, "Every Scripture inspired of God is also profitable for teaching. . . ," verse 15 settles it that the Scriptures referred to were those of the Jewish canon, no more and no less, that is, our own Old Testament. Paul says that *"every* scripture," from Genesis to Malachi, is *inspired of God."* Supposing for a minute, however, that there *is* revelation apart from inspiration, of what *sort* is it? Both Barth and Brunner early rejected the Old Testament narratives of the creation and of early human history. Both of them early subscribed to the evolutionist view of origins. Both of them suavely bypassed that super-event of measureless evidential importance, the bodily resurrection of Jesus, as being relatively unimportant. Well, if that is revelation without inspiration, then instead of rescuing Protestant Christianity from its latter-day troubles, it only pushes it further into the slough. Indeed, that is what it has *been* doing for years now.

But now let me further urge that a supernaturally inspired Bible is vital to *a true Christology.* It is not a bit of use saying, as the theological liberals do, that so long as we have Christ Himself, the inspiration of the Bible is of little moment. Everything we know of Christ, the living Word, we owe (and must keep on owing) to the Bible, the written Word. If our Bible does not carry the guarantees of supernatural inspiration, then how can we be quite sure of the Christ whom it presents to us — whether the Christ of Old Testament prophecy or of Gospel history or of epistolary doctrine?

It is noticeable that when men tamper with the inspiration of the Scripture, it is not long before they tamper with the person of the Savior. The theological liberals themselves illustrate this. With a certain superfine sense of scholarly self-sufficiency, they aver that so long as they have Christ Himself they are above any need for the verbally inspired Bible of the evangelicals and conservatives. But what sort of Christ do they have? He is the "kenosis" Christ handed down by the German radical "higher critics"; a Christ emptied of His divine *pleroma* and reduced to the level of ordinary human fallibility, or even gullibility. It makes one shudder to think of two well-known denominational leaders in this present day speaking thus of our Lord: "Christ was a bastard who rose above the circumstances of His unfortunate birth." "Is not this tendency to deify Jesus more heathen than Christian?" Could men ever speak so if they believed in the divine inspiration of the Bible? And can Protestantism ever be rescued from its present sickliness until such betrayals by prominent leaders are repudiated?

This brings me to another urgent observation: a divinely inspired Bible is vital to *Christian theology.* Brethren, if the Bible is indeed ὁ λόγος τοῦ θεοῦ, the Word of God, then Christian theology is a *science*, for by it we may truly *know*. Indeed it is the highest of the sciences, for by it we may know the truth about God; also truth from God concerning man, physical and spiritual, here and hereafter; also concerning our earth and its kosmos, past, present, future; also concerning human responsibility, and the true morality, and the mystery of sin, and the gospel of redemption.

But if the Bible is *not* theopneustic, or supernaturally God-breathed, then "theology" *(theos logos)* is not a science at all in the classic sense, for we cannot really *know*. Christian theology slumps down into mere philosophizing. Systematic theology, instead of being the constructive classification of ascertained realities, becomes a medley of unprovable assumptions.

That, alas, is just what has largely happened in Protestant Christendom, especially from Wellhausen to Bultmann. There is as much difference between *true* theology and *their* "theology" as there is between scientific astronomy and superstitious astrology. Old Testament prophets, New Testament apostles, all the writers of Scripture, were supposedly bound by the cultural limitations of the age in which they lived; and now our latter-day radical Bible "scholars" (forgetting how culture-bound *they* are!) look upon it as wonderful creativity to develop new "theologies" every new decade or so, based on the so-called religious "experience" of those long-ago culture-bound people in the pages of the Bible. Let us be blunt; their *new* "theologies" are *not* theology in the time-honored and truly Protestant sense.

Modernism is not just a school or phase or fashion; it is a mental *attitude* arising from a spirit of rebellion against the supernatural and the divinely authoritative. Our twentieth-century Sadducees simply cannot stand the thought of an authoritative theology. Before ever they allow the Bible to say a thing to them they come to it with the *a priori* axiom that miracle and supernatural revelation are inadmissible. There is an utterly unscientific foreclosing of the mind against rational *evidence*. They simply will not own a *revealed* theology. Some of them will agree that the Bible *contains* "revelation" after a sort, and they have their so-called theology of revelation, but their theology of revelation is as different from revealed theology as a shadow is from substance.

The result of all this is the present theological chaos of modern Protestantism. As Dr. Carl Henry has said in one of his editorials, "Protestantism so often seems like *the one 'world message' that simply cannot make up its mind.*" If the inspiration and authority of the Bible were a matter merely of theoretic theology, the present breakdown would not be so frightening as it is; but the fearful fact is that the "world message" of true Protestantism is choked in the throats of our large Protestant denominations; and, while they sputter and stutter, souls are living and sinning and suffering and groping and despairing and dying and sinking unsaved into Christless graves.

The World Council of Churches is *not* the big answer to the need of our Protestant world. It is an imposing diversion from the real issue. It blurs the real disease and obscures the real remedy. If the World Council of Churches were half as concerned about denominational infidelity to the Bible as it is about denominational divisions, it would be a hundred times more truly Protestant and spiritually useful. How truly does Dr. Henry add that twentieth-century ecumenism is "more distressed by schism than by heresy"!

Brethren, do I need to persuade you? A Bible uniquely and directly inspired by the Holy Spirit is vital to a true Christian theology. Is it not our duty to think vividly and act with determination in the good cause of restoring the Bible to its true place in our communions? We are not trying to make others believe merely what *we* believe; we want them to believe the Bible as the Word of God. When we criticize the liberal, the modernist, it is not because he differs from *us*, but because he dishonors the *Bible*. We are not asking liberals merely to become evangelicals; we are asking them to come back with intellectual humility to the *Bible* as the truly inspired Word of God.

One thing which has emerged quite decidedly during the past fifty years is that modern critical schools are not necessarily synonymous with intellectuality. Much that passed as brilliant new scholarship forty or fifty years ago is seen as aberrant today. That is *not* so with great works by evangelical scholars. The passing decades have confirmed their stability. At the turn of the century W. L. Baxter's *Sanctuary and Sacrifice* had already made mincemeat of Wellhausen's *Prolegomena to the History of Israel.* James Orr's books display an abler scholarly swordmanship than the extravagant lunges of Vatke, Kuenen, Stade, and the like. But why name more? With a whole new battalion of evidences archaeological discovery has knocked the weapons from the hands of the humanistic critics.

I have always marveled at the irrationality of the neo-orthodoxy, particularly in the way it blandly took for granted critical assumptions which had already been exposed as untrue. Was it not yet another cue that the successive variations of rationalistic Bible criticism are in reality merely new disguises of the one, same, deep resentment against *supernatural* revelation? There cannot be a return to true theological science until that rebellious *spirit* is broken. I have seen the release which comes to men where it *is* broken.

But all that I have said leads to this further emphasis: a supernaturally inspired Bible is necessary to *the preservation of Protestant Christianity*. I need make no apology for repetition here: the inspiration of the Bible is nothing less than the *crucial* concern of our Protestant heritage. There may be a combination of contributory factors underlying the present-day enfeeblement of Protestant witness, but the cause underlying all others is the ragged resentment against the supernatural in the Bible. Never can organized Protestantism go forth again with recaptured initiative, "terrible as an army with banners," until, throughout our well-known denominations, we reavow before all the world our restored faith in the Bible as the revindicated Word of God.

After my last address to a Southern Baptist Pastors' Conference at San Francisco a few years ago, a couple of the brethren, both of them men of scholarly distinction, were discussing with me the disturbance concerning the Bible. One of them said, "We have had all sorts of Southern Baptist crises before, and we have come through them without division or serious hurt; it will be the same again now." My prayer was that his prophecy might prove true. Nonetheless I felt obliged to reply that a crisis over the Bible is not like any other. Here is a handsome building with many good committee rooms, in some of which Southern Baptist committees are having fine old wrangles over this, that, or the other issue; in fact with some of them there is evidently a crisis; yet they are all in the same building and will remain so after their tussles are over. But see, *there* is a group of fellows who have gone down to the basement, and they are hacking away at the very foundations! Unless *they* are stopped, the whole building, classrooms, committees, arguments, and all will come to grief! *That* is the crisis over the inspiration and authority of the Bible. "If the foundations are destroyed, what shall even the Southern Baptists do?" (Ps. 11:3, "Devised" Version!).

A converted Roman Catholic priest stood in the main storeroom of the British and Foreign Bible Society, London, England. For some moments, in thoughtful silence, he looked round that spacious hall, stacked from floor to ceiling with thousands and thousands of Bibles. Then with deep emotion he said, "Gentlemen, this is the only place in the world that is stronger than the Vatican." If only our Protestant leaders and churches today would realize it: *that* is where our real power lies — a Bible really and fully inspired of God. It is not only our bedrock foundation; it is our invincible weapon.

Modernism (in its varied forms) and Romanism (with its unvaried dogmas) are poles apart, but they are equally the enemies of true, New Testament Christianity. They both claim to be Christianity, but both are pseudomorphous species of it. The revealing feature in both is their attitude to the Bible; and on that score we claim that they are both patently self-contradictory.

Modernism, on the one hand, hacks supernatural inspiration out of the Bible, yet is obliged to keep on making use of a source-book which it has rendered no longer authoritative for anyone. Romanism, on the other hand, upholds the supernatural inspiration of the Bible, yet has dishonored it by teachings which flatly contradict it. Modernism subordinates the Bible to man's reason. Romanism has overridden it by a supposedly infallible church. Modernism is a Jehoiakin mutilating the Word of God with a knife. Romanism has been a Judas betraying it with a kiss.

Brethren, from the negations of the one and the perversions of the other the deliverance of our countrymen is long overdue. Numberless people have fled from the bogs of modernism hoping to find solid footing in the authoritarian Church of Rome; but that is a false alternative. The Bible itself needs saving from both. To rescue the Bible from the mutilations of modernism simply to put it under the lock and key of the Vatican is like breaking free from the claws of a panther to be smothered in the coils of a cobra.

One of the strangest surprises just now is the new face of the Roman Church as the encourager of Bible reading. Let us put the best construction on it and thank God for it. It can do nothing but good. The Roman Catholic Church has always proclaimed herself the appointed keeper of the Scriptures: but instead of keeping it *for* the people she has notoriously kept it *from* them. If (as we hope) behind the new change of attitude there is a change of heart we shall be among the first to thank God; but for the time being we must needs wait and see. Is there, perhaps, a touch of opportunism in it? Has Rome waited until Protestant championing of the Bible is almost irreparably broken down before coming out as the new champion of the Bible? Is it a master stroke at a strategic moment? Or is it a genuine change, as we gratefully hope? Is there also divine overruling? Perhaps so, for, as we have said elsewhere, if Protestant infidelity to the Bible persists, God will raise up new Bible champions in the most unlikely places.

This I do believe: that God is now making an eleventh-hour appeal to our Protestant leaders and ministers. It is an appeal, before all else, for a reverent, new acceptance of the Bible in its totality as the one and only authentic written revelation from God, given through Spirit-inspired men, fixed in Spirit-controlled written form, certified and complete. Those brethren who treat the Bible as *less* than that, especially in public ministry, are thereby *continually grieving the Spirit of God.* That solemn truth, so I believe, can be documented beyond question. Weigh carefully the following considerations.

Our Lord repeatedly declared Himself the dominating subject of the Old Testament (see Luke 24:27, 44; John 5:39, 46). Likewise, before the New Testament was ever written He foretold a similar preeminence. In three notable preannouncements concerning the soon-coming Holy Spirit, He anticipatively covered all three areas of our New Testament. "He shall bring all things to your remembrance" (the Gospels). "He shall guide you into all the truth" (the Epistles). "And He shall show you things to come" (the Apocalypse). Then, as if once-for-all to focalize it, He said, "He shall glorify me" (John 16:14).

Brethren, that is the Bible through and through — *"He shall glorify me."* In the Old Testament you have the Christ of *prophecy.* In the Gospels you have the Christ of *history.* In the Acts and the Epistles you have the Christ of *experience.* In the Apocalypse you have the Christ of *coming glory.*

The Old Testament cries, "Behold, He *comes!"* The four Gospels give their sad emphasis, "Behold, He *dies!"* But the Acts follows on with, "Behold, He *lives!"* And the Epistles join in with, "Behold, He *saves!"* And the Apocalypse sublimates it into a Hallelujah chorus with, "Behold, He *reigns!"*

In the Old Testament we have *preparation.* In the Gospels we have *manifestation.* In the Acts we have *dissemination.* In the Epistles we have *realization.* In the Apocalypse we have *consummation.* But it is the same glorious Lord Jesus Christ in successive aspects from first to last and all the way through.

From the time of the Davidic covenant, and on through the pages of the Prophets, we find that miraculous literary phenomenon known as *Messianic prophecy.* How anyone can examine those long-in-advance predictions concerning our Lord's birth, life, miracles, character, atoning death, and ultimate global kingdom without seeing the supernaturalness of the Bible is a puzzle to me. Even the fictitious late-dating of some of the Prophets by the radical higher critics could not destroy the unanswerable evidential value of those predictions and their varied fulfillments in our Lord's first coming to this earth. If *anything* is a divine signature to the Old Testament, *that* is!

Well, now, brethren, how eloquent all this is to you and me as ministers of the New Covenant! Let me quickly mention two challenging upshots. First, *no ministry which desupernaturalizes the Bible can be of the Holy Spirit*. It may be scholarly, clever, eloquent, popular, but it is not of the Holy Spirit. That is obvious from the fact that the Holy Spirit has given Christ to us, not only in New Testament record and doctrine, but also in Old Testament type and prophecy. Old Testament prediction and typology are *supernatural;* they are miracles; they involve direct divine operation.

There is no getting away from this. The first and most unanswerable of all arguments for the inspiration of the Old Testament is the argument of *fulfilled prophecy*. If you establish the presence of only *one* clearly worded prediction, proven to be written long enough in advance to exclude all possibility of shrewd guesswork; and then, if you find unmistakable fulfillment, right down to details, you are obliged to admit, with Pharaoh's wise men, "This is the finger of God," or else you are guilty of irrational prejudice. But when you find genuine predictions of verifiable fulfillments in *scores*, with long centuries between prediction and fulfillment, then, continued refusal by Protestant ministers to accept such evidence is not scholarship any longer; it is an impertinence which grieves the Holy Spirit and breaks the backbone of Protestant witness.

But, brethren, the most wonderful kind of prophecy is not written prediction; it is that amazing phenomenon which we call *typical prefiguration*. Old Testament persons, objects, events, institutions are divinely adapted to prefigure truths which were to be revealed centuries later. The special purpose of such types is to make the truth live and move before us in a way which merely stated doctrine never could. Prophecy in the form of direct statement may make a truth *lucid;* but prophecy in the form of typical prepicturing makes it *vivid*. Paul tells us that Adam was a *tupos* or "type" of our Lord as the "Second Adam." Our Lord Himself says that Jonah's experience in the sea monster typifies the Son of Man's descent into Hades. First Corinthians 10:4 tells us that the rock in Horeb which gave water to the Israelites, as recorded in Exodus

17, was a type of Christ: "That Rock was Christ." These are just random instances representing many.

Now always, when the New Testament refers to such types in the *Old* Testament, it implies their *historicity*. Adam was a real person, not merely a myth. The Jonah episode was a divinely designed actual occurrence, not fiction. Does the Holy Spirit make types of God the Son out of persons who never lived and incidents which never happened? Perish the thought! — and perish the so-called "modern scholarship" which, defying the clear witness of our Lord and the New Testament, keeps on denying the historicity of those persons and records! Brethren, I remind you again: in order to exhibit the deity of our Lord and the divine inspiration of the Scriptures, the Holy Spirit has given us Christ not only in New Testament memoirs and epistles but also in Old Testament prediction and prefiguration. Those Old Testament foretellings and typifyings, taken with their New Testament fulfillments and antitypes, are a literary miracle beyond all refutation. It is the Holy Spirit's Christocentric masterpiece. Therefore, no ministry which desupernaturalizes the Bible, in either of its Testaments, can be of the Holy Spirit.

One further consideration. If, as our dear Lord said, "He shall glorify me," then here we have the decisive test of every movement, every ministry, and every minister. Brethren, if you and I wish to know for certain to what degree we are infilled, controlled, monopolized, by the Holy Spirit, this is the question to ask: To what degree is Christ reflected, recognized, exalted, communicated, in and through my personality and my ministry? The first purpose of the Holy Spirit, when He comes upon us in special enduement or Pentecostal plenitude, is not to awaken ecstatic emotion, or lift us to mystical contemplation, or give us abnormal power, or enable us to speak in tongues, but to make us *Christlike*. Is that what most of us really covet? Wonder of wonders, that same mysterious, brooding, gracious, mighty, sympathetic Holy Spirit who supernaturally communicated divine truth through the tongues and pens of prophets and apostles to give us the Christ-crowned, completed revelation which is ours in the Bible now waits to *illumine* you and me, as ministers of our Lord Jesus Christ, so that we may powerfully rearticulate the treasures of those inspired Scriptures to our own day and generation! My prayer is that all of us may truly know Him as the enduing Spirit of illumination (Eph. 1: 17, 18).

OUR BIBLE: THE KING'S SEAL

Believe it, brethren, God is no respecter of persons: He saveth not men for their coats or callings; a holy calling will not save an unholy man.

Many a tailor goes in rags who maketh costly clothes for others; and many a cook scarcely licks his fingers when he hath dressed for others the most costly dishes. Believe it, brethren, God never saved any man for being a preacher, nor because he was an *able* preacher; but because he was a justified, sanctified man, and *faithful in His Master's work*.

Richard Baxter

OUR BIBLE: THE KING'S SEAL

Brethren, if, as I have urged, the priority concern of Reformation Christianity today is the inspiration of the Bible, then the sensitive center of that issue is the testimony of our Lord Himself. That testimony will surely be final for any man who sincerely calls Jesus "Lord." I would speak with restraint as well as vigor, but it seems to me that to call the incarnate Son of God "Lord" yet politely circumvent or even contradict His clear Word is neither scholarship nor Christian liberty but dissimulation.

Our Lord's witness to the Old Testament is so clear and full that the only way to evade its unanswerableness is somehow to invalidate it, which critics have indeed endeavored to do by three expedients: (1) the *faulty record* theory, which casts doubts on the reliability of the Gospel reports; (2) the *kenosis* theory, which lowers the incarnate Son to the level of human fallibility; (3) the *accommodation* theory, which argues that He accommodated His teachings on such matters to the sentimental suppositions of the day. All three have been exposed again and again as provenly untenable. They need not distract us here. The records have been demonstrated as trustworthy by the most exacting scholarship. They make clear that our Lord's witness springs from divine fulness, not human diminishment (John 1:14; 2:24, 25, etc.). They also show us that our Lord's pronouncements, instead of being accommodated to popular notion, frequently rode right across it, or intendedly collided with it (Matt. 5:20, 32, 38, 39, etc.).

In one short address who could treat so copious a testimony adequately? Yet even in summary form it retains mighty cogency. Our Lord's attitude to the Old Testament may be crystalized in three propositions: (1) He continually quotes it but never once queries it; (2) He always quotes it so as to endorse it; (3) He endorses the whole of it as the inspired Word of God.

1. *Quotation Without Query*

Simply to quote without comment the many verses in which our Lord refers to various Old Testament Scriptures would fill several sizeable pages. He does not merely quote from the Old Testament in a general way; He particularizes. He refers to particular *writers* by name, as Moses, David, Daniel, etc. He speaks by name of various Old Testament *characters*, as Abel, Noah, Lot, Elijah. He refers to particular *institutions;* the Sabbath, marriage, the law of the leper's cleansing. He quotes from different *books;* Genesis, Exodus, and sixteen or seventeen others. He does all this, but what He never does is to betray uncertainty about any part whatever. He was always quoting it, but He never once queried it.

Of course, our Lord recognized that much in the Mosaic economy was incomplete and provisional; that in certain of its regulations it was even concessional (Matt. 19:8). Yet this does not in the least modify the fact that He accepted the whole of the Old Testament Scriptures as being from God, stamped with divine authority, and making known the divine will. He never queries in a single instance the historicity of its records, the supernaturalness of its prophecies, the genuineness of its parts, the accepted authorships of its books, or the divine origin of its doctrines and precepts.

It has been argued that our Lord set aside certain moral standards of the old covenant when, in the Sermon on the Mount, He said, "But *I* say unto you. . . ." That idea, however, is mistaken. In the six places where our Lord says, "It was *said* . . ." He was referring to the Jewish *oral* law, handed down through the centuries. Some of the quoted items certainly *are* in the Old Testament, but our Lord is citing them as they had come down via the oral law. For instance, the first, "Thou shalt not kill; and whosoever shall kill shall be in danger of the judgment," is the sixth command of the Decalogue *plus* the comment of the oral law. So far as His quotations actually concur with Old Testament tenets, our Lord, other than repudiating them, intensifies them, insisting on an inward and spiritual compliance, besides mere outward observance.

It should be remembered that Matthew 5:38 ("an eye for an eye, and a tooth for a tooth") looks back to a ruling which was given to Israel's magistrates, not to private individuals. The old-time command was not that individuals should exact this, as many readers inaccurately suppose. (See Exodus 21 for the context.) It was an injunction to *judges* to ensure that fair play was meted out to both parties in a dispute. It was right then, it is right now, and it will always be right that in a law suit there should be exact equality both as to punishment and as to compensation — "an eye for an eye" and *no more* than an eye! Now our Lord's comment on this is made not to judges but to *individuals*, and He is telling us that although we may rightly *claim* "an eye for an eye" as a matter of administrative justice, we should rather suffer injury meekly, so that if one should smite us "on the right cheek" we should "turn to him the other also."

To say that our Lord was here setting aside the commands of the Old Testament not only fails to recognize the difference between the *written* law and the oral law, it makes our Lord contradict the very purpose He has in quoting, which was to enforce the originals the more fully and inwardly; and it contradicts the very words with which He introduces His Old Testament quotations, i.e., "Whosoever therefore shall break one of these least commandments, and shall teach men so, he shall be called the least in the kingdom of heaven" (verse 19). Indeed, our Lord's whole attitude to the Old Testament may be summed up in the words which just precede verse 19, "Think not that I am come to destroy the law, or the prophets: I am not come to destroy, but to fulfill. For verily I say unto you, Till heaven and earth pass, one jot or one tittle shall in no wise pass from the law, till all be fulfilled." Yes, our Lord was always quoting the Old Testament, but He never once queried it.

2. Unmistakable Endorsement

But second, our Lord always quotes the Old Testament in ways which endorse its truthfulness and inerrancy. Whenever He mentions Old Testament *incidents,* He does so in such a way as to confirm their real historicity. According to the liberals, if there is one place more than another in the Old Testament which is mythical, it is the early part of Genesis; but our Lord has set His seal to all of it as thoroughly factual. We might give a succession of instances, but perhaps a couple will suffice. See Matthew 19:4, 5: "Have ye not read, that he which made them at the beginning made them male and female, And said, For this cause shall a man leave father and mother, and shall cleave to his wife: and they twain shall be one flesh?" Did our Lord found His doctrine of marriage, or His argument against divorce, on a myth? Note especially our Lord's comment, "He which made them said . . ." If that is not accepting the record as of divine authority and historical veracity, what could be? There is equally the same implication in our Lord's references to the Flood and to the destruction of Sodom. Can we think that when our Lord thus sought to alarm men by the centainty of coming judgment He pressed home His warnings by instances of punishment which were merely fictional?

Or take the *Jonah* incident, which, with almost cavalier disdain, has been scouted by many modern critics. Despite efforts to show that our Lord's words in Matthew 12:39, 40 are an interpolation, the manuscript evidence is quite sound; and, in any case, Luke also records the words. See how our Lord applies His reference to Jonah: "The men of Nineveh shall rise in the judgment with *this* generation, and shall condemn it: because they repented at the preaching of Jonas. . . ." Was the very Son of God here teaching (as it is said) that fictitious men in a fictitious story will yet *actually* rise up in the final Judgment and condemn those *actual* men whom our Lord rebuked? Is it not plain that our Lord here endorses the *factuality* of the Jonah incident?

Some of our modern scholars deny outright that Adam, Abel, Enoch, Noah, Lot, even Abraham, had any existence at all: they were mythical figures. Others concede their having lived, but deny any reliable data: all is stray, shadowy tradition. Our Lord, however, accepted them as real persons. We have already noted His references to Noah and Lot: He also says, "Your father, Abraham, rejoiced to see my day." Does He believe that the Jewish race descended from a fictional character, or that the patriarch on whom the Spirit of prophecy thus came was a mere shadow? Or when He refers to David's eating the shewbread, does He treat it as a mere legend? Scarcely, since He appeals to it in order to justify His own conduct, which the Pharisees were criticizing.

Our Lord just as definitely authenticates the origin of the Old Testament *institutions*. According to some of our moderns, few of the laws and institutions attributed to Moses can be traced to him; they originated with this or that or the other personage long afterwards, as occasion required, and were attributed to Moses in order to give them authority (which highly compliments the honesty of those anonymous benefactors!). Or else (as others tell us) the "germ" of the idea came from Moses and was "developed" by much later writers, "under the shelter of Moses' name." Scarcely any of the Pentateuch is directly from Moses. Practically the whole of Deuteronomy is from an unknown writer 800 years later. (It is surprising how many of those "unknown" writers there were in Jewish history, whom the Jews themselves never heard of until a certain type of "modern scholar" unearthed them all — minus their names!).

Now according to our Lord Jesus the various institutions of the Mosaic economy originated exactly when and how the Old Testament affirms. In John 7:22 we read, "Moses therefore gave unto you circumcision; (not because it is of Moses, but of the fathers)." So our Lord not only acknowledges that the rite was a genuine part of the ceremonial law given by *Moses himself,* but He assigns its original institution to the patriarchal period, i.e., to Abraham. In the same paragraph He asks, "Did not Moses give you the law?" — with no hint of mere Mosaic "germs" being later "developed" by unknowns! In another place He replies, *"Moses said:* Honour thy father and thy mother"; which attributes at least one (and by implication all) of the Ten Commandments to the actual Moses. And so we might go on.

Similarly, our Lord endorses the commonly accepted *authorships* of the Old Testament. See John 5:46, which says, "Had ye believed Moses, ye would have believed me: for he wrote of me." Mark the distinction which our Lord makes between what He Himself *said* and what Moses *wrote:* "If ye believe not his writings, how shall ye believe my words?" So our Lord does not mean mere traditional sayings of Moses, recorded by later anonymities, but the actual "writings" of Moses himself. And which were they? Our Lord's hearers knew perfectly well (so do you and I) that He meant the Pentateuch.

The critic says that the Pentateuch is a composite product of *various* writers and redactors. Scholarly analysis is supposed to have revealed that Exodus 20:12 and 21:17, and Leviticus 20:9 are fragments from three different authors; yet our Lord covers all three by *"Moses* said . . . " (Mark 7:10).

Take just one more instance, this time the *Davidic* authorship of Psalm 110. According to experts of a certain kind, that psalm was written as late as the time of the Maccabees, and is a eulogy of Simon on his victory in 142 B.C. Others, who permit it to be preexilic make it the product of some prophet much later than David's time. But what says our Lord? In Matthew 22:43, He asks the Pharisees, "How then doth *David* in the Spirit call him [the Messiah] Lord, saying [in Ps. 110:1], The Lord [Jehovah] said unto my Lord [i.e., the Messiah], Sit Thou on my right hand, Till I make thine enemies thy footstool?" In this one reference our Lord "overthrows the tables" of our newfangled Biblechangers; for all in one He ousts their distinguishing set of ideas concerning Holy Writ. First, He acknowledges the presence of *supernatural prediction,* i.e., David's writing of something over a thousand years in advance. Second, He acknowledges direct and special *divine inspiration,* i.e., that David wrote "in the Spirit." Third, He acknowledges in the Psalms the *Messianic element,* i.e., that David was writing of the coming Christ. Fourth, He plainly endorses the *Davidic authorship* of the psalm.

Truly, it is Christ versus modern critics rather than Christ versus old-time Pharisees, for on all those four points the Pharisees concurred with Him. Indeed, as has been aptly observed, if Psalm 110 was a composition dating only from the Maccabean period, some of our Lord's learned hearers would immediately have said, "It is not David at all who speaks in that psalm; it was written about Simon the Maccabee whom our fathers' grandsires saw as boys."

Do we need add other examples? Is it not clear that our Lord, in His repeated use of the Old Testament, always refers to it in suchwise as to endorse it?

3. *Inspiration, Unique, Verbal, Total*

Thirdly, our Lord endorses the inspiration of the Old Testament as being (a) unique, (b) verbal, (c) total.

To Him it is no mere inspiration in the vernacular sense, a so-called "inspiration" which is merely an extravagant name for human genius or emotion or achievement. It is the supernatural activity of the divine Spirit, through selected human persons, for the purpose of special revelation. It is an inspiration which lifts the Scriptures above all other writings and gives them an authority found nowhere else. While He admits no binding authority in the "traditions of the Elders," the word of Scripture itself is final. When He clashes with Pharisees and Sadducees, the Scriptures are the true test of doctrinal soundness, and He admits no appeal beyond them. Surely, to ascribe such superhuman and final authority to the Scriptures implies their divine inspiration.

Let just one or two of His comments represent all the others. Mark 7:8, 9, 13 says, "Laying aside the commandment of *God,* ye hold the tradition of men. . . . Full well ye reject the commandment of *God.* . . . Making the word of *God* of none effect through your tradition." Can such phraseology mean less than divine inspiration? See also, in John 10:34-36, the passage that says, "the word of *God* . . . the scripture *cannot be broken.*" Or again read in Matthew 5:18, "Till heaven and earth pass, one jot or one tittle shall in no wise pass from the law, till all be fulfilled." Could such imperishability and inviolability be claimed for writings less than divinely inspired?

Beyond dispute, also, our Lord amply indicates His belief that the inspiration of the Old Testament is *verbal.* Right at the beginning of His ministry He repulses the Tempter by that thrice-uttered,

"It is *written*," indicating that the words as well as the substance are important to Him; and it is arresting that the first "It is written" of the trio is, "Man shall not live by bread alone, but by *every word* that proceedeth out of the mouth of God." Nor is it without significance that in His first-recorded public discourse He declares that not "*one jot or tittle*" of that written Word should pass away. In Matthew 22:31, 32, He makes the crux of His argument the *tense* of the verb in Exodus 3:6, "I *am*," not "was." In quoting Psalm 110:1, He puzzles the Pharisees with the little word "my" (i.e., "The Lord said unto *my* Lord"); and in the Hebrew the possessive "my" is simply a Yod, the smallest letter of the alphabet. Certainly that is exegesis based on *verbal* inspiration!

Again, when He makes His triumphal entry into Jerusalem, see how careful He is to fulfill Zechariah 9:9 to the very word — "riding upon an ass, and upon a colt the foal of an ass." Or, further, note how He picks on the words of Jonah 1:17, "three days and three nights," as an exact type of His own burial. So we might go on. This, that, and the other quotation all show the same thing, namely, that our Lord believed the Old Testament to be inspired not only in its *thoughts* (as many today suppose, more or less loosely) but in the very *words* which express the truth.

To crown all this, our Lord bears clear witness that the inspiration of the Old Testament, besides being unique and verbal, is *total*. According to many teachers in the churches today, parts of the Old Testament may be inspired, but not all. According to others, who do not like to commit themselves to such a hard and fast differentiation, it is all more or less generally inspired, only the *quality* of inspiration varies. They speak about "degrees" of inspiration, and "qualitative" inspiration. They tell us that in some Old Testament writings the "supernatural element" is at "maximum" and in others at "minimum." Their powers of discrimination and evaluation are highly developed, no doubt, but the fact is, that although they retain the word "inspiration," they drain away its vital meaning.

Now our Lord Himself knows nothing of this intermittent or variable inspiration. To Him the Old Testament is a unity. He quotes from its different parts with equal deference and equal confidence, which He would not do if its trustworthiness were irregular. In the examples we have given, it will be seen that He quotes from all of the main book-groupings of the Old Testament. And in each instance He does so in a manner which betokens His own unqualified endorsement. Let this be duly weighed by all who would call Jesus "Lord."

As is well known, the Jews of our Lord's time already classified the Old Testament Scriptures into "The Law" *(Torah)*, "The Prophets" *(Nebhiim)*, and "The Psalms," or "The Writings" *(Kethubhim)*. Some of our Lord's utterances about the Old Testament actually particularize it into those three parts and are significant indeed as showing that He puts all three parts on the same level of inspiration and sacredness.

Take the following two pronouncements, the one at the beginning and the other at the end of our Lord's earthly ministry. "Think not that I am come to destroy the *law*, or the *prophets:* I am not come to destroy, but to fulfill. For verily I say unto you, Till heaven and earth pass, one jot or one tittle shall in no wise pass from the law, till *all* be fulfilled" (Matt. 5:17, 18). Here there is reference to two of the main parts of the Old Testament. They are acknowledged as different parts, but not as different in inspiration or authority. Our Lord singles out the Law for special mention because He is about to quote from several parts of it; and there is no doubt that by the "law" He means the whole Pentateuch. Note His reference to it in a total sense: "till *all* be fulfilled." If it should be said that the "law" here means the economy itself, but not the written Pentateuch, the reply is that we know nothing of that economy except through the written record. The economy and the written record are inseparable. To the Jews the "Law" was that which was *written;* and our Lord confirms its divine origin in total.

Now turn to Luke 24:44. Here are words spoken by our Lord after His resurrection. If there were limits to His knowledge *before* His resurrection (as some would tell us), they were certainly discarded *after* He was risen. What, then, does the *risen* Christ say about the Old Testament? He says, "These are the words which I spake unto you, while I was yet with you, that all things must be fulfilled, which were written in *the law* of Moses, and in *the prophets,* and in the *psalms,* concerning me" (my italics).

At once we notice that it is "all things . . . which were *written*"; so it is the actual writings to which Jesus refers. Next we observe that all three parts of the Old Testament are mentioned by name, yet are treated as three equally sacred parts of the triune whole. We note further that in all three parts there is the Messianic and prophetic element — "all things . . . which were written . . . concerning *me*." The predictive element is always an unmistakable seal of divine inspiration. Notice now the word "must" — "all things *must* be fulfilled." Why is there that "must"? Because the law and the prophets and the Psalms are alike of divine origin, and therefore cannot possibly be in error. If such words as these of the risen Christ are not a seal upon the inspiration of the Old Testament in total, what words ever could be?

We might turn to still further examples, but do we need? Those already cited amply establish that our Lord considered the inspiration of the Old Testament to be not only unique and verbal, but total. It has been truly observed that almost *any* reference of our Lord to the Old Testament will support the statement that He regards the old dispensation and its Scriptures as being entirely from God. The impression left on any unprejudiced mind by the manner and frequency of our Lord's Old Testament citations is that they are simply specimens of a book in which God is regarded as speaking throughout.

Surely, even though our treatment of the subject is a mere skimming, it is enough to substantiate our three propositions concerning Christ and the Old Testament, namely, that He continually quoted it but never once queried it; that He always quoted it so as to endorse it; and that He endorsed the *whole* of it as being indeed *the inspired Word of God.*

This clearness of our Lord's witness to the Old Testament may be most inconvenient, even irritating, to those professedly Christian intellectuals who are *determined* to be liberalists in their attitude to those Scriptures. Such brethren, however, cannot do away with that witness or honorably circumvent it. Yet if they reject it, neither can they *genuinely* call Jesus "*LORD*."

ately identify them, or even to realize that they differ. My method follows the common procedure, with some modifications suggested by the need of preserving the historical order, and by the fact that few of my readers are trained experts, and that the materials submitted are necessarily limited.
OUR BIBLE: CRITICAL TACTICS

What an abuse of our Redeemer, that His pretended messengers should make Him seem to judge quite contrary to His holiness and to His law!

For a man, in the name of a minister of the Gospel, to cheat men into such undervaluings and neglects [of His Word] as are likely to prove their condemnation, what is this but to play the minister of Satan, and to work his work in the name and garb of a minister of Christ?

Oh, dreadful reckoning to these unfaithful shepherds when they must answer for the ruin of their miserable flocks!"

Richard Baxter

OUR BIBLE: CRITICAL TACTICS

Brethren, according to the data, our Lord's witness to the inspiration of the Old Testament is clear, full, unmistakable, and I wish we could leave the matter there. We cannot, however, for our latter-day rationalist critics strain to invalidate our Lord's witness by resorting to the three subterfuges which we mentioned earlier.

The first of these three is the *kenosis* theory, which argues that our Lord, in His incarnation, "emptied himself" (Phil. 2:7) in such a way as made Him entirely subject to the ordinary conditions of our fallible humanity, including that which makes our growth in knowledge gradual and limited. "Can we seriously maintain," it is asked, "that as a child He possessed knowledge surpassing that of learned adults on questions of Old Testament authorships?"

We ourselves would be the first to acknowledge that the whole subject of our Lord's psychic nature during His incarnate life on earth is one of delicate mystery. Yet because all that can be known about it is derived from the New Testament, we are the more definite in denouncing that unscientific critical prejudice which would wrest all the data to fit one peculiar interpretation of just one verb in Philippians 2:7. It is a pathetic marvel that men who superciliously sneer at "verbal inspiration" should make so much of *one word* when it suits their purpose, and see in it such decisive finality! It is stranger still that men who charge Paul with making many mistakes should be so emphatic in the case of this one word that he speaks with divine authority! They remind me of drowning men who will grab at anything to keep them afloat a bit longer.

What are the real New Testament *facts?* Well, to begin with, the New Testament has its own commentary on Philippians 2:7. Paul's *ekenosen* passage (Phil. 2:5-8) is paralleled and interpreted by John's *eskenosen* passage (John 1:14-18), that is, "The Word was made flesh, and *dwelt* among us." Corresponding with Paul's definition of the preincarnate Christ as "equal with God" is John's affirmation that prior to becoming flesh "the Word was God." Then, paralleling with Paul's description of the incarnation: "He emptied Himself . . . being made in the likeness of men" is John's "And the Word was made flesh, and dwelt among us, (and we beheld his glory, the glory as of the only begotten of the Father,) full of grace and truth." Note well that the two expressions refer to our Lord *after* His incarnation —

        1. "Only begotten of the Father"
        2. "*Full* of grace and *truth*"

What John means here by "only begotten of the Father" is settled by verse 18, "The only begotten Son [many ancient authorities read: *God only begotten*], which is in the bosom of the Father." What John means by "full of grace and truth" (as shown all through his ensuing chapters) is that our Lord, *after* becoming truly human, was measurelessly above all other human beings in His mental and moral nature. The immortal third chapter of John is preceded with the explanation, "Jesus . . . *knew all men,* and needed not that any should testify of man: for he knew what was in man" (John 2: 24, 25). He not only knew what was in all men as individuals, but He knew what was in *man,* i.e., in our constitution itself. What was that but knowledge supernaturally exceeding all merely human limits? — and it was while He was in His *"kenosis"* condition!

We recall His telling the woman of Sychar all about her past; His telling the disciples that Lazarus had just died, fifty miles away; His predictions about both the near and the distant future, not to mention other such evidences of knowledge transcending all normal human limits. We remember, too, His repeated assumption of the Jehovistic *"I AM,"* and His august asseveration, "I am *THE TRUTH,"* and His tremendous assertion, "Heaven and earth shall pass away, but my words shall not pass away." Can we honestly think that He, the incarnate divine *TRUTH,* was self-deceived, fallible, even gullible, as the *kenosis* theorizers aver? — that He could make all sorts of slips and mistakes about the Old Testament? To say that our Lord's knowledge "did not necessarily extend to questions of literary criticism" is simply throwing dust into the air to avoid the real issue. If our Lord had expressed His verdicts on the Old Testament in terms of literary criticism, denoting that His views were nothing more than conclusions reached by scholarly reasoning, then we would have known that there certainly *were* limits to His knowledge!

What if we now turn to Philippians 2:5-8, and see that "kenosis" verb in its immediate context?

> Who, though he was in the form [*morphe*] of God . . . emptied himself, taking the form [*morphe*] of a servant (RSV).

Surely our interpretation of that verb "emptied" must be determined by the significant double occurrence of the word "form" (*morphe*) just before it and just after it, as if to guard it from possible misunderstanding. According to the lexicon, *morphe* means "form, shape, figure, appearance." It has nothing to do with the nature or the *essence* of our Lord's deity or of His humanity. That unsurpassed Pauline scholar, Bishop Lightfoot, has aptly given the sense: "He emptied Himself, stripped Himself, of the *insignia* of His majesty."

The more one reflects upon it, the more absurdly impossible does it become to suppose that our Lord could have emptied Himself of what He essentially was and is. Nor could he separate Himself from His divine attributes, for they are *involved* in His divine being. He may have suspended the *activity* of certain attributes in some directions during His earthly life, but that He could exist apart from them is unthinkable.

As for those two comments of Luke, "And the child grew, and waxed strong in spirit, filled with wisdom" (2:40); "And Jesus increased in wisdom and stature" (52), they lend no support at all to the liberalist "kenosis" error. On the contrary they indicate a special *filling* with "wisdom," not an emptying down to ordinary human level; and midway between them we find the Jerusalem doctors of learning "astonished at his understanding" (47). Although we cannot probe the mystery inhering in the statement that the youthful Jesus "increased in wisdom," we can at least sense that in the divine-human duality of His mental nature it was the human in Him which thus developed, while all the time the divine personality in Him was carried through the successive stages of the human development, thus gathering round itself the ordinary accessions and experiences of the sons of men.

But even if for argument's sake we were momentarily to grant the "*kenosis*" theorizers those few extra texts which they have wishfully overstressed, would even that give them any mentionable support? No; for even as man our Lord was extraordinarily *anointed by the Holy Spirit*. That supernatural anointing began at His baptism in the Jordan, when the Spirit descended and "abode upon Him." "Jesus being full of the Holy Ghost . . . " (Luke 4:1). "Jesus returned in the *power* of the Spirit . . . " (14). "The Spirit of the Lord is *upon* me" (18). "I cast out demons by the Spirit of God" (Matt. 12:28). "God giveth not the Spirit by measure unto him" (John 3:34). "The Father is in me, and I in Him" (10:38).

"Until the day in which he was taken up, after that he *through the Holy Spirit* had given commandments . . ." (Acts 1:2).

Nor is it a matter only of those verses which directly mention the fact that our Lord spoke and acted under such unique monopoly by the Holy Spirit; the implications of it meet us everywhere. "How knoweth this man letters, having never learned?" (John 7:15). "Never man spake like this man" (John 7:46). All such incidentals press us to the same conclusion. Instead of limitedness there is unlimitedness. Instead of an "emptying" there is a divine filling. Instead of the liberalist *"kenosis"* fiction there is a divine *"pleroma"* — a Christ who is "the fulness of the Godhead bodily" (Col. 1: 19; 2:3, 9).

Accommodation Theory

The *"kenosis"* theory, however, although a favorite of those who desupernaturalize the Scriptures, is only one of their expedients. Checked at one point, they adeptly resort to another, with never an admission of refutation. For as we surely know well enough by now, religious "modernism" in its successive guises is not merely any one school or phase or theory; it is a disposition, a spirit, a set attitude of mind against the supernatural in Christianity. Pride of learning mixed with jealous antisupernaturalist prejudice incapacitates the mind any longer to evaluate evidence logically. What if the *"kenosis"* fabrication crumples before strict exegesis? Why, just this: Jesus, in His confirmations of the Old Testament and of current belief in its inspiration, was simply *accommodating* Himself — quite allowably so, to the cherished suppositions and gullible mentality of His times. It did no real harm; indeed it was necessary in order to expedite rapport with the people.

Such insinuation is horrible insult to the stainless character and guileless motive of the incarnate Son! Furthermore, it is the diametric opposite of all the evidence. Right from the beginning (Matt. 5) when our Master challenged the Jewish oral law by His, "Ye have heard that it was said . . . but *I* say unto you," He ran perilously counter to popular concepts. Right from that first startling shock, "Except your righteousness shall exceed the righteousness of the scribes and Pharisees . . ." He was knowingly the target of top-level animosity. His beneficent but misunderstood contacts with the hated "tax-collectors and sinners" were unapologetically offensive to the conventional morality of that old-time Jewry. The liberties He took with the Sabbath (as He well knew) outraged the narrow formalism of the powerful Pharisees. Yet equally He disappointed those on the lower social stratum who hoped, perhaps, that He would yield them some laxity in His doctrine; for His uncompromising word to them was, "Think not that I am come to destroy the law, or the prophets." His amazing miracles certainly drew huge crowds, while the originality, intuitiveness, independence, authority, of His teaching held them in wonder. Yet His teaching as to the long-hoped-for Messianic kingdom was so spiritual, so ethically demanding, that it rebuked rather than gratified the popular clamor and drove away the more worldly-minded.

Long enough before His final visit to Jerusalem for the Passover observance, He had knowingly incurred the scheming wrath of the Sanhedrin, the Sadducees, the Pharisees, the Herodians, the scribes, the priests; yet it was on that last and tragic visit that He flung down the tables of the moneychangers and the seats of the dove vendors in the temple! It was then, also, that He uttered His scathing indictment: "Woe unto you, scribes and Pharisees, *hypocrites* . . . " Indeed, so outspoken was our Lord that He has been mistakenly charged with purposely aggravating the Jewish leaders to perpetrate the awful crime of His Calvary murder out of their personal resentment.

Yet with all this evidence of our Lord's uncompromising loyalty to the truth, despite bitterest consequences for Himself personally, our present-day Bible scholars of a sort try to make out that He "accommodated" His teachings to the popular fallacies of the day! What casuistry will antisupernaturalist prejudice employ! If there is one thing clearer than another about our Lord's repeated testimonials to the integrity and inspiration of the Old Testament, it is this, that His words are not those of a sycophantic savant or thaumaturge itching after the public ear, but the voice of utter honesty, speaking out of absolute knowledge.

Faulty Record Theory

But, as you know, the deadliest of all the modernist makeshifts to discredit our Lord's testimony is the *faulty record* theory; and by it, more than by anything else, modernism in its successive attires stands self-branded as intransigent unbelief masquerading as biblical scholarship. According to the late professor T. K. Cheyne of Oxford, Eichorn was "the founder of modern Old Testament criticism." Eichorn's greatest pupil was Ewald, who was more piercing in his criticisms. Ewald's greatest pupil was Wellhausen, who with brilliant daring pushed Ewald's principles to their logical rationalism.

The newfangled Bible scholarship which Eichorn christened "the Higher Criticism," despite seemingly innocuous beginnings, does indeed lead just there — to rationalism and an outright denial of supernatural revelation. Although the original purpose of the higher criticism was ostensibly to "remove the difficulties which the historic view of inspiration" supposedly creates, the history of the movement has more and more exposed it as a developing skeptical crusade against the supernatural in the Bible. In this ever-bolder campaign to desupernaturalize the Bible, the supreme target is the incarnate deity and infallibility of our divine Lord. The *kenosis* theory, even stretched to its utmost, cannot entirely negate His witness to the Old Testament and to God, nor can its doubtful ally, the *accommodation* theory. If the authority of our Lord's teaching is to be irrecoverably broken, then the very *record* of it in the four Gospels must be impugned and discredited — *which is to destroy Christianity itself.*

Thus, at the beginning of our twentieth century, Professor Cheyne of Oxford, the English Wellhausen, was already telling the British public, in his *Encyclopaedia Biblica,* that the four Gospels were now provenly untrustworthy records.

> Several of the reported sayings of Jesus clearly bear the impress of a time which he did not live to see (136).
>
> The conclusion is inevitable that even the one Evangelist whose story in any particular case involves less of the supernatural than that of the others, is still very far from being entitled on that account to claim implicit acceptance of his narrative (137).
>
> With reference to the resurrection of Jesus . . . the appearance in Jerusalem to the two women is almost universally given up. . . . The statements as to the empty sepulchre are to be rejected (138).
>
> As for the feeding of the five thousand and the four thousand, so also for the withering of the fig tree, we still possess a clue to the way in which the narrative arose out of a parable (142).
>
> It is very conceivable that a preacher on the death of Jesus may have said, purely figuratively, that then was the veil of the temple rent in twain.
>
> We must endeavour to ascertain how many, and still more what sorts of cures were affected by Jesus. It is quite possible for us to regard as historical only those of the class which

even at the present day physicians are able to affect by psychical methods — as more especially cures of mental maladies. It is not at all difficult to understand how the contemporaries of Jesus, after seeing some wonderful deed or deeds wrought by him which they regarded as miracles, should have credited him with every other kind of miraculous power without distinguishing, as the modern mind does, between those maladies which are amenable to psychical influences and those which are not. It is also necessary to bear in mind that the cure may often have been only temporary (144).

Cheyne even raises the question "Whether any credible elements are to be found in the Gospels at all"! With intellectual magnanimity he manages to salvage nine! During the past fifty years the drive and havoc of the movement have developed into an apostasy the like of which Anno Domino history never knew before. The theological rationalism which had gotten its stranglehold on the religious life of Germany by the beginning of the nineteenth century is now the ubiquitous skepticism which has well nigh ruined Protestant witness, has permeated nearly all our universities, and has vitiated the whole of Christendom.

It is truly said that every kind of attack which worldly infidelity ever hurled against the Bible has now been utilized by men who profess themselves Christian scholars and leaders; and with fatuous irony, as they tear away the very vitals of the true Christian faith, they boast of making Christianity acceptable to the modern mind! Of course, there are varying shades and grades of this skepticism found throughout the larger Protestant denominations, but a typical attitude of the academic modernist toward all such miracles as the Virgin Birth and our Lord's bodily resurrection is the utterly illogical one: "No amount of human testimony could ever avail to accredit such a miracle: therefore I reject it." And a common attitude toward our Lord Himself is: "Only a Christ from whom all supernatural traits are stripped off can be accepted as historical by the 'modern' mind."

Was it ever truer that "a lie travels half way round the world while truth is putting on her boots"? How little does the public at large know the findings of *truer* scholarship as to the veracity of the four Gospels? Even more than the Pentateuch, the four Gospels have been concentratedly scrutinized, tested, sifted. Their rabid ill-treatment by prejudiced higher criticism has provoked a far sounder scholarship to arise in their defense. It is no exaggeration to say that in the light of scholarship equal if not superior to that of the rationalists, the four Gospels have emerged as pure gold tested by fire. We are no longer hoodwinked by the jibe that conservative scholars hold a cherished view of the New Testament without critical investigation. It is the conservative scholars now who know both sides so well as to be able to vindicate the one and to decimate the other, while those of the antisupernaturalist scholarship, once "drunk with the vintage of its own conceit," now sit among the *disjecta membra* of their miscritical speculations and casuistries, only too willing to ignore the erudite conservative answers which have floored them.

I suppose there are half-a-dozen theories or more as to the literary origin of the four Gospels: (1) *mutual dependence*, each one furnishing material for the others; (2) the *documentary theory*, or origin in Greek documents; (3) an original *Aramaic document*; (4) the priority of *Mark* or Mark and a hypothetical Q; (5) an original *oral* Gospel; (6) the *synchronous reporting* of the Master's sayings and doings by the disciples while on travel with Him. But by whichever process they originated, they have enough surface difference to indicate four independent authorships, while at the same time they reveal such basic unity and such fourfold complimentariness as to settle it that they are genuine presentations of the one wonderful Lord Jesus Christ. The truth is, that with obvious naturalness Matthew, Mark, Luke, and John have given us four unique presentations of our Lord Jesus, each having its own aspective emphasis, each being from a point of view peculiar to itself, each being in a real sense complete in itself, yet all four going completively together to make the full portrayal of the God-Man whom the Spirit of inspiration purposes to set before us. One feels pity for those self-blinded "scholars" who miss the fascination of it all. However, the point I make here is the independence and genuineness of the Gospel records, plus this accompanying fact, that although everything in them has been subjected to lynx-eyed scrutiny, although this, that, and the other in them has now been doubted, questioned, resented, denied, *not one single part has ever yet been actually disproved!*

Meanwhile, in addition to an ample refutation of the unevangelical critics by textual, historical, and apologetic scholarship of the conservative school, a flood of archaeological discovery and information has poured in, giving wonderful new verifications of the Gospel narratives. Before that weighty theological thinker Benjamin B. Warfield passed on, only a few decades ago, he was able to write: "Every critical student knows that the process of investigation has been a continuous process of removing difficulties until scarcely a shred of the old list of supposed 'Biblical Errors' remains to hide the nakedness of [the critics'] moribund contention." If that was true then, it is more so today. The divine inspiration of the four Gospels is not the point at issue just here, but only their credibility, truthfulness, and trustworthiness; and if *anything* was ever proved, then *that* has been convincingly proved today for all who have "ears to hear."

Why, then, is it that the other ideas seem to float around so much more easily, spreading their skepticism? The main reason is that modernism in its successive forms, as we have said, is not just a school or a phase: it is a spirit, a set attitude of mind against the supernatural. I have seen men of the modernist type who when they are beaten in argument turn away in anger, determined not to accept the evangelical truth. That modernist set of mind jealously hates to admit any need for supernatural *revelation* and still more for any need of supernatural *salvation*. Alas, that seems to be the preponderating attitude among our Protestant denominational officialdoms today.

Brethren, I put it to you: the testimony of our Lord Jesus to the divine inspiration of the Old Testament is clear, full, and unanswerable. Nor can that testimony be evaded or lessened or in any way nullified by the *kenosis* theory, or by the *accommodation* theory, or by the *faulty record* theory. The critics have been well and truly answered. The records are true. The evidence is one-hundred-per-cent valid. The challenge to us ministers is that of somehow getting this over to the deluded people of our day. Soon after the Second World War, the *Manchester City News* (Oct. 3, 1947) had the following comment.

> We are alarmed at the extent to which sheer materialistic paganism has invaded every sphere of national life. The scientists who preached a godless mechanistic universe in which man was the creature of environment, as in the philosophy of Karl Marx, should have listened to Tennyson's simple warning:
>
> > Leave to thy sister when she prays
> > Her early heaven, her happy views,
> > Nor thou with shadowed doubt confuse
> > The life that leads melodious days.
>
> Not a high ideal of religion perhaps, but when it was destroyed *no new faith was given*. The devil rejoices in a vacuum; and today a faithless people are the destined prey of

any eloquent Fuhrer who comes along with alluring promises. . . . Some deep evil saps the human soul, but God in Christ offers the remedy. Only the supernatural power of a Saviour can lift us from the mire and set our feet on the path which leads from the Slough of Despond to the Land of our Dreams."

Well said, Mr. Editor. If it was clear and disturbing to you then, it is even more so to us now. Marxism and Communism could never have wished for a better ally among our Protestant officialdoms than modernism or liberalism. While communism attacks from outside, the other destroys from within. But, brethren of the evangelical faith, our Lord is "risen indeed," and the written Word "abideth for ever"! More than ever before let us speak out to re-establish the confidence of our people in the Book of Books and in the "faith once for all delivered to the saints."

OUR BIBLE: WHERE ARE WE NOW?

NOTE:

The purpose of the following review is to interpret *"now"* in the light of what *led* to it. However, to readers who are non-ministerial or who are little conversant with the changeful course of theology in Christendom during the past century, it could perhaps seem tedious in parts. Therefore we recommend such readers to postpone this chapter until the end of the book and then read it in the light of our completed argument.

The wisdom of this world must not be magnified against the wisdom of God. Human philosophy must be taught to stoop and serve, while Scripture (as the very Word of God Himself) doth bear the chief sway.

Take heed, therefore, brethren, for the enemy hath a special eye upon you. As wise and learned as you are, take heed to yourselves lest he outwit you. *The devil is a greater scholar than you.*

Richard Baxter

OUR BIBLE: WHERE ARE WE NOW?

During the past eighty years, perhaps as never before, Protestant theology has been characterized by fluidity, indefiniteness, and drift from its former biblicism. Never before, so it would seem, has there been such fateful interplay between human philosophy, natural science, critical scholarship, and Christian theology. Since the New Testament canon was completed, so long ago now, have there ever been such surprise reversals of attitude toward divine revelation? Especially since the time of the First World War some of the developments have become revolutionary, not only in natural philosophy and in Christian theology, but in patterns of human behavior.

Behind the unprecedented shifting and changing there have been three main factors: (1) the influence of Kant and Hegel, (2) rationalistic higher criticism, (3) the Darwin-originated evolution theory, accompanied by the Spencerian synthetic philosophy of mechanistic progress. At times Protestant theology has seemed near chaos. For a spell the "neo-orthodoxy" galvanized it into new vivacity and relevance; but Karl Barth is now gone, and his "new supernaturalism" seems to have tiptoed in melancholy decrepitude to the grave with him.

Are we now at a point where we can look back and see more clearly than ever what happens when we force the biblical revelation to fit human reason, scholarship, and science, instead of letting the biblical revelation be our test of *them?* When the sun is forced to swing around the planets, instead of the planets round the sun, can there be anything but eccentric chaos? As we look back, what are the salient features?

From Schleirmacher, at the beginning of the nineteenth century, on through Ritschl, toward the end of it, the new trend became increasingly distinct, under the influence of Kant and Hegel, i.e., the trend to move Christian theology away from purely biblical foundations. The Hegel-minded broke from the *finality* of the biblical revelation; the Kant-minded disallowed the *possibility* of it. Instead of interpreting God, man, and the world according to the Bible, Christian theology now increasingly judged the Bible itself in subordination to critical philosophy.

Traveling *pari passu* with that was the new, so-called "higher criticism," with its rationalistic re-evaluation of Scripture, its rejection of miracle, its denial of inerrancy, its exposure of supposed error in the Bible, its rearranging of Old Testament documents, and its desupernaturalizing of Christianity.

Another travel companion with similar features was the Darwinian evolution theory which, as the nineteenth century gave place to the twentieth, was firmly in the saddle and riding convincingly. If the radical new philosophy and radical new biblical criticism were reversing peoples' concepts of *God*, the new evolution doctrine was reversing their concept of *man*. No longer was man a direct creation of God, but the product of organic self-development from pre-existing types. Instead of a "fall" of man, as the Bible teaches, there is a long but now wonderfully accelerated *ascent* of man! Instead of "sin" and the need for redemption, there is the evolving victory of man's mighty struggle up from the brute to perpendicularity and ethicism, displaying an innate perfectibility in human nature, leading man on to his own self-achieved "perfect society."

The developing by-product of all this was Protestant theological *liberalism*, with its emphasis on "immanentism," i.e., God is everywhere in the world order, in natural law and the evolutionary process, but moving solely *within* it rather than from *above* it, and operating naturally rather than supernaturally. It was a doctrine of divine immanence which rubbed out divine *transcendence*. Indeed, under the guise of preaching a closer kinship between God and man, it lost divinity in humanity until God was only quantitatively different from man, and Christian theism became blurred almost into pantheism.

Perhaps a reminder is good now and then that evangelicals have never been opposed to investigative scholarship or to the higher criticism *per se:* but Evangelicals *are* opposed to that brand of Bible criticism which fixes its own naturalistic prejudgments as to what *can* happen and what *cannot* happen in the phenomenal universe, and then, on that *a priori* basis, decides which parts of the Bible may be accepted and which parts must be rejected. To us, frankly, that is not reverent scholarship exercised impartially upon a book which makes such claims as lift it above all other literature; it is an apparatus of religious skepticism. When a scholar starts out with the presupposition that miracle and theophany and propositional divine revelation are alike impossible, what truly scientific hermeneutics can there be? Yet that was the kind of higher criticism which developed throughout the nineteenth century.

OUR BIBLE: WHERE ARE WE NOW? 75

Eventually, with critical philosophy seemingly ousting the biblical view of God, and the higher criticism undermining the integrity of Scripture, and the champions of evolution ostensibly demonstrating a non-biblical origin of man, and liberalist theology running at their heels, the whole pressure was to secularize Christianity and base theism on philosophy rather than on the Bible.

For *evangelical* Christianity the tensions became acute, the supreme problem being how to retain an adaquate biblical authority yet admit what then appeared to be the "assured results" of higher critical scholarship and the widely proclaimed validity of evolution as the scientific truth about man. Among thoroughgoing liberalists the trend was to sweep away the miraculous entirely and transfer Christian faith from a biblical to a philosophical basis. Even old-school theologians like Augustus Hopkins Strong shifted their thinking. In his dissertation, *Christ in Creation and Ethical Monism* (1899), Strong welcomed the new idea of the divine immanence, accepted the evolutionary theory as the explanation of divine method, and endorsed the higher critical view of Scripture in considerable degree. How he thought that traditional, biblically based Christian theology could still be upheld with its foundations thus cut away is an unsolved puzzle.

It has been said that the years 1914 to 1946 (from the beginning of the First World War to the end of the Second) mark "the midnight of modern culture." But western culture has deteriorated even more since then. Also, we may well be reminded, it was during those between-war decades that classical liberalism received its deathblow; for that First World War, with its colossal butchery and educated cruelty, badly shook the liberalist gospel of inevitable human progress to a near-at-hand utopia. It was during those interwar years, too, that a new movement, the "neo-orthodoxy," broke in with surprising momentum on the gloomy scene, dealing sledge-hammer blows at humanistic liberalism, and energetically reemphasizing a return to a Bible-based theology.

Yes, "then came Karl Barth" and the "new supernaturalism." In Germany the response was almost meteoric, with powerful effects not long afterward in Britain, America, and elsewhere. It seemed a providential new vindication of the orthodox evangelical faith. Although liberalism with its humanistic theology had by then captured the controlling brains and ministries of the main Protestant denominations, the case for traditionally Protestant Christianity had been so ably defended in Britain and the U.S.A. by unsurpassed scholars like James Orr, P. T. Forsyth, Benjamin Warfield and on the European mainland by such as Bavinck, Kuyper, Lecerf that the flag of fundamental biblicism still waved too proudly for the liberalists to claim complete victory (the more so in America after the fundamentalist secession there in the early decades of our century). When the neo-orthodoxy broke in, it was like the unexpected arrival of new regiments to rescue the hard-pressed evangelical garrison and rout the renegade liberalist forces. According to philosopher Count Kyserling, Barth and Gogarten "saved the Reformation in Europe."

The impact of the neo-orthodoxy may well have seemed such a rescue, because going with the widespread loss of faith in the Bible was a sense of lost *authority*. In matters moral and spiritual the final court of appeal was gone. Yet man is so made that somehow, somewhere he must find moral sanction or "authority." If he does not find it in an infallible Bible he will seek it elsewhere. Intellect and conscience alike demand it. Between the two world wars it was becoming clear that philosophy, science, reason, evolution were not supplying any real substitute for the Bible. Not a few people were turning for refuge to the false authoritarianism of the Roman Catholic church. But among the people at large, and especially among educated thinkers, there was the feeling that Christendom as a whole was now a tottery building on a cracked foundation. Then, suddenly, the scholarly neo-orthodoxy sounded like a trumpet call to reappraisal. It seemed to say, "The foundation, after all, is safe, and the building habitable."

Synchronizing with this, the comparatively new witness of *archaeology* had now reached such dimension, confirming without exception the integrity of the biblical records, that at last, so it seemed, the overdue vindication of evangelical Christianity had come. The critical prejudice which insisted that statements in the Bible were to be doubted until verified was being reversed by palpable evidence which said, "Every statement in the Bible is valid until disproved."

Undoubtedly the neo-orthodoxy wrought a vivid change. Up to the First World War, approximately, there had been just the two main contenders: the evangelical and the liberalist. The basic split, of course, was difference of attitude to the Bible — so opposite as to be irreconcilable. There seemed no likelihood ahead but protracted war between the two when, with surprising force, the neo-orthodoxy broke the duality.

Its acquired name, "neo-orthodoxy," seemed at once to ally it with the conservative faith, and thousands of evangelical leaders hailed it in that light. It came in with new emphasis on the importance of the Bible, apparently putting the Bible back where it belonged. Against the liberalist perverted idea of divine immanence (in some writers almost pantheistic) it strongly rearticulated the divine transcendency and sovereignty. It seemed like Calvin and Luther speaking again in revised version through Barth and Brunner. Over against the "history of religion" schools with their repudiation of Reformation "miserable sinner" Christianity, and such terms as "saved" or "lost," the neo-orthodoxy reasserted that man is fallen and needing to be saved.

This scholarly new emphasis on fallen man as inherently sinful was the more salutary because it coincided with the hour of disillusionment for liberalist humanism. As already noted, the evolution theory of man's now accelerated ascent to a self-achieved utopia had been rocked by global war of such scientific cruelty as had never been before. Crime and violence were increasing just as widely as the education which was supposedly going to cure them. New political and economic ideologies which were coming in as challengers to Christianity — Fascism, Nazism, Communism — were all giving new revelation of basic depravity in man: tyrannical dictatorships with their secret police, fake justice, and elimination by organized murder or mass butchery. Marxist socialist writings were spreading, exposing corrupt money-motive underneath the supposedly objective thinking of the day. Freudian psychoanalysis was a startling new factor, ripping away the draperies of conventional cover-ups and laying bare the sordid "ego" underneath the veneer of "civilization." The gaseous balloon of earlier humanistic optimism was burst. This was the time to listen to the *neo*-orthodox reassertion of man's spiritual plight. It was just the hour to hear the neo-orthodox accent on God as the supreme Mystery-Reality known only by self-revelation; a God of utter holiness, to whom man's only way of restoration is through sovereign grace — by a bridge built from God to man, not from man to God.

It early became apparent through the writings of Barth, Brunner, and Bultmann that the movement was presenting itself as "the new Protestantism," though it later became equally clear that it was as *un*evangelical as it was antiliberalist. Evangelicals had reason enough to be grateful for its reaffirmations, i.e., the divine transcendence offsetting a false immanence; the uniqueness of the biblical revelation; the validity of Christian experience as something beyond mere psychological explanation; the sovereignty of

God — of God qualitatively distinct from man and infinitely above him; the necessity that God be self-revealed if He is to be known; the fact that such divine self-disclosure was given in Jesus Christ; and that we truly know God only by *experience*, not merely at the end of a syllogism. Yet on the other hand the neo-orthodoxy did *not* accept the older view of the Bible as the plenarily and inerrently inspired Word of God, nor would it tie itself to the biblical revelation exclusively. The Bible is not God's Word *written;* it is revelation recorded, but not indited.

Moreover, the neo-orthodoxy largely conceded the "findings" of rationalistic higher criticism and endorsed the evolutionist idea of origins. It rejected the factuality of early Genesis; it mythologized miracles and discounted vital historical events, even our Lord's bodily resurrection, as of little moment, thereby negating prime apologetics of the Christian faith. The liberalist conceit that the Genesis account of the Fall is a blend of primitive myths to explain why snakes do not have legs, why weeds grow on earth, and why human beings wear clothes is too inane to merit comment. In contrast, the neo-orthodoxy said that the fall of man is real enough; nevertheless, the Genesis story, although "theologically relevant," is definitely *not* an historical event, and so on.

Thus, much that the neo-orthodoxy at first *seemed*, it turned out *not* to be. It was another case of "The voice is Jacob's voice, but the hands are the hands of Esau." It came in like a giant warrior on behalf of Protestantism against theological liberalism, but although it had shining new armor, sword, and buckler, it was a Goliath on rubber legs which wobbled and gave way. Like the older, so-called classical liberalism which it came to answer, the neo-orthodoxy is now a spent force; a phase already slipping behind. Why? Because (as many of us think) despite its grand affirmatives it linked arms with the rationalistic higher criticism and the evolutionary explanation of things, thus refusing to build on the Bible as the *written* and infallible Word of God.

And where are we now? Protestantism is more than ever like a limping invalid. Liberalism thought the invalid needed a crutch under his left arm. Neo-orthodoxy put a crutch under his right arm. Both crutches broke under pressure, and the invalid has the staggers. He does not know how to walk firmly or where he is going. The earlier liberalism largely destroyed the reverence and deference which the public at large used to have toward God and the Bible. The neo-orthodoxy has failed to restore it. Again, *why?* It is because, if the Bible is not the provenly genuine and authoritative Word of God, we do *not* have real or saving *certainty* — about God, about man, about morals, about origins, about the future of our race, or about human destiny beyond the grave; we are merely guessing and groping.

What does the "man in the street" care about the continuous wranglings of philosophies and theologies up there among the clouds of lofty debate if the Book on which alone Christianity can be rebuilt is fallacious and untrustworthy? Neither liberalism nor neo-orthodoxy have had a saving message, clear and sure, for the God-conscious, sin-conscious average man.

The liberalists so occupied themselves with "the Jesus of history" that they lost the Christ who is the incarnate Infinite. The neo-orthodox so concentrated on the Christ who is the superphenomenal Infinite that the historical Jesus-event and such questions as the reliability of the Gospel narratives were matters of comparatively small incidence. In both attitudes we see the lingering influence of Kant with his sheer chasm between the phenomenal world which *can* be known and the beyond-phenomenal which *cannot* be known. If Jesus is really historical (says the liberalist), He simply cannot be divine in the ultimate sense, but only in the sense that *all* are divine. If, on the other hand, He is the absolutely divine (as the neo-orthodox says) then the effort to "explain" Him in terms of history is futile.

But if the New Testament documents are provenly genuine (*everything* depends on that), why let Kant drown out what Jesus claimed and taught? Did Kant or anyone else ever make the claims or evince the direct metaphysical knowledge that Jesus did? Have the Gospel *records* of what Jesus claimed and taught ever yet been disproved? (Have we not seen the critics successively disprove each other?) And even if, as Kant said, reason operates only in the realm of phenomena, does that render impossible a sovereign breakthrough of divine self-revelation from the *above-reason* to the lower *within* reason in terms which rational human creatures can understand? Unless we deny outright that God is personal, such revelation is possible, thinkable, probable. And, in our human realm of reason, is not the deciding factor valid *evidence* for such revelation? Must we make reason itself and our basic ability to recognize evidence an illusion? Then Kant himself is an illusion.

It is a settled conviction in my own mind that however brilliant, profound, or theoretically persuasive any philosophy may be, if it contradicts the native, basic, constitutional common sense of our very humanhood, it is somewhere fallacious. God never put His human creatures at the mercy of the abstrusely profound few! In any case, Kant's underlying prejudice that God is beyond the grasp of human concepts is itself highly vulnerable. Admittedly, we do not vitally "know" except by *experience,* as Kant and latter-day existentialists have stressed, but "experience" covers intellect as well as emotion. There *can* be intellectual grasp of objectively revealed truth through reason. In the case of divine self-revelation, a grasp of revealed truth through one's reason and the experience of it subjectively or "existentially" are meant to go together, so that truth becomes *saving* truth. The Lord Jesus Christ of the Bible is the divine in self-revelation. To the open-minded the evidence is clear, valid, full. He is neither the all-human of the liberalist nor the superphenomenal of the neo-orthodox. The Jesus Christ of the New Testament who is the object of saving faith is the uncreatedly divine who became the incarnatedly human; the divine-human Revealer-Redeemer.

As we look back on the succession of liberalist books during the earlier decades of our century, all engaged in what was called "the search for the real Jesus," we see how fantastic that "search" was. They never did find the real Jesus! How could they, if they did not accept the New Testament records as having the veracity which belongs to God-inspired writings? The vague figure they abstracted was a Jesus almost unrecognizably reconstructed to fit liberalist presuppositions. Indeed, they gave us not just *one* "historical Jesus" but *many,* with such contradictions between them that the only thing they had in common was their common rejection of the full New Testament data. Never before had such adulations been heaped upon Jesus as "the highest and completest person" who ever lived, the "completely normal human person," the supreme "religious genius," the one in whom "the Eternal has spoken," and so on. No praise seemed too high, so long as He did not have to be *worshiped.*

But the various representations of Him as the revolutionary, the communist, the pacifist, the bourgeois, even the Aryan and the Unitarian, etc., reached a point where "the search for the real Jesus" lost Him altogether. The desupernaturalizing higher and lower criticism, which was the liberalist's weapon, turned in upon himself; for liberalist Walter Marshall Horton in his *Our Eternal Contemporary* (1943) openly charged that the Jesus of the liberals had now become "irretrievably condemned by New Testament criticism as a spurious modernization which falsifies the Great Master it purports to represent." Thus was liberalism condemned by liberalism!

The liberalist dilemma was twofold. Those who accepted the Gospel records in fuller degree simply could not disunite Jesus from the supernatural, which they fain would have done. On the other hand, the larger number who took the more radical higher critical position gave us a more or less substitute Jesus. With such critical prejudgments as to the biblical documents, how on earth could any such "search for the real Jesus" end in any other way than finding the *wrong* Jesus? To some of us it seems like trying to find the noonday sun in a cloudless sky by using a microscope — and even then a microscope with a cracked lens. Although later the neo-orthodoxy repudiated liberalism it nevertheless clung to the radical higher critical view of Scripture; and it is scarcely surprising, therefore, to find Barth and Bultmann speaking of the historical Jesus as an "elusive figure" about whom "almost nothing can be known."

But we are asking: Where are we now, in this post-Barth juncture? Have we not seen demonstrated again that everything truly evangelical depends on our "Yes" or "No" to the authentic divine inspiration and uncontradictable authority of the Bible? Yet our Protestant officialdoms in general still have not learned. Up and down our Protestant seminaries and ministries we find the outdated and oft-refuted Wellhausen and "history of religion" ideas about the Bible still in vogue. Much in the Bible is untrue (so it is said) but it contains a "theological" or a "spiritual" value. Many denominational leaders and ministers have become ideologically pink, and are equating the kingdom of God with Socialism or a mild form of Communism. That is where the liberalist "social gospel" has landed them. Soon after our century came in, the famed psychologist William James spoke of the effects produced by liberalism:

> We now have whole congregations whose preachers, far from magnifying our consciousness of sin, seem devoted rather to making little of it. They ignore or even deny eternal punishment, and insist on the dignity rather than on the depravity of man. They look at the continual preoccupation of the old-fashioned Christian with the salvation of his soul as something sickly and reprehensible rather than admirable.

If that was true then, how multipliedly so now! Our *neo-liberalists* are still flirting with philosophies which seek to explain human existence on non-biblical premises. Their Bible has no real authority and therefore cannot be a sure basis. Moreover, since this attitude is widespread, it opens the door to strange ministerial compromises and unprecedented excesses which newsmen exploit for lurid publicity, to the shameful hurt of the Church as a whole: Christian ministers openly condoning sexual permissiveness instead of recalling our people to New Testament standards; publicly siding with the use of psychedelic drugs, marrying nude couples, even joining in wedlock pairs of homosexuals in "the Name which is above every name"! Heaven forbid! What next?

That breaking down of public faith in the Bible, the destructive process which began with the radical higher criticism of eighty and more years ago later known as "modernism," has eventually brought upon us a resultant *moral* breakdown which has now reached epidemic disaster-point. Standards of decency long honored are ripped down. Vulgarity is unapologetically obtrusive everywhere. Objective moral authority is gone, since there can be no substitute for the Bible as the written Word of God. In much modern thinking, if man is in any way still responsible, it is only to himself. There is ethical chaos. Morals are at best relative only. Christian chastity and wedlock are labeled "puritanical" by the many. Sexual promiscuity is bringing Sodom back in huge dimension, which means that judgment will not tarry much longer. The powers of evil capitalize on the vacuum caused by destroyed faith in the Bible. Our universities are telling the nation's youth that man is the product of impersonal force plus time plus chance. Human beings are accidents of nature in an existence which has no real purpose or dignity. Even our freedom to make choices is illusory; we are completely under the ever onmoving control of psychological and chemical processes. The philosophy classes of colleges and universities which were originally founded and financed to develop Christian learning and character are now turning out atheists and agnostics galore. Only recently I talked with a man in his thirties who told me he was one of eight young men who had all professed conversion to Christ in earlier years, had all met in the same university philosophy course, and had all come out convinced atheists.

Underneath all the more obvious contributories to the present debacle, the *basic* cause is the latter-day Protestant betrayal of the Bible, with consequent public breakdown of *faith* in the Bible and an increasing breakaway from the *teachings* of the Bible. Today we are witnessing a large-scale tragedy too strange and sad for words. Nations which, during the past three centuries, have become the most advanced and prosperous nations on earth through embracing the true Protestant faith are now falling behind through forsaking it. The loud, loud call of the hour is *Back to the Bible!* Only when that dear old Book is put back where it rightly belongs in the life of the nation will rescue and recovery come. Only when our Protestant denominations reavow their faith in the Bible as indeed the written Word of God will shorn Samson recover strength to pull down Philistine Satan's citadels of social evil, and recapture the respect of our people.

I find rather boring the dismal cliché that today we are witnessing the disintegration of Christianity and the incoming of the "post-Christian era." True Christianity is as indestructible as its divine Author. I verily believe that if there were a commensurate return to the Bible on the part of Protestant leadership and ministry there might well break upon us a *new* Christian era. What we are seeing today is not the demise of true Christianity, but the pathetic failure of an *apostate form* of it. That professedly modernized but apostate form of Christianity has for some time now found its main voice through the World Council of Churches and the accompanying ecumenical movement. To my own mind, the World Council of Churches is an elaborate attempt to dress up a corpse, or a grandiose façade to cover up dry rot and spiritual sterility. The only true life and power of the Christian Church is the supernatural flame of Pentecost which burns through it. Not even the most imposing organizational edifice can be a substitute for *that*. Our ecumenicals, who in general seem far more disturbed about denominational plurality than about unfaithfulness to clear biblical doctrine, may keep telling us to reunite because "unity is strength," but they seem strangely blind to the big difference between vital *unity* and an externally superimposed *union* merely. In itself, no such union is a cure for disease, least of all when it is a combine of cripples and crutches.

There are enough statistics available now to show us that the various denominational fusions already effected have *not* brought spiritual or even numerical increase. The results have been disconcertingly otherwise. It is the *evangelical* churches which are showing dynamic initiative and increase, despite the now widespread confusion of the public mind (thanks to liberalism) as to what Christianity really is. This may be seen not only in yearbook figures but in less tabular ways.

Yes, the voice of the hour is *Back to the Bible!* Millions of people, so I believe, are longing to be shown sure stepping stones from the quagmire of existentialism which leave life minus God and meaning. What would happen if no person anywhere in America could go to a Protestant church without hearing the true gospel preached by a man believing in the Bible as the written Word of God and speaking under the compulsion of the Holy Spirit? It is not merely a "new vocabulary" we are needing (as some continually harp) but the soul-saving, evangelical *truth* based on an infallible Bible, and preached in the power of the Holy Spirit. If only that were what all our churches were providing, there might well ensue the most spacious and transforming Christian resurgence in centuries.

Back to the Bible! Does not the enduring old Book give us more than ample reason? After all the superior snobbery of a scholarly intellectuality which presumed to "know better" than revealed truth, the Bible is still here, as unapologetically and authenticatedly as ever. It weathers the blasts, outlives its critics, survives all changes, and is always one step ahead of the latest scientific findings. But what of those who looked like dethroning it during the latter half of the nineteenth century and the first half of the twentieth? At the beginning of this article we mentioned three main factors in the deterioration of Protestant Christendom: (1) the influence of Kant and Hegel, (2) rationalistic higher criticism, (3) the Darwin-originated evolution vagary. Do those three merit confidence today? Even apart from the *moral* degradation to which they have eventually brought us through turning millions away from the Bible, are they still worthy of *intellectual* homage?

As for Kant and Hegel, far ampler minds than mine have pointed out the gaping fallacies in both. They certainly signaled in a "new departure" in natural philosophy, setting off chain reactions which are now, at length, reaching us in the mongrel existentialisms and doggerel ethics of today.

As for the German-generated rationalistic higher criticism, it is now a flat tire with a hundred punctures and beyond further patching. Not only have its drastic novelties and brilliant blunders been refuted from *within* the Bible by more careful evangelical scholarship, but equally so from *outside* the Bible by the solid, physical evidence which archeology has resurrected from its long burial beneath the silt of centuries. To mention only one aspect of this: one of the basic arguments of the higher critics in their treatment of Old Testament writings was the supposed slow evolution of religion from a primitive polytheism to Jewish and Christian monotheism; but archaeology has completely turned the tables on them, demonstrating that man was originally monotheist, and that he deteriorated into polytheism as he later wandered from a primal divine revelation.

And what of the Darwinian evolution phantom? After Darwin's *Origin of Species* (1859) and his *Descent of Man* (1871), accompanied by Spencer's widely waved banner of inevitable human progress through process of natural law, there was near panic in the minds of many evangelical leaders. It seemed as though the Genesis cosmogony was at last destroyed and the authority of the Bible fatally shaken. Yet where are the Darwin and Spencer champions today? The estimate of Darwin is not only revised, it is reversed. I have before me the latest edition of the *Origin of Species* (A. M. Dent & Sons, 1956) with an introduction by a leading contemporary scientist, Professor W. R. Thompson, F.R.S., the distinguished director of the Commonwealth Institute of Biological Control, Ottawa. I quote from successive parts of that introduction.

> I am not satisfied that Darwin proved his point, or that his influence in scientific and public thinking has been beneficial.

> Personal convictions [i.e., Darwin's], simple possibilities, are presented as if they were proofs, or at least valid arguments in favour of the theory.

> Since no one has explained to my satisfaction how evolution could happen I do not feel impelled to say that it *has* happened. I prefer to say that on this matter our information is inadequate.

> Darwin suggested in the *Origin* that embryological development provides evidence for evolution. . . . This idea, elaborated by other workers, eventually became in the hands of Haeckel the "great biogenetic law" according to which the ontogeny repeats the phylogeny . . . A natural "law" can only be established as an induction from facts. Haeckel was of course unable to do this . . . When the "convergence" of embryos was not entirely satisfactory, Haeckel altered the illustrations of them to fit his theory . . . The "biogenetic law" as a proof of evolution is valueless.

> Darwin in the *Origin* was not able to produce paleontological evidence sufficient to prove his views, but the evidence he did produce was adverse to them; and I may note that the position is not notably different today. The modern Darwinian paleontologists are obliged, just like their predecessors and like Darwin, to water down the facts with subsidiary

> hypotheses which, however plausible, are in the nature of things unverifiable.
>
> A long-enduring and regrettable effect of the success of the *Origin* was the addiction of biologists to unverifiable speculation.
>
> The success of Darwinism was accompanied by a decline in scientific integrity. This is already evident in the reckless statements of Haeckel and in the shifting, devious, and histrionic argumentation of T. H. Huxley. A striking example, which has only recently come to light, is the alteration of the Piltdown skull so that it could be used as an evidence for the descent of man from the apes.

Well, that is the unprejudiced verdict of a front-rank scientist, and is written, of all places, in the Introduction to the latest edition of Darwin's *Origin of Species!* In his well-known main propositions Darwin is now demonstratedly *wrong* — and Moses endures! To this day, not one statement in the Genesis cosmogony can be disproved. But think of the moral and spiritual damage done by the evolution error! It has undermined the Christian faith and morals of millions. That I am not misrepresenting its effects will be seen in two or three more brief quotations from the above-mentioned Introduction.

> Darwin himself, though he once held some rather vaguely Christian views, abandoned them quite rapidly and soon ceased to believe in the Christian revelation.
>
> The doctrine of evolution by natural selection as Darwin formulated, and as his followers still explain it, has a strong anti-religious flavour.
>
> In the *Origin*, evolution is presented as an essentially undirected process. For the majority of its readers, therefore, the *Origin* effectively dissipated the evidence of providential control.

Somehow, I cannot think, as some do, that Darwin was ever intentionally dishonest with the facts. Was it not that his obsession with an idea ran away with sober judgment and exact induction? The one thing which really matters now is that Darwin was wrong and the Bible is still undisproved — as it always will be.

That sets us yet again asking: What *now?* and What *next?* Those two questions may well be asked with apprehensiveness as we see the ominous moral slump today. And can we survey what has happened without asking what is the commensurate *cause* behind such a large-scale reversal? And do not the past eighty or hundred years give the basic answer? Those eight or ten decades of departure from the Bible, in the name of philosophy, science, and religious scholarship have at length dragged us into the dreary morass of *existentialism* (which is a philosophy of irrationalism) and the boggy *"new liberalism"* (which is existentialism in theological copy).

Existentialism marks a departure from rationality to irrationality. Until recently philosophy has always held that the universe, or total reality, is rational and therefore intelligible to human apprehension. From Kant and Hegel onwards the shift has been from "rational" to rational*ism*, i.e., the effort to explain everything on a *purely* rationalistic basis. But the effort admittedly has failed. Reason alone cannot supply all the answers or find the final coherence. At that point philosophical honesty is to admit the need for divine *revelation;* but no, rather than that, our latter-day thinkers still clung to the rationalistic view of the universe in which man is nothing more than the product of chemical forces; and then, *because* man did not make sense that way, they divided all knowledgeable reality into two areas: that of reason and that of *non*reason. They did this, not on the ground of scientific or philosophical induction, but because man simply cannot be fully accounted for chemically and mathematically. There is that in human experience (they said) which is *outside* the field of reason.

But in making that "great divide" between reason and nonreason they did something else almost as unthinkable: they discarded the hitherto uniform assumption of philosophy that the universe is ultimately a total unity; that behind all antitheses there is a final *synthesis,* and beyond all apparent incoherences an all-inclusive *harmony.* Yes, they let go of that, and in its place they averred that philosophy finally leads to irreconcilable *paradoxes:* oppositions and contradictions which are beyond all rational explanation. Total being is *not* a final unity, but unresolvable paradox or nonreason.

Thus "rationalism" (not true rationality) becomes irrational! In the realm of physical phenomena man is a meaningless chemical blob, while all the nonphysical part of man which we call mind, soul, spirit, intellect, volition, emotion, desire, aspiration, love, hate, hope, fear belongs to the area of *non*reason! It is the attempt to give man some worthwhile meaning *outside* the realm of reason, since he has been robbed of any meaning *inside* it. What it really amounts to is that if we view man inside the realm of the objectively phenomenal and seemingly rational we are driven to deep pessimism; while if we view man in the nonreason area we arrive at chaos. Think of it: everything in our human experience which makes life worth living is nonreason! *That* is where rationalist philosophy has at length dumped us. Echoing the late Edgar Y. Mullins, we may well say that such "rationalism" is a blind man in a pitch dark room at twelve o'clock midnight looking for a black cat that isn't there. Is it to be wondered at that such "philosophy" has a devastating effect upon morals and that so many of our younger people who are subjected to such teaching wallow in the mire?

The New Liberalism

The older liberalism is gone, but a new and worse progeny has taken its place. The "new liberalism" is existentialism voicing itself in *theology*. It is a freakish fact that the neo-orthodoxy, which came in to answer the *old* liberalism, originated the *new* liberalism. That is because Karl Barth himself was a mixture of higher critical fallacies and Kierkegaard's existentialism, which insists that truth is known only by experience, that it *becomes* truth only by inward encounter. Experience is the test of everything. Applied to the Bible, that soon begets ambiguity. Indeed, the word which most peculiarly clings around the neo-orthodoxy is "ambiguity." Of all the schemes and schools which have successively appeared, the neo-orthodox has surely been the fuzziest. Even the utmost respect for its scholarly progenitors cannot repress our astonishment that such specialist theologians could lose themselves in such cloudy two-way meanings.

According to neo-orthodoxy the Bible is *not* the Word of God in the clear-cut older meaning, but it *becomes* the Word of God by spiritual impact. Even then it is full of mistakes or "unhistoriographical" myths! Some of us may be impossibly slow, but this has the sound of "What isn't is, yet all the same what is isn't," after the fashion of the French *le roi est mort, vive le roi!* According to neo-orthodoxy the Cross of Jesus is indeed the atonement, yet its significance is not in the historical Jesus nor in the actual blood, for (according to Barth) the historical Jesus is an elusive figure about whom it is difficult to get informatian, and although Jesus died "for us" it is scarcely in the definite older sense that He died in our stead and for our sins. As for our Lord's resurrection, what happened historically at the tomb is quite unimportant. To believe in a bodily resurrection of Jesus is beside the point for Christian faith: the important thing is that in Jesus we can *believe* in resurrection. In Him humanity was taken up into God, and thus the way was opened to Him. To some of us this seems an incomparable blend of casuistry and naïveté. It is saying: We have the *doctrine;* why bother about the fact on which it is built? Apparently this wonderful house does not need foundations; it can float in air! We can retain the *truths* of the gospel even if we cannot believe the *records!*

The "*new*" liberalism" follows suit. According to it the Bible is only the Word of God *somehow;* that is, only insofar as it becomes so in our experience. What is actually written in the Bible has no revelational value in itself, but it becomes "religiously significant" if and as it so registers itself in our experience. The *words* must not be thought of as the *Word*. It is no far cry from that to the further idea that the Word of God may come to us also through writings *other* than the Bible; and, accordingly, we find Reinhold Niebuhr advising us to "let secular idealism speak the Word of God on occasion" and Raymond Panikkar selling us *The Unknown Christ of Hinduism* (1964).

Perhaps, indeed, the title "new liberalism" is already becoming outworn and should give place to "theological atheism"; for that is what it amounts to, since in the realm of reason God is unfindable, and in the nonreason or "philosophic other," God is unverifiable. The belief that God is neither "in here" nor "out there" has already led to the "God is dead" funeral-cry; and now in some quarters, apparently, there is actually an atheistic Jesus-faith advocated. Just recently, in the Saturday religious article of a leading British newspaper, the *Times*, Dr. Alistair Kee, Professor of Theology, University of Hull, speaks of those to whom, in the cultural climate of today, belief in God is not possible, who, nevertheless, have a deep regard for Jesus; who "believe that in him — and in no one else, and in no other tradition — the deepest truths of life were revealed. . . ." The "mystery of life," says Dr. Kee, is not discussed today in terms of a coming Messiah, "but perhaps in terms of what it means to be truly human, and what are the best possibilities for our world." Then he adds, "In these terms, those who believe that the nature of man and the goal of mankind are revealed definitely in what comes to expression in Jesus are by definition 'Christian' *even if belief in God is not possible to them*" (italics mine).

Just as Fabianism, if followed to its logical conclusion, arrives at Communism, so do the premises and presuppositions of theological liberalism, if followed to their logical conclusion, issue in either practical or dialectical atheism. Agreed, liberalist spokesmen still use the word "God" and other Christian terms, but only as part of a religious vocabulary voided of evangelical content yet retained for psychological usefulness. As for God in the sense of a personal, loving God directly concerned about us human beings, "God is dead" indeed. As for our Lord Jesus Christ, in all such neo-liberalist existential reference He is no more the real Jesus of the New Testament than the man in the moon is a real person. His actual Saviorhood is lost in a vapory, sentimental Jesus-idea or Jesus-motivation.

Fourfold Disaster

In summary: we are witnessing now in pretty stark exposure that when human thought and learning reject the Bible as the authentically inspired Word of God in written form, it results in fourfold disaster: (1) a false idea of God, (2) a false estimate of man, (3) moral degradation, (4) pessimism, hopelessness, despair. Take one further brief glance backward over the process.

First, a false idea of *God*. It is observable that from the earliest days of the higher critics, liberalist theology has been the running mate of secular philosophy. Eventually, therefore, the liberalist God became little more than the religious name for natural law in operation; and the universe, instead of being *created* by God, became an *extension* of God. Today, liberalist theology still goes arm-in-arm with nonbiblical philosophy and science, even though it still retains biblical phraseology. But secular philosophy has reached a *terminus* in "existentialism." It can make a *change* and start all over again, but it cannot go any further along the road it has traveled since Kant and Hegel. It has reached the end of *that* road, to find what? A personal, creating, sustaining, caring, loving God is gone forever, and we are given instead a blind dummy in a vast prison from which the only escape for humans is the grave — though perhaps not even there! Yes, "God is dead" — (1) as a philosophical concept, (2) as a theological proposition, (3) as a knowable Being, (4) as an active factor in human life. "God is dead" — except the God of the Bible! In all the history of human thought, was there ever a louder-voiced demonstration of the need for divine *revelation*? And was there ever a louder challenge to us Christian ministers to champion and expound the *FACT* of divine revelation in an authentically inspired Bible?

Second, a false estimate of *man*. When God is extinguished the most-to-be-pitied loser is man. However uncomfortable the thought of a holy God may be to sinful man, a no-God universe is immeasurably more frightening, especially if physical death does not absolutely quench *mental* life at the same time as physical dissolution. Such a universe, from a blank nothing, a mass of blind forces, utterly purposeless, is a monstrosity which degrades man into a pitiable gnat and makes the present pathos of human life a heartless mockery. If everything is an emanation of blind force, then the concept of man as a really personal being cannot stand. How can mind, thought, conscience, free-willed *personal* being be produced by *im*personal force? Man becomes an inexplicable enigma. There can be no conceivable moral responsibility without God; nor yet on the other hand can man be really *free* in such a world: he is altogether the "sport of chance," the helpless, hopeless prisoner of totalitarian chemical and psychological processes. All real meaning and dignity are lost. Was there ever an hour when men needed more to hear again the ennobling, reassuring *biblical* doctrine of man?

Third, *moral degradation*. If anti-biblical philosophy and liberalist apostasy were merely something "done in a corner" (Acts 26:26) the situation would not be alarming; but the sorry fact is that their disruptive concepts largely *dominate* modern thought. The ugly repercussions from this obtrude everywhere. Our younger people, inoculated with such teachings, despair of finding adequate motive or true values in life, and their behavior patterns correspond.

Perhaps the most sickening and ill-boding aspect of the moral slump is the desecration of girlhood and womanhood and marriage. The modern woman has rights, liberties, advantages, and co-equalities with men in business, politics, etc. which her grandmother never knew; but over against all that, and knocking the good out of it all, is the one deadly development that she has lost or is fast losing, the respect of the male. More and more today, men look upon her as a means of animal gratification rather than as the God-appointed trustee of all the higher, tenderer virtues, the object of respect and reverential affection whose love is to be honorably sought and cherished and safeguarded. There is less and less chivalrous love, but more and more sexual lust. Among our girls and women never were there so many venereally defiled bodies and broken lives. No nation or civilization ever rises higher than its womanhood. That is the frightening aspect. When the rot eats its way in *there*, disintegration soon follows. It is no mere "prophet of gloom" who says so. It is the lesson of history, written in the rocks with a pen of iron.

Fourth, *pessimism, hopelessness, despair.* The old saying, "A lie travels half way round the earth while truth is putting on her boots," has been echoed again in the rapidity with which the faith-destroying higher critical, or "modernist" ideas of the Bible have permeated Christendom. In a comment on this, back in 1909, P. T. Forsyth said, "Extremes are always easier to grasp and to sell." At that time the daring, stunning new ideas of the critics about the Bible were boldly invading Protestant seminaries and pulpits; and it is that discrediting of the Bible which has torn down our ramparts, allowing degenerating philosophies of life to wreak their moral havoc in our society. Or, in other metaphor, deep down beneath all upper and outer symptoms of our multiple disease is the repudiation of the biblical revelation, which repudiation has at length provoked such erratic excesses as the sleazy hippie movement, the dementing drug culture, the erotic "new morality," the frantic rock 'n roll mob, the new black magic cults, the corrosive coarseness, the anarchic violence and vandalism of these days. Most onlookers see the syndrome rather than the originating cause.

Our young folk, growing up amid this, are far more an imbibing part of it than we older ones can realistically grasp. They have never known other and better with which to compare. Things which were mentioned only in *sub voce* abhorrence a generation ago — lesbianism, homosexuality, rape, pornography — are brazenly flaunted or publicly discussed without indignation today. Wickedness is apologized for. Criminals now, instead of being "enemies of society," are explained by our behavioristic psychologists as products of body chemistry or of an environment for which all the rest of us are to blame. Youths swinging switchblades and bicycle chains are "innocent victims of our cruel society." Is the spiraling crime rate or the vicious contempt for the law to be wondered at?

Yet very many of our younger folk need sympathy as much as censure, for they have been deliberately misguided. Their bad behavior faithfully reflects the thinking of present-day authors, teachers, professors, artists, actors, playwrights. And whatever guidelines for *better* conduct may be given to them are not based upon any *real* moral authority, for there is *no* real moral authority outside a God-inspired Bible. The best that non-biblical thinkers can offer is *determinism,* with its Freudian teaching that men are not really free and therefore are not really responsible; or *hedonism*, with its insistence that pleasure is, after all, the true objective of human choice and behavior; or *utilitarianism*, with its higher motive of "the greatest good for the greatest number." But all these have in common the belief that there are no absolute standards of right and wrong, that in the ultimate analysis each individual works out his own moral code. Even if society as a whole makes laws and rules which must be obeyed, they are for self-preservation or "the common good"; they do not make murder or robbery or perjury *intrinsically* wrong, but only prohibitions necessary for collective protection. "Crime" is not *sin*.

Pragmatists, positivists, idealists, materialists, existentialists, where have they all brought us? Look at the mess we are in! The "permissive society" is already the *decadent* society, the *self-destroying* society. Nothing placards it more pityfully than the debasement of womanhood by girls and women themselves: well-known women parading with bravado their unchastity for all to see, even holding press conferences to announce pregnancy from anonymous fathers; young girls still at elementary school displaying before teacher and schoolmates the sign of imminent childbearing. Heaven pity us! Unless mighty change is near, major catastrophe *is!* That is no mere alarmist cry of a screech owl!

Hear again the sob of disillusionment from higher intellectuality. Robert Maynard Hutchins, recently president at the University of Chicago, has said, "We do not know where we are going, or why, and we have almost given up the attempt to find out. We are in despair because the keys which were to open the gates of heaven have let us into a larger but more oppressive prisonhouse. . . . These keys were science and the free intelligence of man. *They have failed us.* We have long since cast off God. To what can we now appeal?"

Never was there a more tragic irony than when, in the opening years of our century, the liberalist breakaway from the older view of the Bible was palmed off on the public as a *release* — a release from dingy old biblical ideas that had kept us all tied to outworn credulities which impeded man's progress to a finally evolved self-fulfillment, a release being brought to the public, at last, through our wonderful new "scientific scholarship" as it now showed us the foolishness of the old superstitious reverence for the Bible. What a release! a release from the guardian wings of an angel to the coils of a cobra, from a well-marked highway to a trackless jungle, from liberating truth to depraving error, from fresh mountain air to a malarial swamp, from God-given hope to the profound failure and starless night of rationalism!

There comes a point in any deteriorating civilization beyond which recovery is impossible. The will has become too flabby for the mighty exertion needed to turn back the down-driving current. Are we at that point today? I do not think so, though I think we could be much too near it. There are hope-renewing aspects. Although the forces of evil were never more rampant, and although they may fight the truth, veil it, misrepresent it, they cannot destroy in men that inborn, constitutional recognition of truth when it is clearly borne in upon them. "Deep calleth unto deep." Wide travel, careful observation, news reports, statistics, conversation with youth leaders all "add up" to convince my own mind, at least, that we might be even now on the verge of some big, new-patterned spiritual awakening bringing large moral recovery.

In that connection a glance back is encouraging. No review of Protestant Christendom through the past century can be in true perspective if it overlooks the meaningful fact that just when the liberalist "new theology" and the evolutionist scientists were striking their hardest blows at the public thinking and pushing evangelical theology with its back to the wall, God was incepting a counter-offensive in the rise of powerful new agencies as dynamic apologists of the gospel: the incomparable voice-and-pen ministry of C. H. Spurgeon eradiating the saving message from London, England, throughout the English-speaking world; the unprecedented world-wide evangelistic sweep of Moody and Sankey, to be followed by the similarly widespread Torrey-Alexander and Chapman-Alexander campaigns the founding and prairie-blaze spread of General Booth's "Salvation Army" salvaging the down-and-outs of city slumdums; the emergence of the Plymouth Brethren movement with its new insistence on a solely and wholly biblical Christianity and appealing more particularly to the upper middle classes, the Cambrian revival which set the whole of Wales ablaze with spiritual fervor; the birth of large Bible-centered "conventions" like the *Die Heiligungsbewegung,* or "Sanctification Movement," in Germany, and the "Keswick" counterpart in Britain; and in America the "fundamentalist" revolt against the "modernist" invasion — a revolt and secession and recapturing of evangelical initiative often misrepresented, but now becoming more truly appreciated as that which "saved the day" for uncompromising evangelical witness in the U.S.A. and gave it new impetus.

There is a heartening parallel to that today. Although, in the words of Isaiah 59:19 (K.J.V.) the enemy has "come in like a flood," the Spirit of the Lord is lifting up "a standard against him." In many minds disillusionment with humanistic philosophy is evoking new cry after the divine positives of the Bible. All over the U.S.A. and spilling over into other countries are the remarkable new women's Bible fellowship movements and new interdenominational Bible fellowships for men — in both cases reaching thousands who have had no church connections. The large-scale Billy Graham campaigns continue to be crowdedly attractive and persuasive, notably to younger people. There is the "Campus Crusade" progenitored by Bill Bright a score of years ago, having now an annual budget of some eighteen million dollars, and some 350 workers on 450 campuses. There is "Young Life" with 1300 "clubs," and "Youth for Christ" in 2000 high schools, and Inter-Varsity Fellowship with growing appeal among the more intellectual types. Evangelical voices, also, are ringing clear and continuingly through radio and T.V., with immense audiences in the aggregate.

And now, since 1967, we have the new "Jesus People" movement, a sudden, incandescent evangelistic witness in one of the darkest problem areas of modern youth. Already it has grown large enough to claim nationwide comment and seems likely to proliferate internationally, for like the Indian banyan tree its branches seem to send down new roots sprouting new trees. *Time* magazine, June 21, 1971, says of it:

> It is a startling development for a generation that has been constantly accused of tripping out or copping out with sex, drugs and violence. Now, embracing the most persistent symbol of purity, selflessness and brotherly love in the history of Western man, they are afire with a Pentecostal passion for sharing their new vision with others. Fresh-faced, wide-eyed young girls and earnest young men badger businessmen and shoppers on Hollywood Boulevard, near the Lincoln Memorial, in Dallas, in Detroit and in Wichita, "witnessing" for Christ with breathless exhortations. Christian coffeehouses have opened in many cities. . . . Communal "Christian houses" are multiplying like loaves and fishes. . . . Bibles abound: . . . they are invariably well-thumbed and often memorized. . . . The revolutionary word is also spread by a growing, literally free Jesus press that now numbers some 50 newspapers across the country. . . ." Already there are 600 such "Christian houses" scattered across the U.S.A.

One of the commonest questions being asked just now is, "What should be the attitude of the Church to the Jesus Movement?"

The question, however, is off keel; for insofar as the leaders and members of the movement are bringing souls into regenerating union with Christ, the Jesus Movement *is* the Church, just as truly as any other group of the "born again." Through earnest young leaders and workers with a "passion for souls," the enterprise is one more outreach of the Holy Spirit through the "body of Christ." The question should be, "What is the true attitude of all local evangelical *churches?*" It should be one of gratitude, intercession, cooperative encouragement, and practical help if invited, which need not mean any compromise of sanctuary decorum. The leaders of the Jesus People movement themselves know that some of *their* necessary methods are not suitable *inside* the fellowship of a local Christian church. They are using ways and means by which alone they can reach the kind of young folk they are after; and once those young folk are won for Christ, *we* should be immediately ready to "take over from there."

At the time these lines are being written, the "rock" musical "Jesus Christ Superstar" has hit Broadway and is creating a major sensation. The record sales of it have broken all earlier figures in America. In its title, style, quality, concepts, language, to most of us it is *repulsive*. I mention it only to point up the strange new interest in our Lord Jesus. It is saying all over again that although He may be rejected, opposed, misrepresented, He simply cannot for long be *ignored*. As one of the Jesus Movement underground newspaper posters puts it: "*Warning: He Is Still at Large!*" There is no one else like Him. We have to keep coming back and taking another look at Him. "Jesus Christ Superstar" is a revolting caricature of Him who (overwhelming thought) is GOD INCARNATE; but seen in the context of the astounding new interest in JESUS it is strangely eloquent. As for the cynosure "Jesus People" movement, at this time of writing it is too early to assess its meaning and potential, but it is spreading contagiously and bringing thousands of misguided, perverted young people and others to a saving experience of the true gospel. Could it be a surprise turning of the tide, an unorthodox lead-up to spiritual renewal in large dimension?

One feature, however, which is anything but consoling is, that the exciting new back-to-the-Bible and back-to-Jesus movements are *outside* our organized Protestant denominations. Is the divine Spirit bypassing those religious bodies because of their disloyalty to the Bible? Such movements as we have mentioned are doing what the churches are *not* doing, but *should* be doing. This much is predictable: if our Protestant bodies in general continue in their betrayal of the Bible, God will raise up *other* champions of it. He is showing us so. One of the big surprises of our time is that the Roman Catholic Church, which for centuries has withheld the Bible under Vatican lock and key, is now openly advocating free reading of the Bible among its members. Yes, God will raise up new promotion of His Word in least likely quarters.

Is not this a crisis hour when all of us Protestant ministers should be coming back to our Bible with new loyalty, new convincedness, new eagerness to master the arguments for its divine origin, and with new resolve to become able apologists in its behalf against the no-God, no-good philosophies which have benighted men? This is the time for clerical critics of the Bible to become critics of the critics, for the Bible remains true and its presuming critics are found wrong.

This is a time, also, for a clarion recall to the *validity of evidence*. The deadliest artifice of secular philosophy and liberalist theology was the making of miracle an *a priori* impossibility, thus short-circuiting the validity of rational proof. It was that which heralded the "flight from reason" in modern thought. This is the time for a recall from the gauzy webs of nonreason to *reason:* from irrational rationalism to real *rationality*. The well-tested laws of logic are sound. The phenomenal universe is real and rational. The human mind is correspondingly rational. Our senses of perception are not a lie. They do not deceive us. All scientific experiments carried out on that basis prove the *reciprocal* rationality existing between the outer world of phenomena and the inner world of human reason. We may see and perceive, test and experiment, weigh and analyze, deduce and *know* by repeated test and check.

When we contemplate *metaphysical* and *spiritual* realities, human reason reaches the mysterious boundary line, not between reason and *non*reason, nor between reason and *anti*-reason, but between reason and *above*-reason. Beyond that point human reason cannot go alone; it needs help. If it is too proud to admit this it takes a "leap in the dark" and flounders about in the indecipherable; but if it is humble enough to *ask* for help there is a Voice of *Super*-reason speaking from the other side of the metaphysical. We do not have to *reject* human reason, but at that point human reason needs divine *revelation*.

That revelation is THE BIBLE. That inspired book is divine omniscience speaking to human reason — not contradicting it, but enlightening it. There is the same reciprocal rationality between the biblical revelation and the human mind as there is between the human mind and the phenomenal world. Thus, when human reason *receives* that revelation, instead of a "leap into the dark," there is a leap into light! And, mark, it is not only a leap of *faith;* it is an act of *intelligence.* Why? Because reason accepts the revelation on the ground of *valid evidence.* Thus, through the operation of *reason* we enter that *above*-reason realm of the DIVINE WISDOM.

Christian faith, therefore, is not nonrational. It is not credulity. It builds on verifiable fact. Reason is *not* an antithesis of faith; it is an *ingredient* of it. Faith without fact is fancy. True faith is a union of reason and trust. Faith is reasonable *because* it builds on fact; and the fact is valid for faith because *reason* has ascertained so. The big question which faith asks is: "Has God spoken?" When *reason* answers a clear "Yes," faith acts and begins to move in the realm, not of nonreason, but of the divine *super-reason.*

That, assuredly, is the big, big question: HAS GOD SPOKEN? Human philosophy today says, No. The Bible says, Yes. Which shall we hear? Well, judged by their influence on human nations and society, I should say the Bible. But there is more to it than that. All our present-day philosophies and ideologies begin with *ideas:* but the Bible projects great, originating *facts* — as the investigable foundation on which all its moral and spiritual truths rest. The Bible itself challenges investigation of the facts. It appeals to *evidence.* It asks no credulity. It encourages no presumption. The solid evidences are there. The argument of fulfilled prophecy never spoke so loudly, so unanswerably as now. The witness of archaeology grows bigger as the spade digs deeper and the decipherers translate. The testimony of Christian experience, crowned by transformed character, confirms it as unmistakably as ever.

Such is the critical situation today. It seems to me that the clock of destiny strikes the hour of a dramatic challenge. Somehow, with a mighty effort, undergirded by the promised help of God Himself, we must put the *Book* back where it rightly belongs. Let our watchword be *Back* to the Bible! *Out* with the Bible! *On* with the Bible! The Protestant pulpit was *built* on the Bible. If only that pulpit might now be *rebuilt* on it, who knows? There could happen, even yet, a twentieth-century Reformation as epochal as that of four hundred years ago.

Part Two

PENTECOST

Perhaps it should be stated here that the following five addresses on aspects of Pentecost were delivered to the Annual Ministers' Conference of the Southern Baptist Convention, held at San Francisco, California, some years ago, under the chairmanship of my esteemed friend, Dr. Carl E. Bates. That will account for certain incidental references, especially in the fifth of the series. They are here reproduced practically as they were then given.

J.S.B.

It is the Holy Spirit who hath made us overseers of His Church, and therefore how it becomes us to take heed! The Holy Spirit makes men overseers of the Church in three several respects: (1) By qualifying them for the office, (2) By directing the ordainers to discern their qualifications, (3) And by directing them (pastors and people) for the affixing them to a particular charge. All these things were done then (i.e., in New Testament times) by inspiration. The same are done now (today) by the ordinary way of the Spirit's assistance. But it is the same Spirit still: and men are made overseers of the Church (when they are truly called) by the Holy Spirit *now* as well as then.

Richard Baxter

PENTECOST AND THE PRESENT HOUR

When the first preachers of the gospel went through the Roman world of long ago, they could not sow the seed of Christian truth on virgin soil; the ground was already full of other growths. The human mind of that era was the very opposite of a religious vacuum. Everywhere men's minds were full of religious and philosophical ideas, and the famous "mystery religions" had penetrated into practically every part of the Roman dominions.

Some of those ancient "mystery" cults, in their doctrines of the *taurobolium*, or blood bath, bore strange likenesses to the new Christian doctrine of redemption through the blood of Christ; and in certain other particulars, also, they shared incidental correspondences to the gospel of Christ. Of course, they did not have the factual veracity, the evidential validity, the ethical transcendency, the spiritual purity, the experiential reality, or the divine authority which we have in the Christian revelation; yet nonetheless the points of similarity between them and the new Christian message are remarkable.

We need not hesitate to admit this. Nay, should we not rather claim it? For if we have discerning eyes, we may perceive in it a superintending divine providence, gradually preparing men's minds, not only through inspired Hebrew prophets, but in a lesser way through groping heathen mystics, for the day when the glad tidings of *true* redemption through the incarnate Son of God should break upon the ears of mankind.

However, there was one striking feature of the new Christian message which at once fundamentally differentiated it from all other faiths. What was it? It was *the Christian doctrine of the Holy Spirit*. That was something historically unprecedented, theologically all-eclipsing, dynamically unique. And what *is* the Christian doctrine of the Holy Spirit? In concentrated brevity it is this: that the very life of the Eternal, having become historically incarnated in the divine Savior, Jesus, is now regeneratingly *communicated* by the Holy Spirit to all those human beings who, through simple but vital faith, become united to the Savior.

That, I repeat, at once fundamentally distinguished Christianity from all other faiths. It meant and it *still* means that Christianity is not merely a creed, or a code, or a cult, or a philosophy, or a system of ethics, or a way of behavior, or a school of thought, or an ideology, or even a religion. Christianity is a *life;* a life which, if a man possess it not, he is dead while he lives; but which, if a man possess it, he lives even though the body dies. Christianity is not merely an ethic; it is a soul-saving, life-changing, character-transforming experience of God, through Christ, inwrought by the Holy Spirit.

Surely that is the conspicuous emphasis of the New Testament. What was the subject uppermost in our Savior's mind just before He went to Gethsemane and Gabbatha and Golgotha? It was the imminence of the *Holy Spirit,* as the later chapters of John show us. What was His first word to the apostles, immediately after His resurrection? John 20:22 tells us: "He breathed on them, and saith unto them, Receive ye *the Holy Spirit."* What was His last word just before He ascended to heaven? Acts 1:8 tells us: "Ye shall receive power, after that *the Holy Spirit* is come upon you." What was the first exercise of His high-priestly ministry in the heavenly sanctuary? Acts 2:33 tells us: "Having received of the Father *the promise of the Holy Spirit,* he hath shed forth this, which ye now see and hear." What was the first promise Christianity ever made to men when it came out onto the platform of historical publicity? Acts 2:38 tells us: "Repent, and be baptized every one of you, in the name of Jesus Christ for the remission of sins, and ye shall receive *the gift of the Holy Spirit."* What was the first test question which was asked in apostolic days to ascertain whether a person was or was not a true Christian believer? We have it in Acts 19. Paul meets twelve professing believers at Ephesus. He has some doubt about them. What does he ask? "Do you believe in the triunity of the Godhead?" No; before any creedal catechizing comes this: "Did you receive *the Holy Spirit* when you believed?" In other words, "Have you the new *life?"*

A New Life From God

All these factors accentuate this first big significance, that Christianity is not merely a new law, but a new *life;* not merely a new and higher ethic, but a life-imparting dynamic.

Let me peal it out again: *that* was the vital feature which distinguished Christianity from all those other faiths of long ago; and that is what vitally distinguishes it today from Confucianism, Hinduism, Buddhism, Mohammedanism; yes, and from Communism. All the non-Christian systems can give us a philosophy or an ideology, but they cannot impart new spiritual life. They may fascinate, but they cannot regenerate. Their philosophies may float among the clouds, but they cannot lift fallen men from the gutter. Communism may violently excite the brain and disturb the nervous system; but Communism has never yet saved one alcoholic from his wretched slavery; it has never yet cured one moral leper of his sin-disease; it has never yet raised one dead Lazarus from his grave and given him new life. Only Christ, by the Holy Spirit, does that.

Brethren, this needs new emphasis today. Christianity is not merely sound biblical theology, or militant Protestantism, or Trinitarian orthodoxy, or even Evangelicalism, or Fundamentalism. Christianity, in its first-flush meaning for mankind, is new life, new *spiritual* life; new life from God as revealed in Christ, and now savingly communicated by the Holy Spirit.

Let me not be misunderstood. I believe more than ever that the conservative evangelical faith is the true Christian faith, the faith once for all delivered to the saints. I believe in the need for a systematized theology. I believe in the usefulness of a creed as a concentrate and safeguard. I believe in the need for efficient church organization. What I am here insisting is that without this supernatural life, this regenerating energy, this transfiguring power, this vital, glowing experience of the Holy Spirit, our theologies are clanking skeletons, our creeds are shibboleths of denominational corpses, and our best-organized churches are valleys of respectable dry bones.

At the beginning of the Christian era, Christian experience did not grow out of theology. It was largely the other way round. Christian theology grew out of Christian *experience*. It was not merely a new theology which conquered the Roman world of twenty centuries ago, but the irrepressible new *life* imparted by the Holy Spirit. That is a fact which needs reemphasizing today. Our ministers and churches are needing a fresh experience of this transforming new life. I believe that if there were a new insurge of this liberating, sanctifying, dynamic spiritual life throughout the churches of America, the scaffoldings of Communism would crumple before it.

A New Fellowship With God

But further, Pentecost means not only a new life from God; it means a new *fellowship* with God. In that sense Pentecost is the historical culmination of ages-long dispensational preparation. Down through the avenue of the centuries, God has been seeking to come nearer and yet nearer to the heart and love of man. Travel back in imagination to that first paradise in Eden. See that first human pair, unsullied by the slightest moral default, walking in uninterrupted fellowship with their benign Creator amid the blemishless loveliness of that pristine paradise. What a delectable picture it conjures up! Over that brief but exquisite Edenic dispensation we may write, emphasizing the preposition, "God *with* man."

Alas, there came the sorry tragedy of the first human sin. The hiss of the serpent fouled that first lovely harmony, and the slime of the tempter smeared the fair paradise. But after the expulsion from Eden, did God utterly forsake His fallen creature, man? Thank God, no, in the gracious condescension of heaven there now commenced an illuminating series of divine self-revealings, or *theophanies,* to the first fathers, or patriarchs, of our human family; and over the patriarchal period we may write, again emphasizing the preposition, "God *to* man."

Next followed the period of the Israelite theocracy, at the inception of which we find God saying to Moses, "Make me a tabernacle, that I may dwell among my people." Over the period of the Israelite theocracy we may write, again emphasizing the preposition, "God *among* men."

Then ensued the national history, idolatry, and apostasy of the covenant people. The nation fell foul of its high calling and involved itself in pitiable calamity, judgment, and disintegration. But amid the declension and wreckage, God raised up a succession of mighty messengers, the Hebrew prophets, through whose supernatural inspiration He addressed the decadent people. Over the period of the prophets we may write, again emphasizing the preposition, "God *through* men."

At last, in the "fulness of the time," God "sent forth His Son, begotten of a woman"; and over that matchless manhood we may write, "God *as* man."

Yet even that is not enough; God would come closer still. Toward the end of His earthly ministry, our Lord began to tell His disciples of the Comforter, the Holy Spirit, who was soon to come to them. "At that day," He said, "ye shall know that I am in the Father, and the Father in me, and ye in me, and I *in* you." Again, "If a man love me, he will keep my word; and my Father will love him, and we [the Father and the Son] will come unto him, and make *our abode within him."* Oh, the matchless wonder of Pentecost — the Father and the Son together abiding *IN* us by the Holy Spirit!

Think back now, over that kaleidoscopic development. The Edenic dispensation, God *with* man; the patriarchal period, God *to* man; the Israel theocracy, God *among* men; the Hebrew prophets, God *through* men; the Incarnation, God *as* man; Pentecost, God *in* redeemed and regenerated men, making them His living, human habitations! Oh, the never-ending wonder of it! God forgive us that our surprise at it ever for a moment subsides! Well may we be ever exclaiming,

> Oh, gift of gifts! oh, grace of grace!
> That God should condescend
> To make my heart His dwelling-place
> And be my bosom Friend!

A New Filling From God

Once more, Pentecost means a new *filling* from God. The words of Ephesians 5:18, "Be filled with the Spirit," articulate the intendedly normal experience of the Christian believer. "Be filled with the Spirit"; this is our covenant provision, our redemption right, our spiritual inheritance, our scriptural prerogative in Christ. It is our duty, our need, our privilege. We Christians are meant to be Spirit-filled and Christ-communicative. The Holy Spirit seeks the full monopoly of our personalities that He may interpenetrate them with the life and love of Jesus. Away with any such immature and unscriptural notion as that we have not had the Spirit's suffusion unless we "speak in tongues"! Speaking in tongues, apart from transformation of the character into Christlikeness, is a counterfeit and a deception. When the Holy Spirit fills a consecrated heart, whatever spiritual gifts He may or may not impart, He always comes to fill that heart with the love of Christ and with power for witness to Him. Different believers have different gifts, but *always* four things happen, whoever the believer may be, when there is a real yieldedness and filling. First, there comes a wonderful new consciousness of Christ. Second, there comes a wonderful new aliveness in prayer. Third, the believer begins to exhibit more plainly than before the graces of Jesus. Fourth, there begins to develop in and through the believer the "joy unspeakable," and the "peace that passeth understanding," and the "life more abundant," and the "enduement of power from on high." This is the blessing we all need and which we should all prayerfully seek. Especially do you and I need this blessing in our sacred work as ministers of Christ and as leaders among the companies of His people.

Whatever other Godward or manward meanings may inhere in the phenomenon of that historic Pentecost which signaled in the Christian dispensation, the three main meanings which live on through the centuries and should be revivified to us today are those which I have emphasized: (1) a new *life,* (2) a new *fellowship,* (3) a new *fulness.*

All of us who are born-again men have that new life. No man without it is a true minister of Christ. However scholarly, religious, or well-intending he may be, if a man is in the ministry and yet a stranger to the new birth he is a counterfeit. Whether knowingly or unknowingly he is an imposter; his profession is a masquerade. But, beloved brethren, in the words of Hebrews 6:9, "we are persuaded better things of *you.*" Gratefully do I presume that I am now addressing true brethren in the ministry; men whose hearts blend with my own in thanking God for the "precious blood" which has redeemed us, and for the regenerating Holy Spirit through whose supernatural operation within us we have become spiritually reborn. Yes, brethren, you and I have that new *life* from God; but how much do we know about the new *fellowship* with God, and the spiritual *fulness* which Pentecost is meant to effect?

Am I right or wrong in suspecting that many of us who verily have the new life know little about a heart-to-heart *fellowship* with God? Through the gracious miracle of our inward renewal God has "begotten us again" to sonship, and the voice of that sonship within us cries heavenwards, "Abba Father"; but we allow the competing clamor of public demands continually to divert us. Our ministry becomes desultory; prayer becomes spasmodic; and communion with God a faltering flicker. I know, of course, that communion with God does not consist only in set times of prayer; it is a reciprocal intercommunication which continues uninterruptedly through all the pressure and clamor of daily work hours; yet it cannot survive, much less thrive, *without* regular, set seasons of secret prayer.

Think again of John Wesley and his first four hours every day alone with God and the Bible; of Martin Luther and his three hours of similar daily retirement; of Charles G. Finney and his long withdrawals alone for prayer; and of other such whom it would take too long even to mention. What a delight were all those men to God! — and what a delight was God to them! To those men prayer was their "vital breath" and communion their "native air." They *walked* with God, as truly as Enoch did. They *knew* God as truly as a man knows his friend. They had earthly troubles in plenty, but they had learned a high level on which they rode above earth's cloudy tempest. From glowing experience they could say with John, "Truly our fellowship is with the Father, and with His Son, Jesus Christ."

Those men really knew God and lived in sanctifying communion with Him. They experienced a kind of fellowship with God which has become possible only since Pentecost. During Old Testament times, even in the covenant nation, there was no such open fellowship with God as there now is through the "new and living way." From time to time there were specially chosen men on whom the Spirit came in an abnormal way; yet even they did not have the continual "access" which we now have through "the blood of the everlasting covenant" and as reborn "sons of God."

Oh, brethren, are you and I truly living toward God as His blood-redeemed, Spirit-born *sons?* He has "begotten us again" for *fellowship* with Himself. Through continual fellowship with Him each of us is meant to become what every Christian minister should long to be: *"a man of God."* If only we would give God opportunity! If only we were men of prayer! The Holy Spirit, given in fulness at Pentecost, waits to make it all "come alive."

But finally, besides *fellowship* with God through Pentecost, there is the new spiritual *fulness* which we are all meant to know. "They were all filled with the Holy Ghost," says Acts 2:4 of the disciples away back *then.* "Be filled with the Spirit" says Ephesians 5:18 to you and me *now.* So it is proper for me to ask: Brother minister, do you know the experiential reality of being *"filled with the Spirit"*? Is the Pentecostal provision a proven verity to you, or only a side theory? Maybe there is another question I should ask: Are some of us nowadays so afraid of "Pentecosta*lism*" that we are shying away from Pentecost itself, with its supernatural flame and fire and force and fulness? Are some of us so fond of self-management that we shun the complete hand-over to God which alone makes a Pentecostal infilling possible? Are some of us so busy that we are almost empty? Gentlemen, I pay you tribute. You are the most energetic people on earth. You put some others of us to shame. How generous, how well-organized, how collectively efficient you are! But (if I may dare ask without any seeming disrespect) is the missing quality (with many) spiritual *depth?*

Brethren, if my estimate of you is right, you would sooner I came to you with the rebukes of a prophet or the wounds of a friend than with the hollow flatteries of a sychophant. Let me be fraternally frank: I believe that one of the things (perhaps the *main* thing) which the evangelical denominations and churches and ministers of today are needing to relearn is the ultimate futility of the cleverest organization and the most elaborate "programme" apart from a real and continuing experience of Pentecost.

But if truly Pentecostal sanctification and infilling are to be known among our evangelical churches, how may a new moving of the Holy Spirit be engendered? Must it not begin with us ministers? You and I, brother minister, must seek the fulness, and do so with godly resolve. It will have to be another case of "when the iron bar is in the fire, the fire is in the iron," or "when the sponge is in the water, the water is in the sponge." We possess by being possessed. When the fire has all of the iron bar, the iron bar has all of the fire which it can hold. When the sponge is fully in the water, the water fills the sponge to capacity. There must be a complete hand-over. There is no other way: and every man of us must make choice. The Holy Spirit must really possess us if there is to be His saturation of our personalities. What I give to Him He *takes*. What He takes He *cleanses*. What He cleanses He *fills*. What He fills He *uses*. That is the fourfold formula. It always works. It never fails. May you and I, all of us, know its reality in our own experience! It is futile for us to start "claiming" the promised infilling (as we are often told to do nowadays) unless we have first allowed *Him* to claim *us*. "Claiming" by the incompletely yielded is a valueless presuming which is never honored from the heavenward side. But once we are indeed yielded *entirely* to our Lord, *then* there thrills into our living experience the truth that He never leaves a fully surrendered vessel unfilled. Let our prayer be:

> Break through my nature, mighty heavenly Love,
>   Clear every avenue of thought and brain;
> Flood my affections, purify my will;
>   Make all I am Thy sanctified domain.
>
> Thus wholly mastered and by Thee possessed,
>   Forth from my life, spontaneous and free,
> Shall flow a stream of grace and tenderness,
>   Loving because *Thy* love lives on through *me*.

PENTECOST AND THE LOCAL CHURCH

I know that we have a knotty generation to deal with, and that it is past the power of any of us to change a carnal heart without the effectual operation of the Holy Ghost; yet it is so usual with God to work by means, and to bless the right endeavours of His servants, that I cannot fear but great things will be accomplished, and a wonderful blow will be given to the kingdom of darkness by this work, if it do not miscarry through the fault of the ministers themselves.

Richard Baxter

PENTECOST AND THE LOCAL CHURCH

Organized Christianity originated two thousand years ago on that historic "day of Pentecost" which is graphically described in the second chapter of the Acts. The local Christian assemblies of those New Testament times have an undying significance for the organized Christian Church throughout the present age. We do well to turn back to the records again and again, lest we wander from the Spirit-wrought original.

I would not go so far as to argue that in every detail the occurrences of that Pentecost long ago were meant to continue in perpetual recurrence. At that point I respectfully but decidedly differ from those brethren who would have us believe that Pentecost in every detail was meant to be the abiding *norm* of the Church's experience throughout the present age. I hold that some of those miraculous efflorescences such as "speaking in tongues" and the startling abnormality of raising the dead were meant as temporary "signs" for the time which then was, rather than as continuing phenomena for the time which now is.

Examination of Scripture convinces me that many brethren fail to distinguish adequately between the two Greek words, *sēmeia* and *charismata*, that is, between "signs" and "gifts" — the difference being that "signs" are merely temporary, whereas "gifts" are permanent. Those supernatural wonders which accompanied the Pentecost described in Acts 2 are specifically called "signs" — including the "speaking in tongues." They had special reference to the suspense period covered by the Acts of the Apostles, in which our Lord Jesus, now crucified and resurrected, was being offered for the *second* time to the nation Israel, as the long-promised Messiah-Savior.

If we would know what the Holy Spirit's permanent *"gifts"* to the Church are, we must consult the New Testament Epistles, especially the "Christian Church Epistles" (i.e., Romans to 2 Thessalonians). When we do so, we find that from beginning to end of the twenty-one epistles in our New Testament, "speaking in tongues" appears in only one passage — 1 Corinthians 12 to 14; and even there it is assigned a subordinate place.

These words of mine may be frank, but they are spoken with respectful charity. We must surely distinguish between the incidental and the fundamental; between the outwardly circumstantial and the inwardly all-essential. Once for all, let us get clear on this point: that thrilling "day of Pentecost" and those days of apostolic "sign-miracles" which signalled in the present dispensation were never meant to constitute a *detailed outward* "norm" for the Church's subsequent history; yet just as certainly they *were* meant to be a *spiritual* pattern — a continuing spiritual pattern right on from that first coming of the Spirit to the second coming of Christ. *

With that in mind, let me direct you to a few verses in Acts 5, where we have a remarkable snapshot of the first local Christian assembly or "church" in history.

> And by the hands of the apostles were many signs and wonders wrought among the people; (and they were all with one accord in Solomon's porch. And of the rest durst no man join himself to them: but the people magnified them. And believers were the more added to the Lord, multitudes both of men and women.) Insomuch that they brought forth the sick into the streets, and laid them on beds and couches, that at the least the shadow of Peter passing by might overshadow some of them. There came also a multitude out of the cities round about unto Jerusalem, bringing sick folks, and them which were vexed with unclean spirits: and they were healed every one. Then the high priest rose up, and all they that were with him, (which is the sect of the Sadducees,) and were filled with indignation, And laid their hands on the apostles, and put them in the common prison.

At that point a troublesome interval began for the apostles and for the Church. But see the outcome of it, at the end of the chapter, in verses 40 to 42:

> And when they had called the apostles, and beaten them, they commanded that they should not speak in the name of Jesus, and let them go. And they departed from the presence of the council, rejoicing that they were counted worthy to suffer shame for his name. And daily in the temple, and in every house, they ceased not to teach and preach Jesus Christ.

---

* I sympathetically realize how annoying a brief reference like this can be to brethren who advocate speaking in tongues as belonging to today. For fuller treatment may I respectfully refer them to the three chapters on "A Re-survey of the Acts" in my recent book *The Strategic Grasp of the Bible*.

Those verses photograph three arresting features belonging to that sanctified Christian band of the first days: (1) power to repel; (2) power to attract; (3) power to surmount. Pause for a moment at the first of these.

Power to Repel

That first of all local churches had *power to repel*. See again verse 13, "And of the rest *durst no man join himself to them* . . ." It reminds us of Deuteronomy 28:10, "All the people of the earth shall see that thou art called by the name of the Lord; and they shall be *afraid* of thee." When a church is possessed and controlled by the Holy Spirit, it not only spreads joy, it creates awe. It not only sheds the light which saves the contrite, it flames with a fire which frightens pretenders. Spurgeon never said a truer thing than, "A holy church is an awful weapon in the hand of God."

I suspect that many of us pastors are needing to halt at those words again: *"No man durst join himself to them."* Most people nowadays seem to think that the only power needed by the Christian Church is the power to *attract;* but they are wrong. They cannot see the difference between a Gideon's "three hundred" and a mob. The modern drive after numbers needs reconsideration. Bulk can never be a substitute for power. Growth is never the same as obesity. Some of the biggest bodies are the sickliest. The Church needs power to *repel* if it is to maintain that holy separation in which alone the Holy Spirit can do His most God-glorifying work. Our local churches today need to recover that separateness, that holiness, that overshadowing divine presence which creates God-conscious awe and strikes fear into the insincere. Our churches need again the power to repel. They need again that holy flame which scorches the hypocritical fraternizer; that awesome presence which scares away the "mixed multitude" of compromisers — Satan's quislings and the world's plausible Judases.

One of the main reasons why the churches in many parts have lost their power to attract is that they have lost their power to repel. They have doted on mere statistics, and in doing so have shuffled from separation into compromise. They have lost the passion for holiness, and in losing that they have also lost the supernatural flame of the divine Spirit.

During recent years it has been my privilege to preach the Holy Scriptures up and down both hemispheres and in all five continents. I have been graciously permitted to occupy well-known pulpits among Baptists, Methodists, Presbyterians, Congregationalists, Lutherans, Episcopalians, Anglicans, Christian Alliance churches, and other Protestant groups. In review, I set my seal to this, that nowhere have I found any combine of churches more agog with zest and verve for evangelism, recruitment, expansion, and territorial outreach than you Southern Baptists. In that sense you "lead the van"; and I, for one, am minded to learn all I can from you. Yet (if I may follow up my sincere compliment with sincere concern) could your very point of excellence be your peak of peril? Could there be any danger of strangulation by overorganization? To be humanly *galvanized* is very different from being divinely *energized*.

Brethren of the Southern Baptist Convention, after moving around among you somewhat I want to ask you: Is there an overawing awareness of the divine majesty and holiness in your sanctuaries? Is there a solemnizing, purifying reverence among your people? Is there such a haunting, clinging, subduing God-consciousness that the unconverted are afraid to take liberties with you? Are the pastors, especially the younger ones, becoming too bland to denounce sin with a prophet's thunder? Are the members becoming so harmlessly affable that they are losing the capacity for "righteous indignation" at moral evil? Is the master passion of the Southern Baptists *holiness?* — or mere numerical size? Alas, I think there is *cause* for my asking that question.

Brethren, time was in America when communities had a healthy *fear* of the Christian pulpit and pew. Why has it largely disappeared? Never was there better or bigger organization than now; but the awe-inspiring flame of the unmistakably *divine* seems missing. In some places churches have been denominationally organized until they have become spiritually paralyzed. Many a minister today is looking for success in *numbers,* when the real solution is in *exodus* — a turning out of those who should never have been taken in! Thousands of people are amiably cajoled into church membership who do not have the vital prerequisite for it. There ought to be such holy life and power and fire and divine presence among us that all such are either broken down before God or frightened away. I am the last person to underrate the importance of planning and expediting, but in my judgment the peril just now is that of *organizing* instead of *agonizing;* of pressing a human *programme* rather than pleading the divine *presence.* There is a new challenge upon us today which can only be truly met by the tongue of fire in the pulpit and the heaven-born flame in the pew. We are needing a new accent on separation, on sanctification, on enduement by the Holy Spirit. We are needing this because we are desperately needing again today the power to create fear, the power to repel the false, for the sake of safeguarding and demonstrating the real. Let us never forget it: the first feature of that early church was its *power to repel!*

Power to Attract

But now let me underline the second prominent feature belonging to that primitive Christian group in old Jerusalem. It had the *power to attract.* It did not try to coerce. It did not seek to beguile. It had neither whip nor wand. It indulged no publicity stunts. It advertised no catch titles. It boasted no academic scholarship. It had scant administration. It had no millionaire members. Yet it had victorious power to attract which dumbfounded the hostile bigots at the head of the *status quo.*

It specially attracted two classes of persons. It attracted (1) *believers* and (2) the *sick.* The former came for fellowship. The latter came for healing. Glance again at verse 14: "And believers were the more added to the Lord, multitudes both of men and women." Those "believers," I repeat, came for fellowship, and they found it.

Every truly born-again believer reaches out for fellowship with other members of the "household of the faith." Christian believers are not merely a society, they are a *family;* for the one same Spirit of new birth is in all of them. They long for fellowship with one another because that same Spirit of life in each of them yearns toward all the other members of the family.

Alas, one of the dreariest tragedies today is that spiritually minded Christians believers *cannot* find this family fellowship in many of those buildings and congregations known as "churches." Almost anything *but* fellowship can be found there! Many of our congregations are mere Sunday audiences rather than Christ-conscious *fraternities* of the regenerated.

Even among our evangelical churches, real "fellowship of the Spirit" is comparatively rare. As a result, thousands of Christians are fighting their battles in lonely isolation, often disheartened and unaware of the resources which would be theirs if only our local "churches" would learn to be churches after the New Testament pattern. Our local churches should be fellowships where "perfect love casteth our fear," but many of them are little more than religious depots or rendezvous of social hobnobbing.

Yes, there is a breakdown in local church fellowship. Why?

Well, perhaps in America some of our churches are too *big*. Individuals often feel lonesomely lost in the anonymity of the large modern congregation. Or, maybe, in some of our sanctuaries we are now so sophisticated, so etiquettically "proper" that we are politely closed to each other. Perhaps we are needing to rediscover the importance of the small Christian group, and of open-hearted reciprocity such as John Wesley's "class" meetings engendered.

But why "beat about the bush"? The real reason we do not have the magnetic fellowship of the early church is our *spiritual superficiality*. Most of the preaching is sermonic rather than prophetic, and the evangelism is anecdotal rather than Pentecostal. The hymns are sentimental more often than doctrinal, with a pleasing lilt rather than a profound truth. And the members say, "Now wasn't that good?" so long as the preacher is orthodox and interesting. Oh, brethren, I would not misuse time in merely criticizing — any quack can do that — but with deep concern I contend that most of our local churches today need rescue from *spiritual superficiality*.

That world-girdling American evangelist, the late Dr. R. A. Torrey, tells how, when he was a young pastor, he became weary with blustering around in zealous inefficiency, until at last he stopped short and rather desperately vowed that he would not enter his pulpit again until he knew by experience the promised enduement by the Holy Spirit. There were hours of intense praying in secret, of heartsearching, of struggling to the point of utter surrender, and of waiting, waiting, waiting. But the mighty envelopment came, and Torrey was never the same again. Nor was his church. He began to get his leaders and some of the members low before God in similarly tenacious yielding and praying. By and by, the whole band of believers was in the lovely grip of spiritual revival! Is it not time for something of the same sort to happen among present-day ministers and memberships?

But now, look again at verse 16 and see how that early church attracted the *sick:* "There came also a multitude out of the cities round about unto Jerusalem, bringing sick folk and them that were vexed with unclean spirits: and they were healed every one."

Maybe today some of us are needing to reread those passages in the Epistles which speak about divine healing for the body. As for myself, I am persuaded, after thoughtful examination of the New Testament, that those noisy, self-boosting faith-healing movements of our time which offer bodily healing to anybody and everybody as part of the "whosoever" gospel are exegetically wrong.

Inquiry has shown, also, that many of their supposed cures are spurious. I do not believe that the Scripture warrants us to include healing for the body in the Church's message to the miscellaneous public. Yet I do believe that healing for the body is included in the Spirit's gifts to the *Ecclesia,* and that it is appropriable among those who are truly the Lord's own people. I believe, also, that if we were rescued from our present spiritual shallowness and were living abundantly in the rich life of the Holy Spirit, we might see a delightfully spontaneous reappearance of various healings among us.

However, for the moment I am content to let those sick folk who came to that Jerusalem "church" long ago represent those all around us today who are sinsick, or fearsick, or worrysick, or heartsick. They are on every street in this century of frantic rush, urban congestion, nervous tautness, domestic intricacy, and psychomatic strain. Many who wistfully frequent our churches need saving almost as much from the druggist as from the devil. There are no tranquilizers sold over the druggist's counter to compare with the healing tranquility shed in the believer's mind by the Holy Spirit. Many people who supposedly need psychiatry are in reality needing *Christopathy,* the healing which only Jesus gives.

There is a verse in the Gospels which says, "It was noised abroad that Jesus was in the house." There is another place which says, "And the power of the Lord was present to heal." If our local churches were Pentecostally living and operating in the "fulness" of the Holy Spirit, it would be continually "noised abroad that *Jesus* is in the house" and that "the power of the Lord is present to *heal.*" I believe that such churches today would be just as magnetic *now* as that first "church" of two thousand years ago was magnetic *then.*

Power to Surmount

Finally, that church of the first days had the power to *surmount.* Glance back at the narrative again. Verse 17 spells trouble: "Then the high priest rose up, and all they that were with him (which is the sect of the Sadducees,) and were filled with indignation, and laid their hands on the Apostles, and put them in the common prison." So at one stroke all the church leaders were dumped into custody; and that was but the beginning of rough handling. There was to be inquisition and flogging. But see how the chapter ends: "They departed from the presence of the council, rejoicing that they were counted worthy to suffer shame for His name. And daily in the temple, and in every house, they ceased not to teach and preach Jesus Christ."

Yes, that church had the power to overcome. New difficulty meant new opportunity. New trial meant new triumph. A church filled by the Spirit can never be killed by the devil. Even its martyrdoms become conquests, for at the stoning of every Stephen there is some onlooking Saul who becomes a Paul. It is because that young church of those early times had such resilient power to surmount and flourish that we are here today in the goodly succession.

But there is one big question left. What was it which gave that first church its power to repel, its power to attract, its power to surmount? The answer is threefold.

First: it was a church in which *all the members had become witnesses.* They were not merely believers holding certain redeeming truths. Nor · were they merely disciples learning certain spiritual disciplines. They were witnesses to saving facts and to a transforming experience of Christ. (See Acts 2:32; 3:15; 4:33; 5:32).

Second: it was a church in which *owners had become stewards.* In Acts 4:32 we read, "Neither said any of them that aught of the things which he possessed was his own." I am not suggesting that in our socially different present day we should resort to the communal pooling adopted during that abnormal Jerusalem situation; but I *am* insisting that today, just as much as then, we should cease to be owners and become stewards — with every one of our possessions laid at the Master's feet.

Third: it was a church in which *all self-interest was sunk in one holy passion to exalt Christ.* Unlike our modern World Council of Churches, which (at least to some of us) seems to be always talking about the Church, the Church, the Church, *that* local church in old time Jewry *never* preached the Church, but only and always Christ, Christ, CHRIST.

Nowadays, in our denominational assemblies, one hears about the Baptists this, and the Baptists that, and the Baptists the other: or the Methodists this, and the Mehodists that, and the Methodists the other. I am not criticizing necessary denominational references; but today we are so denominationally self-conscious and voluminously self-advertising that we are obtrusively blocking men's vision of *HIM.*

It is the same in much modern evangelism, where, instead of a lowly man of prayer, the evangelist is a sort of glamorized religious "star." Pictures and posters, write-ups and boosters bedeck him with human plaudits until one wonders whom the people are coming to hear — the meek and lowly Jesus with nail prints in His hands or the loudly publicized big boy who takes the platform. I am not speaking in a sarcastic vein, but I could not help thinking about a certain type of modern evangelist when I recently saw a notice over the main entrance of an automobile repair shop: "Enter and blow horn!"

Brethren, it is wrong. A thousand times, it is wrong. Far too much glory is given to human leaders. Worldly methods of promotion and propaganda have reached a point where the true spirituality of the Church is impaired and the supernatural operations of the Holy Spirit are prevented.

Somehow, we must get back to the New Testament pattern. What is the first step? Awhile ago I was deeply challenged by a comment which I came across in my reading. It said: "The first duty of every minister is to beg God, very humbly, that all which he, the preacher, wants to be done in his hearers may first be *truly and fully done in himself.*"

Brethren, hear my final word. In a vital, spiritual sense the local Christian church seldom, if ever, advances further than its pastor advances *on his knees*. I therefore ask each one of you: Do you know the experience of being "filled with the Spirit?" Have *you* waited on God and continued with steady tenacity until you knew the "enduement of power from on high"? That is the biggest need of the modern evangelical church and its pulpit.

It is all so important because the local church is so important. Wholeheartedly am I in favor of mass evangelism. In this industrial age, with its ever-multiplying urbanization, mass evangelism seems more needed than ever. Yet if my own reading of Church history is right, not the evangelist but the *local church* is the vital cell in the preservation and propagation of the Christian faith. How wonderful it would be if this minister and that minister, if this local church and that local church, caught again the pure flame of truly Pentecostal Christianity, and then the fire here and the fire there wafted together until a prairie blaze of spiritual revival spread across the land! Is the Lord's arm shortened? Does not God still fill the earth with summer where winter has held grip? Has the Holy Spirit been withdrawn? Is He not still looking for consecrated ministers and churches? If revival is to come it *must* begin somewhere. Could it begin in *you*, and in *your* church? R. A. Torrey, for one, would say, "YES!"

PENTECOST AND THE PULPIT TODAY

A sermon full of mere words, how neat soever it be composed, while it wants the light of evidence, and the life of zeal, is but an image, or a well-dressed carcase. In preaching, there is a communion of souls, and a communication of somewhat from ours to theirs. As we and they have understandings, wills, and affections, so must the bent of our endeavours be to communicate the fullest light of evidence from our understandings to theirs, and to warm their hearts by kindling in them holy affections, as by a communication from our own.

Richard Baxter

PENTECOST AND THE PULPIT TODAY

I am addressing preachers, and I want to say something timely to preachers. I shall not commit the effrontery of even attempting anything oratorically brilliant, or philosophically profound, or theologically novel. On the contrary, I am thinking that it would do us all good, once again, to take a humble, careful, steady look at the apostle Paul as a significant example to all of us who would be true ministers of Christ and prevailing preachers of the divine Word. If preachers are to be estimated according to impact and results, then from the beginning of the Church until today there has never been a greater than Paul.

The indomitable apostle is a challenging example to Christian believers in many ways, but he is especially exemplary to all Christian preachers who would fain be in the true apostolic succession. So then, at the moment we are thinking of him as *Paul, the pattern preacher.* For our present purpose I turn to one passage only: 1 Corinthians 2:1-5.

> And I, brethren, when I came to you, came not with excellency of speech or of wisdom, proclaiming to you the testimony of God. For I determined not to know anything among you, save Jesus Christ, and him crucified. And I was with you in weakness, and in fear, and in much trembling. And my speech and my preaching were not in persuasive words of man's wisdom, but in demonstration of the Spirit and of power; that your faith should not stand in the wisdom of men, but in the power of God.

It seems to me, after long and thoughtful observation, that there are two crises through which each of us must go, in one way or another, at one time or another, if we would be convincing and prevailing preachers of Christ. The one crisis is intellectual, the other is spiritual. They are both evident in the Pauline autobiographical flashback which we have just quoted.

The Intellectual Crisis

The intellectual crisis is indicated in verses 1 and 2.

> And I, brethren, when I came to you, came not with excellency of speech or of wisdom, proclaiming to you the testimony of

God. For I determined not to know anything among you, save Jesus Christ, and him crucified.

This is all the more remarkable when we reflect what Corinth was in those days. Think again what it meant for Paul to renounce oratory and philosophy at Corinth of all places. The Corinth of Paul's day, even though it was a sink of voluptuous sensualism, boasted that its institutions of learning excelled those of Rome and that its philosophers outshone the most brilliant thinkers of Athens. Its cosmopolitan populace, an exotic conglomeration of peoples, were of the flamboyant, floridly emotional type, tropical in disposition, vivid in their reactions. They were easily enamored of the brilliant, the flashy, the demonstrative. It was there (need I remind you?) that the golden-tongued orator Apollos gate-crashed into immediate acclaim. Paul knew well enough that if there was one place more than another where "excellency of speech" and "philosophy" would be impressive, it was Corinth. Yet it was there that he most resolutely discarded them!

Why, then, did Paul renounce the accoutrements of learning at the very place where they might have been the most impressive? Here is his reason: "I came ... proclaiming unto you the *testimony of God.*" Brethren, either our gospel *is* or is *not* the "testimony of God." If it *is*, then our trying to give it power or make it work by academic arts or prowess of learning is like holding up candles to help the sun to shine. Is our gospel really divine in its origin and authority? Then human intellect and eloquence must be completely subordinated. The divine message itself must be allowed to do its own work and prove its own power.

That is where the *intellectual* crisis arises. Is the Bible really the Word of God? Is Jesus Christ really God the Son incarnate? Is the gospel really the truth of God? Those are the big, all-determining questions which must be answered within each of us. I call attention to that word "determined" — "I determined not to know ... ." It indicates cogitation, mental wrestling, and emergent resolution. We evangelicals believe that Paul was inerrantly inspired in all that he *taught,* but we do not necessarily believe that he was thus inspired in all that he *thought.* He was a man of like passions with ourselves, and I can well imagine that he had sleepless hours during the night as he contemplated his visit to Corinth. He decided that if the gospel was really the "testimony of God," then it ought to prove itself just as truly in problematical Corinth as anywhere else.

Maybe there are others of us who need a similar inward struggle and iron-willed resolve. Could it be that even among ourselves there are brethren who secretly doubt? I am frequently told that there is a place for honest doubt. So there is, but not in the Christian pulpit. The more honest a man's doubt, the sooner he will vacate the ministry. The Christian pulpit was never built for doubting Thomases, nor was it ever built *by* them. I can sympathize with sincere doubters. In the second year of my own ministry I almost quit through doubts. I am grateful to say that amid my quagmire of uncertainty I found the stepping stones back to a firmer faith in the great Christian verities. I remember how the increase of doubt corresponded with the decrease of power, and how, with a restoration to a new certitude, there came a new sense of vitality. At any rate, brethren, this is the first big question, this is the intellectual crisis: Is the Christ whom we preach really God incarnate? Are the Bible and the gospel, which we preach, really and truly and fully *divine* in origin, nature, and authority? Each one of us has to settle it one way or the other. We come through this crisis in many different ways; some suddenly, others gradually, some earlier, others later, some mildly, others tumultuously; but there is never any real preaching power until, like Paul, we emerge with the deep-plowed conviction that our gospel is the "testimony of God."

See the twofold result in Paul, consequent upon that conviction. First, he puts himself completely out of the picture — "I came not with excellency of speech or of wisdom." Second, he puts Christ right in the forefront — "I determined not to know anything among you save Jesus Christ . . ." Nor is even the Christ of Galilee enough; it must be the Christ of the Calvary stigma — "Christ and Him *crucified.*"

Brethren, have you and I traveled at least that far with Paul? Are we really convinced as to the divinity of our message? Have we put "self" completely out of the picture? Is Christ continuously and conspicuously right in the forefront? Are we preaching the whole message? — or are there reservations, withholdings, and deletions? Not so long ago the young son of a Baptist minister in England stole into his daddy's study. A new sermon was being prepared. The little boy peered at his daddy's preliminary jottings and then asked, "Daddy, do you get your sermons from God?" Daddy thought he had better reply, "Yes." Whereupon the little invader asked, "Daddy, if you get your sermons from God, why do you do so much crossing out?" What a lot of crossing out we do today! Are we giving our people the whole "testimony"? Have we pushed "self" right out of the picture? Is Christ always in full view? Most of all, are we prayerfully, feelingly, urgently preaching that wonderful divine-human Savior, the Christ of the *cross?*

The Spiritual Crisis

Look now at the spiritual crisis:

> And I was with you in weakness, and in fear, and in much trembling. And my speech and my preaching were not in persuasive words of man's wisdom, but in demonstration of the Spirit and of power.

So brethren, it is not enough in itself even to have the *message* right — with all display excluded and Jesus supreme; the *method* must be right as well. The Christ of Calvary must be preached in the power of Pentecost. No matter how true the sermon or how earnest the speaker, there is no dynamic counterpart in the hearer except by the Holy Spirit.

That is where the *spiritual* crisis arises. Many a preacher who preaches Christ and is bravely prepared to preach the "offense of the cross" is not prepared to give up his own way of doing it. Brethren, there is to be no reliance on anything of self or anything human. This is a delicate point and not too easy, perhaps, to express with fine exactness, yet it is vital to spiritual effectiveness. There may be a place for cultivated speech, organizing, advertising, and other means, but the minute they are relied on for spiritual results they become fatal. There must be utter abandonment to the heavenly Spirit. It is that which brings what Paul calls the "demonstration of the Spirit and of power." The "power" is in the preacher; the "demonstration" is in the hearer. The Holy Spirit is the connection between the two; and that alone is how vital spiritual effects are wrought.

See the frank, startling words in which Paul discloses his own reliance on the Holy Spirit: "I was with you in *weakness,* and in *fear,* and in much *trembling."* What a trinity of surprises — "weakness," "fear," "much trembling"! Was *that* the sort of preacher who would impress the Corinthians, or you, or me? Well, it was because Paul had so really come to the end of himself that the Holy Spirit could use all that he really *was.* Oh, for more such weakness and fear and trembling in our modern pulpit! — and for more of the same results! I have sometimes heard conference preachers tell us that the cure for nervousness is to be filled with the Holy Spirit. Was

Paul filled with the Holy Spirit? He certainly was, yet he speaks of "weakness," and of "fear," and of "trembling." It was not fear of men or of physical suffering. The infilling of the Holy Spirit will indeed give us victory over weakness and fear and trembling, but that does not necessarily mean His taking them away from us. Some of those who have triumphed most have trembled most, as did Martin Luther before the congregated German nobles. Perhaps many of us are needing such a revivified consciousness of the eternal issues hanging upon our preaching that we too shall know this apostolic weakness and fear and trembling. I have heard of a newly ordained young Presbyterian minister in Scotland who went to take the morning service at a certain church. In the absence of the resident minister, the kind old verger asked if he could be of any assistance, but the young minister conceitedly replied, "Not at all, sir; I am a fully ordained and degreed minister." In that spirit he went into the pulpit and made a complete failure of the service. Afterward he came down from the pulpit in a confusion of humiliation. The verger's comment was, "Young brother, if you had gone into the pulpit the way you came out, you might have come out the way you went in."

It is often said, "The truth will do its own work if it is preached, even if the preacher himself is not all he should be." That, however, is a deceptive error, all the more dangerous because it is a mixture of right and wrong. The truth we preach has no real spiritual effectuality in the hearer unless vitally applied by the accompanying power of the Holy Spirit. The degree to which that vital power is transmitted through our preaching is determined by the degree to which we ourselves are controlled by the Holy Spirit. It is well worthwhile, brethren, to suffer with Paul in his weakness, and fear, and trembling, if thereby we may also experience in and through our preaching the "demonstration of the Spirit and of power" as it operated in and through Paul.

Try to picture the scene as Paul lectured in the house of Titus Justus at Corinth. Imagine yourself sitting there, next to a couple of curious Corinthians who have been coaxed into hearing the little Jew. When Paul appears behind the desk, you overhear one of them remark, "Very poor appearance," to which the other responds, "Looks consumptive to me." Paul is rather pale, and his opening remarks are faltering. You overhear the further comment, "Not much of a speaker. Why, look, he's trembling. He can't disguise it! He's nervous and afraid! Let's go; we shan't get much here." However, the two visitors linger a few minutes; and now they notice a peculiar change in the speaker. A dash of color flushes his cheeks. A prophetic flash is in his eyes. A compelling tone of authority rings in his voice. The seeming weakness has given place to a thrill of power which grips and sways his hearers. The early hesitancy has given place to an eloquence which pours forth like a torrent of fire flakes on hearts and consciences. There is an irresistible utterance now, altogether different from that of the chattering pundits in the Corinthian debating halls. There is a *presence* in the room; an invisible but unmistakable *presence*. What is it? The two visitors do not know; but that little speaker is clothed with a supernatural power never encountered before, and something is happening inside them which they had never dreamed possible.

That is how it happened again and again. That is how thousands of souls were supernaturally converted and the first Christian churches formed. Brethren, I believe that the saddest tragedy of our modern evangelical pulpit is the *lack* of that power — that which grips and sways and saves. It is the Spirit of God who alone imparts power to the Word preached. Without that power, all the truths we preach will be no more than "thunder to the deaf, or lightning to the blind." You may have plenty of good sealing wax and a finely cut seal, but the metal seal will make no impression on the wax unless there is a hand to apply it firmly. So is it in the preaching of the gospel; if the fine-cut seal of the Word is to make vital imprint in human minds, it must be impressed there by the Holy Spirit as the executive of the Godhead.

In our days, the common idea seems to be that in order to attract and hold the people we must devise new methods. Well, I suppose there is always a need for adaptation; yet that is comparatively of lesser importance. Back in the days of D. L. Moody, the commonest remark heard after his meetings was, "Nothing new; nothing new; but what *power!*" Is it mere accident that Paul, Wesley, Whitefield, Spurgeon, Finney, Moody, and many other mightily used preachers of the Word have all shared the same idea as to the first-important prerequisite in preaching the gospel with supernatural effectiveness? They all had that same Pauline idea: "And I, brethren, when I came to you, came not with excellency of speech or of wisdom, proclaiming to you the testimony of God. For I determined not to know anything among you, save Jesus Christ, and him crucified. And I was with you in weakness, and in fear, and in much trembling. And my speech and my preaching were not in persuasive words of man's wisdom, *but in demonstration of the*

Spirit and of power; that your faith should not stand in the wisdom of men, but in the power of God" (1 Cor. 2:1-5).

Finally, see Paul's *motive* in it all: "That your faith should not stand in the wisdom of men, but in the *power of God.*" That is why apostolic Christianity flourished despite both intellectual and physical opposition. It needed no propping up by the artificial scaffolding of human science and philosophy, so-called. It throbbed with the manifested power of God, and that was its all-victorious, pragmatic apologetic which conquered the ancient world. One of the most depressing spectacles today is the wonderful amount of faithful gospel ministry which is destitute of power. In all the Bible there is no more pathetic sight than Samson shorn of his locks; and there is nothing more pathetic today than vital Christian truth preached without Pentecostal power. Look at Elijah on Mount Carmel: all the rhetoric, all the threatening, all the irony of Elijah would have failed if the fire of the Lord had not fallen to consume the sacrifice. When the fire fell, that was the convincing demonstration. So is it with the preaching of the gospel; it does not reveal the "power of God" without the fire of Pentecost. The fire must fall. The Spirit must burn through our words. *He* must make the Word mighty in the hearer's mind. Is it not time for many of us who are public preachers of the holy gospel to get alone with God, to search our hearts, review our ministry, and seek to know that heavenly enduing which brings into our preaching "the demonstration of the Spirit and power"?

PENTECOST AND PERSONAL WITNESS

If you would prosper in the ministerial work, be sure to keep up earnest desires and *expectations* of success. If you long not to see the conversion and edification of your hearers, and do not study and preach in *hope*, you are not likely to *see* much success. . . . I have observed that God seldom blesseth any man's work so much as his whose heart is set upon the success of it. Let it be the property of a Judas to have more regard to the bag than to his work, but let all who preach for Christ and men's salvation be unsatisfied till they have the thing they preach for.

Richard Baxter

PENTECOST AND PERSONAL WITNESS

My dear brethren, in this present address I am to speak on the subject of Pentecost in relation to our witness-bearing for Christ. As a beginning, I ask you to turn with me, once again, to the well-known words of Acts 1:8:

> But ye shall receive power, after that the Holy Spirit is come upon you: and ye shall be witnesses unto me both in Jerusalem, and in all Judea, and in Samaria, and unto the uttermost part of the earth.

To us Spirit-born believers, who comprise the true Church, God has given the greatest mission in the world, the greatest message in the world, and the greatest Master in the world. Our mission is to *save* men. Our message is the *gospel*. Our Master is the risen *Christ*. Never was there more urgent reason than now for us to fulfill our divine mission. Never was there more cogent reason than now for us to proclaim our divine message. Never was there more poignant reason than now for us to obey the grand commission of our divine Master.

In our time such winds of evil have heaved their foul breath over the earth as have never been known before. False ideologies spread specious deceptions over the nations, under the pretence of accelerating human evolution. Ambitious despots with an atheistic totalitarianism have usurped a tyrannical dictatorship over hundreds of millions of our fellow humans; and millions more seem likely to fall a gullible prey to the hydra-headed communist monster. The free nations are cursed by corrupt politics and a demoralizing psychology. Priestcraft and dead orthodoxy and heretical cults jeopardize Protestant Christendom as never before. The call of the hour to us of the Protestant and evangelical churches is to break free from the parasitic entanglements of secondary issues and less important absorptions which sap our strength and foil our progress, and to get back to the unrescinded, original mandate in its august simplicity:

> *But ye shall receive power, after that the Holy Spirit is come upon you: and ye shall be witnesses unto me, both in Jerusalem, and in all Judea, and in Samaria, and unto the uttermost part of the earth.*

That is how the whole adventurous story of the historic Church began: Christ went up, the Spirit came down, and the Spirit-anointed witnesses went out. Think of it: twelve men, twelve unlettered men, twelve men without any college brogue or academic degrees or cultural finesse, twelve men without any civic prestige, or monetary reserves, or state backing, twelve men destitute of all those impressive accoutrements which are supposedly necessary for world conquest; twelve seemingly incompetent men and their equally unimpressive-looking compeers went out to preach the new religion of a publicly executed Jew — a crucified Jesus who was stigmatized by His own nation as the blaspheming Nazarene and was regarded elsewhere as a disgraced felon. Yes, those twelve seemingly unqualified men went out to preach that strange-seeming new religion against all the imperial might of ancient Rome, against all the myriad sophistries of the intellectual Greeks, and against all the unbending religious bigotry of old-time Jewry. Their enterprise seemed ludicrously impossible. Yet those same twelve Jesus-men and their growing brotherhood of helpers had not been on the job for more than a few decades before there was a hue and cry: "These men that have turned the world upside down are come hither also!" How did they do it? They did it in the enveloping power of the Holy Spirit, and in fulfillment of our Lord's promise: "Ye shall receive power, after that the Holy Spirit is come upon you: and ye shall be witnesses unto me, both in Jerusalem, and in all Judea, and in Samaria, and unto the uttermost part of the earth."

Yes, brethren, that is how the dramatic adventure of Christianity began; and it drives us back in upon ourselves again today with some heartsearching questions. Are we reaching out today with the old initiative? Are we witnessing today with the old irrepressibleness? Are we experiencing today the old empowerment? The New Testament ideal is: every Christian a soul winner and every local church an evangelizing center. But in most instances we are far removed from that today! In view of the vast and ominous international developments of our time, we are needing, more than ever, a new invasion by the Holy Spirit, a new immersion in the compassions of Christ, and a new revival of individual soul winning.

The acutest need of late-twentieth-century Christendom is a new encounter with the risen Christ through a new relay of witnesses under a new compulsion of the Holy Spirit. It would do far more to relieve the fuddled problems of our times among men and nations than all the best-laid schemes of economic and political theorists. It would give a new slant, a new vision, a new approach, a new interpretation, and a new kind of solution such as comes only to a spiritually enlightened people. It is still true, and more pertinent than ever: the gospel of Christ makes new men, who in turn make a new society. It did that in the first centuries A.D. It could do it again in the twentieth. Superficially the twentieth century is widely different from the first, yet fundamentally it is much the same. There is the same heart need, and the same heart cry; and there is still the same unchanging, all-sufficient answer: Jesus Christ. The one true hope of turning the tables on the Communist menace is a widespread new epidemic of Spirit-endued witness-bearing to the living Christ; but the most pathetic picture of ineffectuality in Protestant Christendom today is the preaching of Christ by preachers *without* the power of Pentecost. How urgently do we need to consult again our Lord's searching challenge!

> BUT YE SHALL RECEIVE POWER, AFTER THAT THE HOLY SPIRIT IS COME UPON YOU: AND YE SHALL BE WITNESSES UNTO ME, BOTH IN JERUSALEM, AND IN ALL JUDEA, AND IN SAMARIA, AND UNTO THE UTTERMOST PART OF THE EARTH.

Looking at the text homiletically for a moment, we may say that the subject of it is Christian witnessing, and that there are three notable features indicated: (1) Christ is the *focus* — "Ye shall be witnesses unto me." (2) The world is the *scope* — "Jerusalem . . . the uttermost part of the earth." (3) The Holy Spirit is the *power* — "Ye shall receive power, after that the Holy Spirit is come upon you." Yes, Christ is the focus, the world is the scope, the Holy Spirit is the power.

There is always the need to reassert this, that in all our witnessing *Christ must be the focus.* This is a day of conceited passion to magnify denominations. All too many evangelistic endeavors seem to be motivated by denominational considerations. Sometimes membership in a certain denomination is made the practical equivalent of membership in the spiritual body of Christ. We betray ourselves into a deceptive false emphasis through an hypnotic enchantment with statistics. How blameworthy this is! A study of the great historical revivals which have periodically swept through the churches shows that in all such visitations from heaven the Holy Spirit entirely disregards denominational boundary lines.

More than ever in these days Christ must be the focus. We are not trying merely to make people religious. We are not trying to make Baptists or Methodists or Congregationalists or Episcopalians or denominationalists of any other kind. Much as we abhor the perversions of Romanism and its oppressive hierarchy, we are not trying even to make Protestants. We are seeking to bring men and women, youths and young women, boys and girls into regenerating union with the Son of God Himself. All merely denominational aspects must be depressed into a severely subsidiary place.

May I remind you that even apart from the eternal issues involved in this Christ-centered witnessing, we cannot do a more patriotic thing than seek to bring our fellow nationals into this revolutionizing experience of our Lord's Saviorhood. Some time ago, I heard of an amusing incident in a British railway train. In one of the eight-seater compartments there were just three occupants — a gentleman trying to read a book, and a youngish woman with an obstreperous little boy who simply would not stop talking nor sit still. The gentleman sat in a corner trying to read his book. The young mother and her unruly junior were at the far corner on the opposite side. The book reader did his best to concentrate. The boy did his best to distract him. The mother did her best to maintain respect for the one and restraint over the other. They were all doing their best in one way or another, but it ended in a major disaster. The would-be reader kept looking up with annoyance at the interrupting youngster. The mother kept up a running commentary of "Sit still!" and "Be quiet!" Eventually, all her powers of nonviolent subjugation being exhausted, she seized the cantankerous young rascal, laid him over her knee, and soundly spanked him. At this the outraged bookman started up, took off his spectacles, and with a look of intellectual agony in his eyes, exclaimed, "Oh, madam, have you not heard about the new methods of psychology?" The woman replied, "Yes, sir, I'se heerd all about that; but *this is quicker!*"

Yes, it was "quicker" — and, by a sharp rebound from the humorous to the serious, we claim that this one-by-one plan of winning souls to the Savior is a quicker way of social betterment than any other. In these days of disturbingly increased juvenile delinquency and adolescent criminality, various countermeasures such as clubs, societies, sports groups, camps, and classes are advocated by anxious leaders. We have nothing but goodwill for all such well-conducted activities, but, if our leaders and people will believe it, the quickest and surest way to transform human character is conversion to Christ. When a man becomes truly born again through conversion to Christ, he becomes a better husband, a better father, a better workman, a better citizen, a better all-round man. To those who complain that the one-by-one method seems "so slow," we reply that it is only slow because so few are doing it. If there were a large-scale rededication to this business of individual evangelism, what mighty changes would be wrought! Yes, I believe indeed that mighty changes would be wrought by a sufficient twentieth-century resurgence of first-century individual evangelism, though I am not blind to this, that soul winning is perhaps more peculiarly problematical today than in any former generation. The increase of difficulty arises from certain disadvantageous developments which now beset us. I mention four of them in particular. (1) The *changed attitude* to the Bible, which no longer regards it as a divinely inspired court of appeal. (2) A correspondingly increased *ignorance* of the Bible, which is another setback in bringing its truths to the unconverted. (3) The misleading nature of much modern *religion* which goes by the name of Christianity but is a perversion of it. (4) The multitude of *distractions* which beset men and women today, preoccupying their minds with worldly gaiety or strain as seldom if ever before. All these make the task of winning souls for Christ more difficult.

On the other hand, besides peculiar difficulties there are unique *opportunities* today. Oh, for enough hands to seize them! What we here stress is that, be the competing obstacles and opportunities what they may, this vital business of individual witness and soul winning is that which more than all else must go on! It is our Master's sacred trust to all His followers throughout this present age. It is the *supreme* service for the following three reasons. (1) It fulfills the highest of all functions to our fellow creatures. (2) It obeys the last and most sacred of all our Lord's commands. (3) It receives the highest of all promised rewards.

However, brethren, what I want to emphasize concentratedly in this present brief address is that our onniscient Lord, who foreknew all the difficulties peculiar to the present time, has made one great all-sufficient provision for our equipment. It is this: *"Ye shall receive power, after that the Holy Spirit is come upon you."* Beloved brethren, I am reminding you again in simplest language that while every local Christian minister is meant to be an apostle and a prophet and a teacher and an evangelist and a counselor and a pastor, nothing is more important than that he shall be a firsthand *witness* to a living experience of Christ, and that he shall enunciate it in the enduing power of the Holy Spirit. It is not enough just to be a herald. Each of us is meant to be a witness. A herald is the mouth of a message. A witness is the mouth of an experience. Once again I find myself shaken by the conviction that most of us ministers are needing to rescue ourselves from exhausting entanglements with the merely administrative and mechanical incidentals of the pastorate, to get alone with Christ and to *stay* alone with Him until we know in transforming experience the reality of this promised *enduement* by the Holy Spirit.

Fellow minister, do *you* know this enduement as an experiential reality? Remember, you, as a Christian minister, are to be our Lord's "witness" not only outside the pulpit as one witness to one person, but also *inside* the pulpit as one witness to many persons, week after week. You therefore need a continuing firsthand *experience* of the living Lord, and a continually *replenished* enduing by the Holy Spirit for the communication of that experience through your ministry. This does not mean frequent pulpit reference to your "experience" or to yourself in any way (on the whole the less of that the better), but it does mean that your experience of Christ will express itself through this enduing in all your exposition of the Word, in your evangelism, your instruction, your exhortation, your pulpit prayers, and indeed in your very leading of the sanctuary services. Your personal experience of Christ and your knowing (or not knowing) the promised "enduement from on high" inevitably, though indefinably, makes itself "felt" through all your pulpit ministry. You all know Phillips Brooks' definition of preaching as "truth through personality." Perhaps that is not an entirely adequate definition (have you ever seen one?) but it gives the quintessence. When truth communicates itself through personality steeped in rich experience of Christ and imbued by the heavenly Spirit, it has found a voice, an appeal, a persuasive penetration which it finds nowhere else; and *all who listen know it*.

"Ye shall receive power, after that the Holy Spirit is come upon you." Brethren, unless we are victims of a strange torpor, our Lord's words must surely stir us deeply. It gives us the secret of a *spiritual eloquence* which sublimates even mediocre ministerial speaking ability into powerful speech for God; an eloquence of the Spirit compared with which the adventitious talkativeness of much modern pulpit showmanship is as "a noisy gong or a clanging cymbal." How many of us never become compelling spokesmen for God because we want to become preachers! I once heard a fashionably fluent preacher say, "One of my biggest troubles has always been my ease of utterance. I could always say something until I had something to say." He described himself truly, for to a discriminating ear that was the impression he not infrequently gave — an intriguing volubility articulating a disguised vacuum.

How little power there is in much of our preaching! We "wave our censor" between the living and the dead, as someone words it, but "the plague is not stayed." Like Gehazi, we lay our staff on the face of the dead child, but there is no returning of life. Like the seven sons of Sceva, we exorcise the demon by the name of Jesus, but he still holds his victim. We warn dwellers in Sodom, but our words are as idle tales. Like king Canute, we command the waves to come no further, but they still roll in over us with foaming defiance. Every Lord's day, thousands of sermons are preached which are "the truth, and nothing but the truth," yet they are poignantly powerless. As I have said elsewhere, there is no more pathetic spectacle in our evangelical churches than powerful truth preached powerlessly. Brethren, unless the Holy Spirit endues the preacher and moves in the hearers, our most energetic preaching is like trying to bounce a ball on sodden sand. Apart from Him we can no more produce truly spiritual responses than we could move a yacht by puffing at the sails with our own breath.

Brother minister, I ask you again: Do *you* know this "coming upon you" of the Holy Spirit for power in witness? It is unwise, perhaps, to make too rigid a cleavage between regeneration and sanctification, yet there *is* a difference. It is one thing to be "*born* of the Spirit"; it is another thing to be "*filled* with the Spirit." The former infuses new spiritual *life;* the latter equips with spiritual *power*. It is one thing to receive Christ as Savior; it is a further, deeper, fuller response of soul to Him when, without one subtle reservation, we put every domain of our being underneath His scepter. When that scepter has absolute control, *then* we begin to find His word indeed coming alive to us: "Ye shall receive *power*, after that the Holy Spirit is come upon you: and ye shall be *witnesses* unto me." In the experience of that enduement our whole ministry contracts and diffuses a "spiritual glow," a heaven-imparted glow which, although it has many counterfeits, has no substitute. Oh, for a truer experience of its rich reality!

> Come, wondrous Fire of heaven,
>   Burn in my soul today;
> Let self-bound aims be riven,
>   All falseness burned away;
> Come, all my doubts expelling
>   With Pentecostal glow,
> Until Thy rich empowering
>   I truly, fully know.

Come, mighty wind of heaven,
  Break in, o'erwhelm my soul,
In all Thy promised fulness
  My heart and mind control;
As ne'er before sweep through me,
  Tear up deep-rooted sin;
For service cleanse, renew me,
  In fulness dwell within.

PENTECOST AND INNER EXPERIENCE

One of our most heinous and palpable sins is *PRIDE*. This is a sin that hath too much interest in the best of us; but which is more hateful and inexcusable in us than in other men. Yet it is so prevalent in some of us, that it enditeth our discourses, it chooseth our company, it formeth our countenances, it putteth the accent and emphasis upon our words. . . . O what a constant companion, what a tyrannical commander, what a sly and subtle insinuating enemy, is this sin of pride! It goes with men to the draper, the mercer, the tailor; it chooseth them their cloth, their trimming, and their fashion . . . But, alas! how frequently doth it go with us to our study, and there sit with us and do our work! . . . And when pride hath made the sermon, it goes with us into the pulpit — it formeth our tone — it animateth us in the delivery — it taketh us off from that which may be displeasing, how necessary soever, and setteth us in vain pursuit of vain applause. In short, the sum of all is this, it maketh men, both in studying, and preaching, to seek themselves and deny God when they should seek God's glory and deny themselves. . . . O, therefore, be jealous of yourselves; and, amidst all your studies, be sure to study humility!

Richard Baxter

PENTECOST AND INNER EXPERIENCE

My dear brethren, the subject designated for our present consideration is Pentecost and our inner experience. We are to reflect upon this particularly from a Christian minister's standpoint, and, with this in mind, I begin by submitting three germane propositions.

The first is this: Of all vocations, the Christian ministry is that in which a man most needs to *forget himself*. No man who has not trampled upon all self-seeking can fully preach the Christ who gave Himself in tears and blood on Calvary. Some brethren may think they can, but they are deluded. That bruised and broken Redeemer can be sympathetically preached only by men who, for His dear sake, have said a resolute *NO* to "self." A man who is full of himself can never preach the Christ who "emptied Himself."

Scotland never produced a finer Presbyterian theologian than the late Dr. James Denny. I am reminded of some heartsearching words which he once uttered to a group of seminary graduates going out to their first pastoral charges. "My young brothers," he said, "never forget this: no minister can be continually giving the impression that he himself is clever, and at the same time truly preach Christ." That may well make some of us ponder.

More than any other calling, brethren, the Christian ministry demands selfless humility. No mere professional modesty or unctuous obsequiousness can be a substitute for it; nor can the Uriah Heep brand of humility, which fawningly advertises itself. Spurgeon once said about a budding young preacher, "We all thought he was humble – till he said he was." Brethren, you and I can never be the prophet voices to our generation which in our truest moments we long to be until we completely rid ourselves of that seductive temptress *selfism*.

During one of my earlier visits to America, a minister told me the following tidbit concerning a friend of his, at whose church the President of the United States was a member. A certain evangelist wrote, wanting to conduct meetings there. In his letter he said, "For your information, I am one of America's greatest ten preachers"! The minister replied that the church calendar was already too full. "But," he added, "I am interested to learn that you are one of America's greatest ten preachers. Could you tell me who are the other *eight?*" It was a priceless application of Proverbs 26:5, "Answer a fool according to his folly." Yet while we are amused at the naive egotism of that inflated evangelist, do not some of us have ample cause to weep as we think of the subtle vanity and touchy pride and obtrusive self-importance which disfigure and debilitate our own ministries? Brethren, I verily believe that no man has ever really seen the cross of Christ until he has wept the words of Isaac Watts:

> My richest gain I count but loss,
> *And pour contempt on all my pride.*

I come to my second theorem: Of all vocations the Christian ministry is that in which a man finds it *most difficult* to forget himself. In other occupations, so long as a man does his job efficiently, he receives his wages, and the employer does not inquire into the employee's private life. The man and the job are separate. Nor does it considerably matter in most cases whether the employee is good-looking, amiable in disposition, prepossessing in manner, or likeable in personality. The sole requirement is that he does his job well.

In the Christian ministry, however, the minister and his ministry are indivisible. The man and his job are one. This peculiarity has most delicate implications. If a minister himself is disliked for some reason, his *ministry* correspondingly suffers. If he gives offense to church members, his preaching of the Word has a diminished effectuality. Or if for any other reason he provokes personal antipathies, there are adverse repercussions upon his pulpit and pastoral endeavors. Every minister knows how important it is that he himself, the man, should be *persona grata* to the people among whom he labors. Also, because of this, every minister knows how fatally easy it is, bit by bit, to become hypersensitive as to what people think about *him.*

There is another reason, too, why the ministry makes it harder than other occupations for a man to lose sight of himself. If a minister has personal charm, popular gifts, public success, he is the center of adulations which can easily breed conceit. If, on the other hand, despite his sincerest efforts things go wrong and the work wilts or flags, he is the inevitable center of criticisms. But whether it be flatteries or captious faultfindings, too much of either is bad for any man; it keeps chaining his thoughts to *himself*. Under such circumstances it is the easiest thing in the world to become, by imperceptible stages, a chronic case either of self-praise or self-pity.

The late Sir Charles Brenton once remarked about J. N. Darby, progenitor of the Plymouth Brethren movement, "I never knew a man in whom the two Adams were so strong." I do not know to what extent that comment was justified, but I do know this, that unless you and I "watch unto prayer," the "old Adam" in us, alias Mr. Ego, can become woefully self-obtrusive amid the peculiar aggravations of the Christian ministry. Tantalizing contrariety though it may be, our holy calling, which more than any other requires a man to forget himself, is that which more than any other tends to provoke the very opposite effect.

This brings me to my third proposition. Of all vocations, the Christian ministry is that in which a man most needs to be *a living reproduction of Christ*. Brethren, look back again over our Lord's life on earth. Get an impressionist, overall view. What are the salient perspectives of His disposition? There are three: (1) intensely spiritual, (2) perfectly natural, (3) thoroughly practical. Yes, that was Jesus — intensely *spiritual*, but perfectly *natural*, and always thoroughly *practical*. We see the byproducts of these all the way through: dignity with humility, manliness with gentleness, severity with sympathy, joyfulness with seriousness, power to command with meekness to serve. He was the center of adulation and devotion even to the point of being worshiped, yet there was never a breath of self-praise. He was equally the center of wicked criticism and vituperation, even to the point of being crucified, yet there was never a breath of self-pity. He was loved as no other. He was hated as no other. Through it all, there was nothing but selfless outreach of heart to heal and mend and bless others.

Brethren, such was our Master. Each of us who dare to represent Him in the ministry of His church is meant to embody a replica of His character. What the worth of anything else if we fail there? What will anything else have mattered when at last we meet Him face to face?

But if we are to be thus like Him, *how?* There is only one answer: we who are the public representatives of Christ need *an experience of the Holy Spirit at continual maximum*. Nothing less than that can break our innate selfism and liberate our highest capacities. Nothing less than that can transform us into the moral image of our Master. Nothing less than that can give us the "tongue of fire" in the pulpit, the "enduement of power" for witness-bearing, and the voice of the prophet in our communities.

Yet although that is our "priority number one," it is what we rarely ever find in the modern ministry. Many among us, even the most evangelical, seem to be forgetting the essential supernaturalness of Christian experience. True conversion to Christ is no mere phychological turnabout; it is a supernatural operation of the Holy Spirit which regenerates a soul into the new humanity in Christ. Similarly, *sanctification of the character* is a supernatural work of the Holy Spirit, by which, in answer to our complete self-yielding, He floods our inner being with the life and love of Christ, renewing us in the "spirit of our mind," refining our tastes, purifying our predispositions, enlarging our spiritual capacities, transforming us in the very basis of our personality, and infusing His own energy into our Christian ministry.

Sympathetic observation persuades me that comparatively few ministers nowadays know much about this postconversion crisis. What most of us are needing, more than anything else, is to get really alone with Christ day after day, and to linger alone in heart-searching conference with Him until we know by unmistakable evidence that this infilling by the Holy Spirit is ours. That is the way to a transformed character and to a transformed ministry.

Some of you may be asking if I am preaching what used to be called the "second blessing." My answer is both a "No" and a "Yes." If by the "second blessing" you mean the supposed eradication of a so-called "old nature" in us, I answer, "No." If you mean any kind of surgery upon a so-called "body of sin" within us, I answer, "No." Examination of Scripture has convinced me that those vagaries are unexegetical. If by the "second blessing" you mean "speaking in tongues" or some other such abnormality, I again answer, "No." But if you ask me, do I believe in a post-conversion crisis or special experience such as Finney and Moody and Torrey had, in which the Holy Spirit infills us, sanctifying the mind and expansively vitalizing our testimony, I answer, "Yes."

Brethren, if only there were a new and vivid experience of *that* among truly Protestant ministers today, it would rescue the evangelical pulpit from its present-day dilemma. South Africa's famous General Smuts complained that his statesmen kept applying "second class remedies to first class crises." The same may be said of the organized Church today. It keeps looking for new techniques, whereas God is looking for *new men* — transformed men whose personalities have the "spiritual glow." An ambitious combine like the World Council of Churches may look dimensionally imposing, but no such denominational coalition can be a substitute for a Spirit-baptized pulpit. If you bring a lot of diseased bodies together, that does not make them all healthy; they only die together instead of apart. The vital need is a new experience of the Holy Spirit; and if we fulfill the conditions, He will come upon us, first individually and then collectively.

The center point of my "case" just now is this: Our inner experience of the Holy Spirit is far more important than any outward multiplicity of ministry. The inner is always more important than the outer, because the inner determines the *quality* of the outer. Our Lord said of John the Baptist, "He was a burning and a shining light." The "burning" was inward. The "shining" was outward. If there had been no inward burning, there would have been no outward shining. The inward burning was the Holy Spirit. The outward shining was sanctified and Spirit-empowered preaching of truth.

Brethren, just because you and I are living in such days of challenge as never before, and because we all must soon give account to the living Christ who holds the seven stars in His hand, I am asking you: Do you know that post-conversion experience in which the Holy Spirit does a never-to-be-forgotten something within you, after which you are never the same again? You may run away from Pentecosta*lism*, but do not run away from Pentecost. You may shy away from "speaking in tongues," but has the one tongue which you possess been touched by the "live coal" from heaven's altar? You may disapprove such phrases as "the second blessing," but are you letting cheap prejudices cheat you out of that unique crisis-experience which transformed Wesley, Moody, Chapman, General Booth, and a host of others whom God mightily used? I am the last man ever to plead for mere shibboleths and passwords; but I am greatly concerned that we should know the *experience*. In this critical hour of history the two all-eclipsing needs of the Protestant pulpit are a new loyalty to the whole Bible as the authoritatively inspired Word of God and a new pervasion by the Holy Spirit.

With all my heart I believe that the explosive freshness of Christianity from age to age is not in big amalgamations but in the supernatural flame of Pentecost through Christ-monopolized men. I also believe that the teaching of the Bible and the witness of the saints are one in urging every present-day evangelical minister to wait on God until he knows in deep reality the promised "power from on high."

Could it be that some of us are asking even now: How may I know this deeper work of the Spirit? Then perhaps the first part of my answer may occasion some surprise. Many of us are needing to bring ourselves to a crisis before God which must be intellectual before it can become spiritual. We are needing to acknowledge *the intellectual lordship of Christ*. Face it squarely: No man can truly call Jesus "Lord," yet at the same time dare to contradict the clear testimony of Jesus to the Old Testament. With unmistakable definiteness our Master has set His imprimatur upon the genuineness of the Old Testament authorships, the integrity of its histories, the supernaturalness of its prophecies, and its divine inspiration as a whole. As already observed, when He refers to the Jonah episode He lets us know quite clearly that He is *not* referring to it merely as you or I might refer to a fictional personage or incident in one of Sir Walter Scott's historical novels or in John Bunyan's *Pilgrim's Progress*. No; He says, "The men of Nineveh shall stand up in the Judgment with this generation, and shall condemn it, for they repented at the preaching of Jonah." Will anyone irreverently pretend that the incarnate Son of God was committing the effrontery of teaching such nonsense as that fictitious men in a fictitious story will *actually* stand up in the *actual* Judgment and condemn the living men of our Lord's own day?

In equally unmistakable syllables our Lord endorses the Mosaic authorship of the Pentateuch, the genuineness of the Genesis cosmogony, the origin of the human race in that one man, Adam; the individual creation of Adam and Eve; the factuality of the early Genesis chapters; the historicity of Noah and the antedeluvians, also of Abraham, Isaac, and Jacob, not to mention others. Therefore, no man who contradicts this clear testimony to the Old Testament can truly call Jesus "Lord." Nay, if Jesus could be mistaken about those historical matters, how can we be sure that He was not mistaken in matters spiritual and eternal? Let there be no blurred thinking on this vital point: there cannot be such an absolute Lordship without infallibility. Nor can any man ever be filled by the Holy Spirit who dares to differ with Christ or to impugn His infallibility. An accredited Christian minister may be scholarly, polished, persuasive, and impressive in other ways, but until he surrenders his intellect to Christ and accepts all that Jesus clearly taught, he *cannot* be filled with the Holy Spirit, for the Holy Spirit never contradicts Christ.

You can easily test what I am saying. Think back over the German-originated radical "higher criticism" of the Old Testament, issuing successively in the so-called "New Theology," "modernism," "liberalism," "existentialism," "neo-orthodoxy," and now "Bultmannism." Recall the earlier champions of this so-called "new biblical scholarship" — Eichorn, De Wette, Vatke, Wellhausen, Ritschl, Scholz, Karl, Holtzmann, Wernle, Clemen, Pfleiderer, Windesch, and others. All those men accepted the "documentary theory" of the Pentateuch. They all championed those shadowy phantom-figures, "J" and "E" and "P" and "D" and their fuzzy X.Y.Z. "redactors" in preference to the God-appointed Moses. They all treated the facts of early Genesis as myths of primitive credulity. They all desupernaturalized the histories and prophecies of the Old Testament. They presumed even to correct Paul and to contradict our Lord Himself. All this in a benign concern to make the Bible "acceptable to modern reason!"

And what did they do for the following new generation in Germany? They turned it *away* from the Bible. Along with other humanistic concomitants, they so weakened faith in the basic Christian verities that the new young Germany fell prey to the evolutionary philosophy of Nietsche and its ugly by-product, the Nazi cultus of Hitler, which soaked three continents in blood.

These are the men who gave us the "kenosis" Christ, a Christ emptied of His divine *pleroma* and reduced to the level of human limitation. Whatever may be the purely scholastic contributions of "higher criticism" *per se,* those men and their rationalistic successors have brought about the most divisive apostasy in Protestant Christendom since it originated. They have shorn the Protestant Samson of his locks and are betraying him to the Vatican Delilah or the Dagon of materialism. They have stolen away our virile positives and left us only sterile negatives.

Around the time of the First World War, as I vividly remember, this issue as to the Bible forced itself squarely upon our evangelical leaders in Britain. They were "good men and true," but they were not prepared to separate or cause a split. They did not like turning their backs on comrades in the ministry who had succumbed to the new higher critical schools. They wavered, palavered, stayed in, and compromised; from which time onward the evangelical cause in Britain has gradually shrivelled, until now in many parts it is scarcely existent.

I am saddened to find that over here, in the South, you are being subjected to the same old pleas which we heard back in Britain forty years ago. You are being told that nothing must break the denominational unity, that it is uncharitable to disparage those whose views differ from ours, that those who hold the newer views of the Bible are "such sincere brethren," and that we Baptists have always stood for liberty in interpreting the Bible. Yes, we have heard these pleas again and again. It will be the easiest thing for you to forget that the only *true* way to conserve denominational unity is to maintain staunch loyalty to the divine inspiration of Holy Scripture and the infallible authority of Christ. It will be easy, unless you are watchful, to forget that the first kind of sincerity required in a Christian minister is sincerity toward the intellectual lordship of Christ, including His endorsement of Genesis. Yes, we Baptists *have* always been champions of that great Protestant tenet, "the right and duty of private judgment in relation to the Scriptures"; but liberty to *interpret* the Bible never meant license to *discredit* the Bible or to contradict the clear dictum of Jesus.

Brethren, you must listen to me. All the trouble which modern biblical radicalism has brought upon Protestantism began with the "documentary theory" of the Pentateuch. It might almost have been with the present epoch in view that our Lord said, "If ye believe not *his* [Moses'] writings, how shall ye believe *my* words?" (John 5:47). Millions of Christian believers around the world have their eyes on you Southern Baptists. Millions of us have thanked God for your loyalty to the written Word and the living Word and your attitude to issues such as the World Council of Churches and to "the faith once for all delivered to the saints." We are praying that you may *remain* the great evangelical body of believers which you have been through many years.

Brethren, I say today, as I have said before: the creeping paralysis which besets Protestant Christendom in our time results from a chaotic disloyalty to the Bible. The biggest and best restorative would be for the large, well-known Protestant denominations officially to reavow their faith in the divine origin, inspiration, completeness, and authority of the Bible.

As for ourselves, am I not right when I say that some of us, before ever we can know the deeper work of the Holy Spirit in us, are needing the *intellectual* crisis of which I have spoken? I am thinking cautiously and speaking reverently when I utter my conviction that the Holy Spirit never fills a Christian minister who refuses or evades the lordship of Christ over our human *intellect*. To differ with the incarnate Son of God about the Old

Testament is not only strange presumption; it effectually grieves away the Holy Spirit who inspired those "living oracles." No scholarship which contradicts the clear Word of Christ is of the Spirit. To think that we become more scholarly by accepting the dicta of *any* school which runs contrary to our dear Lord's "verily I say unto you" is an unspiritual delusion which in the end can bring only spiritual sterility.

What can I say, brethren, to prevail on some of you who may be yielding to the enchantment of specious modern "scholarship"? I would counsel you to reject *any* scholarship which belittles or evades or contradicts the teaching of our Lord, for in the end it will either dump you in boggy doubt or land you in a spiritual desert. I have now lived long enough to see this happen in some of the choicest men who ever entered the Christian ministry. Younger brethren, beware of the mirage! Stay close to Him who said, "I AM THE TRUTH"! Beware of Satan in the cap and gown of new-fashioned scholarship. Stay with the Bible as the inspired Word of God, for in the end it will prove to be imperishably true. Make Christ indeed the Lord of your intellect. Kneel before Him as the king of your life. Give Him absolute "right of possession." Then, in the stillness, wait on Him for that most wonderful of all spiritual enrichments, *"the fulness of the Spirit."* If you really make Him your LORD, He will most surely make you His "chosen vessel," and your ministry a well of "living water" to many.

Part Three

PUBLIC WORSHIP

NOTE:

If any British reader should happen to be traveling through these pages, perhaps it should be pointed out that much in the following *third* group of chapters does not apply to the churches in Britain. That is because ecclesiastical and national features differ enough in the two countries to require correspondingly different approach, especially in the matter of public worship.

All our work must be managed reverently, as beseemeth them that believe the presence of God, and use not holy things as if they were common. Reverence is that affection of the soul which proceedeth from deep apprehensions of God, and indicateth a mind that is much conversant with Him. To manifest irreverence in the things of God is to manifest hypocrisy, and that the heart agreeth not with the tongue. I know not how it is with others, but the most reverend preacher who speaks as if he saw the face of God doth more affect my heart, though with common words, than an irreverent man with the most exquisite preparations. Yes, though he bawl it out with ever so much apparent earnestness, if reverence be not answerable to fervency, it worketh but little. Of all the preaching in the world (that speaks not stark lies) I hate that preaching which tends to make the hearers laugh, or to move their minds with tickling levity, and affect them as stage-plays used to do, instead of affecting them with a holy reverence of the name of God.

Richard Baxter

REVERENCE, PLEASE!

On the first day of January, 1955, my dear wife and I left Liverpool, England, for our eighth visit to the U.S.A. and Canada. I had now resigned from my eighteen-year pastorate in Edinburgh, Scotland, and was venturing forth on a wider ministry of itinerant Bible teaching. It felt strange to be making such a break from our British moorings, but we felt sure of divine guidance; so, in the words of Paul, we "thanked God and took courage."

It was our thought to spend two years in America, then to move on to engagements in New Zealand, Australia, South Africa, India, and Japan. Little did we foresee that our two years in America would lengthen indefinitely! Let me pay grateful tribute to the many evangelical ministers who, with their churches, have warmly welcomed us and responded to our ministry of the Word. Everywhere we have been received with cordiality. I verily believe that the American people, taken as a whole, are the friendliest, the most generous, the most open-minded, the most inventive, the most hard-working, the most playful, the most gifted in organizing, the most go-ahead people in the world — and in some ways (dare I?) the most gullible.

Now just because I am a guest (my legal status now is "Resident Alien") and have been treated with such unmerited kindness, and because my love for America grows greater the longer we stay here, I am the more diffident to say anything which might seem discourteous. Also, we slower-moving Britishers have so much to learn from you fast-moving Americans, with your genius for "promoting," that I rather hesitate to offer suggestions, let alone indulge criticisms. Sometimes, when I hear of disrespectful remarks about America which are made by visiting preachers of a certain sort, I get a red face. When they come over here you appreciatively fuss them up and remunerate them with such characteristic liberality that they turn into heady little pundits pouting about all the wrong things over here which need putting right. They would even alter the tilt of Uncle Sam's top hat if they could.

Let me assure you that most of us who come over here appreciate your magnanimous reception far too keenly ever to be impolitely corrective. Admittedly, America is a land of strangely mingling opposites. There is an extreme of crime; yet I know this, also, that the most sacrificial and Christlike godliness which we have ever met has been on *this* side of the Atlantic. Of all lands on earth this is the land of most colorfully diversified interests; but again and again that which strikes us most is American generosity and American willingness to listen. So with genuine esteem and in capital letters we say, THANK YOU.

Yet now, brethren, if I shall not seem *too* much like John Bunyan's "Mr. Facing-both-ways," and if I am not trespassing too clumsily on your forbearance, please help me pluck up courage to criticize you! I risk uttering my deeply respectful criticisms only because I now have three seemingly good qualifications: (1) During my eight visits here, and especially during this more than eighteen years' itinerary, we have traveled all forty-eight states of the U.S.A. mainland, and Canada from Atlantic to Pacific; so we can speak from wide enough background. (2) During these extended years of perambulation in this most wonderful natural and political geography lesson, we have had prolonged opportunity to observe, review, and reach some thoughtful conclusions, more particularly concerning the *evangelical churches* over here. (3) Having lived fifty years in Britain and had three pastorates there covering twenty-five years, we can make comparisons with sufficient familiarity to be in at least some measure reliably constructive. And to this perhaps I should add that all our criticisms spring from a fountain of sincere concern for the preservation and true advancement of the evangelical cause in this beloved land of the Stars and Stripes.

I prophesy that you will chafe at some of the things which I shall dare to say. You may even resent them; but I ask you to receive them, for I speak with a real burden on my heart.

All of us know that in the U.S.A. and Canada, present-day developments have reached a point at which evangelical revival is an acute need. We all realize, too, that if such revival is to come there must be more protracted prayer, more loyalty to the Bible, more Spirit-endued evangelism. But there are also *other* prerequisites which need attention if we are to cease grieving the divine Spirit.

PUBLIC WORSHIP

Let me first refer to public worship. Brethren, we must all agree that in public Christian worship the first essential is *reverence*.

My own conviction is that we preachers never get far with a man and never get deeply into his soul for God unless he has first been made God-conscious and correspondingly reverent. True reverence is vital to our sanctuary services if there is to be persuasive soul winning, rich spiritual life in our church members, and a moving of God's Spirit among us. Yet my lengthening years of travel all over America have shown me that if there is one thing more than another lacking in our evangelical churches it is reverence.

Please try not to be angry at my next observation. It is this: in my own judgment the average church service among the evangelical churches over here is ragged and undignified. I realize that there is a false dignity which should be avoided, but there is also a true dignity which should be preserved. I am utterly one with you in your characteristic American detestation of ecclesiastical starchiness and stuffiness, but often I am far more revolted by the laxity over here. Ironically enough, when my wife and I long for the uplift of a really reverent service we often have to slip away from the evangelicals and go to some more formal type of church. There may be little for us in the talk from the pulpit, but the worshipful atmosphere, the more orderly conduct, and the richer hymns — all these are healing balm to the mind and wings to one's devotion.

Now of this I am sure: the evangelical churches pay dearly for their defaulting in this matter. They are failing to draw and hold the better class of people socially and intellectually. Let me give you just one illustration. Not long ago, when I was holding meetings in a certain city, I noticed a distinguished-looking gentleman and his wife attending. I learned that he was one of the most respected citizens in the community. Not only was he well-educated and a well-to-do businessman but he and his wife were true Christians. For some seventeen years he had been chairman of the central committee coordinating all the churches of his denomination in that area. Yet more and more his spirit had become grieved by the liberalism in his denomination, until eventually, much to the surprise of his associates, he had resigned his chairmanship and even his membership in that denomination. He and his wife were now going from church to church, seeking a spiritual home where the Word of God was truly honored. I suggested to them, "Would you not think of joining *this* church? The minister here is one of the best preachers, and he certainly preaches the Word." I can still see the pained look which spread over their faces as he replied, "Thank you. We know that the Word is preached here; but we could never really *worship* here. There is such irreverence, gossipy whispering, interruption by squirming or crying babies with mothers who are apparently quite unconcerned at the distraction their babies cause; and there is such a poor type of hymns, and such lack of proper behavior that we could not feel we were in the house of God." As he gave me this reply there was no disdain, but only regret. So that evangelical church lost a couple who could have been a wonderful power for good in it, spiritually, intellectually, financially.

The same sort of thing is happening in numberless other instances all over America. Just as much as any of you I am alive to this, that our evangelical churches must never kowtow to wealth or social rank, for all souls are equal in God's sight; yet it is egregious folly to be repulsing such people by the unaesthetic deformity of our services.

This default in reverence has other effects as well. It gradually lessens respect for the pulpit, for the minister, for the message, and for the church building. It also engenders superficiality and presumption. It is time some of us gave up boasting about liberty and informality and free style in our services. It is time we trembled again in self-abasing worship before the divine majesty. It is time we got our people down low before Him, too. Think again of those sinless, flaming seraphs on high. See their six wings — two to cover their faces, two to cover their feet, and two to fly. Yes, four wings for adoring worship, and only two for active serving! Many of us are so occupied with the wings for serving that we are forgetting the "Holy! holy! holy!" of worship without which religious activity is presumption.

Somehow we simply must bring a more reverent worship into our gatherings. There is a certain type of building which aids worship in a certain type of mind. We should remember that when we are building. This also is true, however, that in the least conducive building there can be as reverent a worship as in an ornate cathedral. Much depends on the minister. Some of the most reverential hours I have ever known have been with small groups in buildings without any Gothic arch or stained-glass window.

It is well to ask what are the engendering factors in this lack of reverence which I am criticizing. Let me mention some of the incidentals which are more important than many seem to think. In other Christian lands, when persons go to a service in God's house, their first act as they sit in the pew is to bow in prayer.

With some this may be only formal, but with many it is devout, and with *all* it is a betokening of reverence. When the minister comes into the pulpit to lead the service, his first act is to bow there in a moment of silent prayer. Thus the service commences reverently. Over here, at least among the usual evangelical churches, neither do the people bow in preliminary prayer nor does the pastor bow in prayer on entering the pulpit. To me, that is not only a careless omission, it is an impertinence and can only tend to diminish reverence.

Further, I frankly deplore the lax way in which many members *dress* for Sabbath day exercises over here. Except during excessive heat the men and male youths should all be required to wear suits with jackets. It is worse than disrespectful to enter Zion's courts in sloppy or ranch-type trousers and the kind of hang-out shirt more fit for a football match than attendance at divine worship.

Only recently I was at a Sunday morning service in which about eight new members were being welcomed at the Lord's table. Most of the eight were teen-agers, and as they stood facing the Communion Table with their backs to the congregation, what a sight some of them looked! One of the young fellows had on a brilliant short shirt which left part of his bare back showing! I dread to seem wrongly severe, for the dear Lord knows how we rejoice to see young men and women coming into our fellowships. But the church is not a hotel parlor, nor is the Lord's table a buffet counter! Is it not time evangelical ministers and officials taught many of the members and young people, both by word and *example*, the way to dress when they come to worship? If it means offending the few for the sake of the many, then are not the many more important than the few?

The mention of that prompts me (with genuine respect) to ask: When are we going to do something about the *children* in our gatherings? As a preacher I am not easily put off by minor distractions in an assembly (open-air preaching helped cure me of that), but again and again over here, in the middle of the preacher's exposition of divine truth, boys and girls will get up and walk out to the rest rooms, and their trek is nearly always from one of the front pews, which adds to the interruption. Believe me, this is no playing off Europe against America, but over there that sort of behavior is just not known, even though boys and girls over there are physically just the same as Americans! Nor over there must all boys and girls be armed with chalk, pencils, paper, or gadgets to fill in the time. These things have become so common among evangelicals over here that it really needs an outside observer to jolt churches about them. Sometimes in my own preaching, when I have built up my message to a climactic point of appeal, just at that very instant the attention will be drawn off by a couple of youngsters suddenly deciding to leave their places for the usual excursion. A free-and-easy tolerance of these usually needless interruptions may pass as American "good nature" (which I sincerely compliment) but they *all* contribute to a bad lack of reverence.

My next scapegoat is *the electric organ.* What my auricular nerves have suffered from electric organs during the past years tongue cannot tell. How often have we wished those instruments had never been invented! How I have sighed that a law might be passed interdicting church organists from everlastingly using that exasperating tremolo, with its pathetic dither making the most robust tunes trembly and squeamish! One Sunday evening as Mrs. Baxter and I were walking to the church where I was to preach, we were sorry to hear what seemed like a fairground going at full swing with jiggy-joggy tunes and tinny squeaking blare such as is their usual din. It became louder as we neared the church. Can you imagine our dismay when we found that the raucus medley was issuing from the open windows of the church where I was to preach and where the young organist was now playing introductory music for our service?

The metallic electric organ of course (though some are much better than others) can never have the soft, rich timbre of a good pipe organ; nevertheless the real fault, more often than not, is with the organist. I *have* heard electric organ music sound almost like the appealing strains of a pipe organ when the proper registrations are fingered with sympathetic restraint; but, oh, the ghastly opposites we have endured! Usually the playing is *much too loud* for sanctuary purposes. In a score of instances, before delivering my message in a Sunday service, I have wanted to join heartily in the hymn-singing, but the organ has been so loud and the competition so tiring that I have given up the unequal struggle and lapsed into dumb defeat. Also I have observed individuals in the congregation bravely contending in the same warfare until with despairing look at the organist they too have suddenly quit and stood silently waiting till the organ of torture should desist. What makes it harder to bear from time to time is the gleam of triumph in the dear organist's face!

Nor is that all. Far too often the playing is swingy, almost jazzy, with chromatic slurs and vamping thuds, and instead of pure chords the inclusion of the crazy sixth. Sometimes when both organ and piano are going together it is almost a rant. (In any case, Sunday mornings are far better *without* piano, if an organ is used.) My inward ears still register agony from a recent playing of that precious hymn, "I Am Thine, O Lord," as though it were a dance-hall number, and "Sweet Hour of Prayer" with jarring modern discords which outraged all the canons of true harmony. Far better have the choral pieces *a cappella* and let the congregational singing rely solely on the old-fashioned tuning fork than allow sacred hymnody to be desecrated by such unbecoming organ-antics!

Nor is even that all! Over in Britain and other countries, after the closing benediction is pronounced, the custom is for worshipers to tarry a moment with bowed heads until the organ begins softly playing a gentler type of postlude. There is something finally helpful about leaving the house of God to the accompaniment of those subdued and sympathetic strains. But over here: oh, no! the instant the service is through the organist lets go with a loud, grandiose march or some other exultant blare, as though the supreme ambition of musical art is to burst eardrums, or wind up a service in a way which seems to shout, "Well, folks, that's it: now let's shake it off!" Sometimes when persons have wanted to talk with me about spiritual concerns I have had to send word to the organist, "Could you please allow us to hear each other talk?"

Brethren, instrumental music was introduced into public worship to *assist* congregational praise, not to smother it! I realize that correction is in many cases a delicate problem because the naughty culprits are such delightful persons; yet if *reverence* is to survive in our evangelical Bethels, such organ behavior and habits *must* be corrected.

Dear me! By now I have lunged myself really "amid stream" in this gurgling river of animadversions. I cannot turn back nor can I stay here; I must struggle through to the far bank. Some of you may be pretty exasperated already, but you cannot turn away yet, for you do not know what I am going to say next! My mention of electric organs reminds me of other present-day features, all militating against reverence in the sanctuary.

One of these is *streamlining:* short hymns, short prayers, short sermons. Hymns sung fast, with no break or pause between the verses. Brethren, rush and reverence never cohabit. Just as we should not bring the noise of the outer world into the sanctuary, nor its type of tune, nor its style of singing, nor its colloquialisms, nor its showmanship, nor its television exaggerations, so neither should we open our doors to its hurry. More than ever, in these days, wearied minds are needing escape, retreat, haven, from the fagging pace of the outside world. Our sanctuary services should strike a contrast to the present-day world, not a likeness to it. There need be no lackadaisical drag, but there should not be hurry, for hurry destroys rest and undermines reverence. The very passion nowadays to pack corporate worship into just one neat hour is fleshly; and when, in addition to hymns, Scripture reading, prayers, and sermon, the one-hour hurry has to be decorated with choir anthem and one or two solos or duets, it is absurd as well as irreverent.

Only recently I was preaching in a Sunday morning service where there were two contributions by the choir and two solos which were both of poor quality and added nothing at all of spiritual value (one of them was merely a semi-religious song with fancy accompaniment). I had gone there after much prayer, my heart gratefully burdened with a word which I believe God had given me. But after all the needless solo and choral padding the time left for my message was about sixteen minutes! My reaction was no mere impatience: it was sincere anger. It is that sort of Sunday morning menu which is destroying the power of American evangelical church services. There had been no time for an unhurried pastoral prayer, no time to get the congregation really bowed down before Almighty God and then lifted up into adoring worship around the heavenly throne; no time for intercessions on behalf of Christless outsiders and God-forgetting cities, but choir pieces and solos — then a hurried curtailment of the message from the Word. Oh, how wrong it is! How can we expect the heavenly wind and fire to break in upon us?

At this juncture it will be diplomatic on my part to remind you of my admiring tribute to America which I uttered at the outset! Also, let me seize the opportunity of sincerely assuring you that I am not forgetting features of the evangelical churches over here which merit highest eulogy. Nor am I conveniently forgetting the plight of our British churches today, still struggling to recover from the impoverishing and dislocating wreckage inflicted by two world wars, still reaping the sorry harvest from the wild oats sowed by earlier modernism, and still far behind your American churches in organizing efficiency. No, I am not forgetting any of those things, but my one concern at the moment is this matter of *reverence*, or rather the *lack* of it, for I am certain it is one of the most serious hindrances to spiritual depth, growth, and revival.

I shall not be deterred if you are momentarily amused when I now add that loudspeaker systems and printed or mimeographed "order of service" forms tend to distract from worshipful quietness. In the days before the "mike" appeared at the front of the pulpit, most congregations *had* to be quiet in order to hear the minister clearly, which, although a disadvantage in other ways, induced silence, concentration, reverence. Also, before the typed or printed "order of service" came into vogue, audiences *had* to focus attention on the pulpit so as to catch each hymn number or Scripture passage. I have repeatedly noted that when the loudspeaker system is too loud its influence is *against* quiet attention.

My conscience forbids me to linger longer with these criticisms pertaining to reverence; so let me simply add a few questions and then leave it. Brethren, do you really think the organ should be playing during your public prayers? Why should you have to talk over *that*? Should there not be complete silence while you publicly address God on behalf of the congregation? Sometimes the playing is an aimless drift of chords, which is unedifying. Sometimes it is somewhat too loud, which is annoying. Sometimes it is the soft playing of a well-known hymn tune which has an irresistable tendency to lure the mind from the pulpit prayer to the words of the hymn. The whole sanctuary, including organ, should be in complete *silence* during the pulpit prayers.

Again, do you not think that there should be (as there almost invariably is in other countries) a suitable curtain just around the organist, so that the movements of hands and feet at keyboard and pedals are not distractingly on view? I am sure most organists would gratefully play a *Te Deum Laudamus* to have such an etiquette of coverage! Details of that kind, even in the smallest churches, contribute to an overall decorum.

Again, do you not think that after the opening prayer of invocation there should be a congregational saying of the Lord's Prayer? Doing so always solidifies the feeling of *congregational* worship. It always best sums up and expresses congregational desire toward God and always fosters congregational reverence. In American evangelical churches there is now almost an entire absence of *congregational response,* which omission is a decided fault.

There are those who say that public repetition of the Lord's Prayer is "vain," according to Matthew 6:7, but they are wrong. What our Lord discountenanced was not repetition but *"vain* repetition." There are some compositions *made* for repetition, and the Lord's Prayer is one of them (6:9), given to His disciples for the whole of the present age as the perfect *pattern* for prayer, and a perfect *summary* of supplication.

I have even heard some ministers and dispensationalists object that the Lord's Prayer is not for present praying because it is dispensationally out of place and belongs to what they call "kingdom truth." But when the kingdom actually comes at the glorious return of our Lord, it will be too late then to start praying "Thy kingdom come"! The time for that prayer is *now*. (A comical contradiction is that those who will not pray the Lord's Prayer in public pray every day in private for the coming of the kingdom!).

Others will not pray the Lord's Prayer because (so they say) the words, "Forgive us our trespasses as we forgive those who trespass against us" are *"legal* ground," making God's forgiveness of us dependent on our forgiveness of others. That objection is an evasion. We are not saved *by* good works, but by grace alone; yet we cannot be saved *without* good works, for that would be sinning in order that grace might abound. Similarly, neither are we forgiven *because* we forgive others, yet we cannot be forgiven *without* forgiving others; for it we are unforgiving to others we are not truly converted; we have no inward right to assume that God has forgiven us. We never enjoy an inward assurance of our own forgiveness (however dispensationally correct we may be!) while we refuse forgiveness to others.

Alas, I have slipped into the interpretative and argumentative, which is the last thing suitable here. My concern is not to defend an incidental viewpoint, but to urge both the exclusion of the vulgar and the inclusion of the finer in the public worship of our evangelical churches. A denominational leader lamented to me a few months ago, "The spirit of worship has declined in our churches." Yes, it has; and it is because the average kind of service, instead of cultivating worship, stultifies it. Brethren, do I need even *try* to convince you that I say these things with only deepest esteem for yourselves and with unfeignedly sincere concern for our evangelical cause? We long for spiritual revival? Then I am certain we must correct such disfigurements of our public worship as I have here deplored. I say it again: if there is to be real revival, then a first requirement is *reverence, please!*

CONCERNING HYMNS

Is it nothing to be brought up to learning, when others are brought up to the cart and the plough? and to be furnished with so much delightful knowledge, when the world lieth in ignorance? Is it nothing to converse with learned men, and to talk of high and glorious things, when others must converse with almost none but the most vulgar and illiterate? But especially, what an excellent privilege is it, to live in studying and preaching Christ! — to be continually searching into His mysteries, or feeding on them!

Whether we be alone or in company, our business is mainly for *another* world. Oh, that our hearts were more *tuned* to this work! What a blessed, praiseful life should we then **live!**

Richard Baxter

CONCERNING HYMNS

Most ministers realize that hymns are important in public worship, but comparatively few realize *how* important. The Roman Catholic leaders ruefully complained that Martin Luther had sung far more people into Protestantism by his hymns than he ever preached into it by his sermons, which complaint may well remind us that Christian hymns are meant to express *great truths* in the form of worship and witness.

The late Dr. Harry A. Ironside told me that on one occasion a few years back, as he sat in the waiting room at a railway station, he could not help overhearing a conversation between two ministers. One of them was saying, "Do you know, I had been at the church over ten months before the young people's group even asked me to their meeting! When I went in, what do you think? They were singing those old Sankey hymns about 'saved by grace,' and 'There is life for a look,' and other such stuff. My! didn't I lunge at them and their outworn ideas! But, would you believe it? The minute I finished, the young chairman said, 'Let's get right back to that favorite hymn, 'A ruler once came to Jesus by night'!'" There was a pause, then this comment: "I'll never get anywhere with those young folk *till I do away with those hymns*"!

How much some of us owe to "those hymns" of our childhood and youth! They became bone and marrow to our early understanding of divine realities. Through them the goodness of God and the grace of Christ reached into our hearts as no pulpit discourse or Sunday school class ever could have done apart from them. What an impoverished mistake it is that thousands of younger boys and girls today in our Sunday schools are deprived of them in favor of catchy choruses!

Oh, the power of great hymns down through the centuries of the Church's history, especially since the Protestant Reformation! Even a rough review here would become another book, rather than a digression; but let me risk one or two general observations. Overleaping the hymnal desert (comparatively speaking) of the "dark ages," it may be said that up to the time of the Methodist revival Christian hymns were mainly expressions of adoration, contemplation, and devotion. The Methodist revival marked an epoch.

Through the pen of that consecrated genius Charles Wesley, strong, evangelical *doctrine* and vividly versified spiritual *experience* suddenly leapt full-grown into Christian hymnody.

Then, as our twentieth century was coming in, the river of Christian song (excuse my sharp change of metaphor!) took another turn and assumed still wider spread through that remarkable pioneer of musical evangelism, Ira D. Sankey. Like a river in spate came a new class of hymns, largely of the verse-and-chorus type, all *preaching the evangel,* or uttering Christian *testimony,* or giving *exhortation* on the Christian life.

To our rising generation of today Moody and Sankey have receded into a misty yesterday, but not even yet have we taken the full measure of Ira D. Sankey. Those mighty Moody and Sankey evangelistic campaigns were far more than ably organized human effort; they were a veritable visitation from God. They shook the English-speaking world. Up to about A.D. 1908 the book which had achieved the largest circulation of any outside the Bible was Sankey's twelve-hundred edition of *Sacred Songs and Solos!* That circumstance alone eloquently attests the tremendous impact of Sankey. Cities and towns all over Britain, America, Australia, New Zealand, and other lands were set singing Sankey's great compilation. As never before, Christian hymnody now became a definite and popular way of preaching and pressing home the welcomes and warnings of the gospel. Beyond a doubt, Sankey marks a turning point. He, more prominently than any other, pioneered the new era of *the gospel in song.*

The new era, however, is not a cloudless sky. Since Sankey, American hymnody has painfully deteriorated. I am not blaming Sankey, though it was he who spearheaded the new *style* of hymn. Sankey is no more to blame for the paltry cheapening of that new mode by subsequent hymnists than Calvin is to blame for the later extravagances of some hyper-Calvinists. Sankey, though, did "open the door." From then onward, American popular hymnody has drifted from its true moorings — from the objective to the subjective, and from the doctrinal to the sentimental. Some of the sentiment is good. Much is poor. Too often it is sickly exaggeration. Instead of poetry there is mere rhyme and lilt; instead of thought progress through the verses to an edifying completeness, you are no further at the end of a hymn than at the beginning.

Nearly all the *evangelical* churches in America seem to be singing only from three groups of hymns: (1) a very few hymns of praise or worship — on Sunday mornings only; (2) simple gospel hymns; (3) a large area of hymns, practically all subjective, and often fulsomely sentimental. The results are bad. More and more, in our travels my wife and I have observed (especially in the Southwest and Texas and the deep South) many people in church do not bother to sing. Some never even pick up the hymnbook. I confess to a sneaking sympathy for them. When one keeps singing the same gospel hymns and the same subjective or sentimental hymns week after week, they grow stale; they keep the heart's gaze on oneself, in one way or another. They cease to edify. Why keep singing them? By contrast, the great old *objective* hymns which lift the soul out of itself into contemplation of God or of lofty divine *truths* never, never grow stale; they become dearer with use. Somehow the older they grow, the fresher they stay! To cite just one, as a classic representative, let me ask you to read slowly through *this* old treasure again, letting it lift you out from yourself and yet bring Christ right to your heart:

> Jesus, the very thought of Thee
>   With sweetness fills my breast;
> But sweeter far Thy face to see,
>   And in Thy presence rest.
>
> Nor voice can sing nor heart can frame,
>   Nor can the memory find
> A sweeter sound than Thy blest Name,
>   O Saviour of mankind.
>
> O Hope of every contrite heart,
>   O Joy of all the meek,
> To those who err how kind Thou art!
>   How good to those who seek!
>
> But what to those who find? Ah, this,
>   Nor tongue nor pen can show:
> The love of Jesus, what it is,
>   None but His loved ones know.
>
> Jesus, our only joy be Thou,
>   As Thou our prize wilt be;
> Jesus, be Thou our glory now,
>   And through eternity.

Here, however, we are faced with a frustrating realization that although the hymn just quoted is in most American hymnals (usually minus one verse or two) those hymnals which are used by the conservative evangelical bodies are sadly deficient in well-written, good-quality hymns of the deeper, spiritual sort. How few hymns there are on the enduing ministry of the Holy Spirit! How few on the deeper aspects of our union with Christ! How few on inwrought holiness! How few on fellowship with God the Father!

Perhaps the biggest problem which confronts me is that most whom I now address have never known the rich world of hymns to which I refer. In line with the proverb, "What the heart has never known it never misses," many are content with the poorer through unawareness of the better. When I talk about a more worshipful order of hymn, they suppose that I mean the staid, formal, and "churchy" compilations in the heavier denominational hymnals of some two generations ago. Yet that is hardly my meaning — though some of the purest gems *are* found in those now largely deserted treasure mines. Perhaps the nearest to what I mean are the Presbyterian and Methodist hymnbooks — the earlier rather than the present edition (though the trouble is that *they* lack an intermixture of the *other* kind which I will call the "Sankey" genus). There is now in existence a combined wealth of *both* kinds and a whole in-between territory of choice hymns, *all* of which our evangelical churches should be using but are not.

My dear American brethren, I mean every syllable when I say that *you* can teach others of us *far* more than *we* can offer you in return, but if there is one area where we can perhaps make a needed contribution, it is in this matter of hymns. We are not singing over here the really great and enriching hymns; consequently the quality of our public services suffers, our pulpit ministry loses a wonderful ally, and a vital means of spiritual education is denied to the members. Indeed, the whole fellowship suffers; for undoubtedly the hymns of the sanctuary are among the main factors which set the level of spiritual experience among our people.

I am a pastor, and after twenty-five years in the settled ministry I simply cannot help looking at all such concerns from a pastor's standpoint. I am jealous on every pastor's behalf that his ministry may be of maximum effectiveness. Much itineration has shown me that in general the American evangelical pastor is at a disadvantage compared with his overseas counterpart in this, that the earlier part of the average American church service does not engender the favorable atmosphere or prepare his people for the pulpit message nearly so much as the type of service in certain other countries — and this is noticeably so in the different class of *hymns* used. I keenly dislike hearing the earlier exercises of a service referred to merely as the "preliminaries"; they are all meant to be *preparatories*, all preparing a "highway in the heart" for the expounding of "thus saith Jehovah" from the Book.

Will you think it an impropriety if I here refer to my own ministry by way of illustration? During my eighteen-year pastorate in Edinburgh, Scotland, almost always the Sunday morning service was devoted to teaching believers the deeper truths of the Word; the evening service was usually evangelistic. For the morning service we used our Baptist Church Hymnal (an excellent book), and for the evening Sankey's (1200 edition), so we had a copious supply which allowed continual variety. During a summer vacation among the Perthshire highlands my wife and I went right through both hymnbooks, choosing all those hymns which we considered best in their respective categories, and then selected the hymns for our services through a full four years ahead, leaving ample scope for any needful readjustments. We determined that our people should learn and sing and profit by all the good-quality hymns in both books (four or five hymns for each service). Not long afterward Mrs. Baxter began coming to me bearing the appreciative comments of the many who were being enriched. One of the commonest was, "I never suspected there was such treasure in the hymnbook."

Imagine yourself there one Sunday morning. At eleven o'clock the vestry door opens and the pastor ascends the pulpit stairs. While he bows in a moment of silent prayer at the pulpit desk, the choir sings one verse of a devotional hymn or some other brief, worshipful introit. Then the pastor beckons the congregation to bow in an opening prayer, followed by the blending of all hearts and voices in the Lord's Prayer (our congregations sit or kneel during prayer, and stand for the hymns). Then the first hymn is given out, the first verse being read in suchwise as calls attention to the words. It might well be the following (usually sung to the tune, *Dalehurst*): —

> I would commune with Thee, my God,
> E'en to Thy throne I come;
> I leave my joys, I leave my sins,
> And seek in Thee my home.
>
> I stand upon the mount of God,
> With sunlight in my soul;
> I hear the storms in vales beneath,
> I hear the thunders roll.

> But I am calm with Thee, my God,
>   Beneath these glorious skies;
> And to the heights on which I stand
>   Nor storm nor cloud can rise.
>
> Oh, this is life, oh, this is joy,
>   My God, to find Thee so!
> Thy face to see, Thy voice to hear,
>   And all Thy love to know!

Or it might well be another favorite — surely one of the greatest hymns ever written in its class: Thomas Binney's,

> Eternal Light! Eternal Light!
>   How pure the soul must be
> When, placed within Thy searching sight,
> It shrinks not, but with calm delight
>   Can live, and look on Thee!
>
> The spirits that surround Thy throne
>   May bear the burning bliss;
> But that is surely their's alone,
> For they have never, never known
>   A fallen world like this.
>
> Oh, how shall I, whose native sphere
>   Is dark, whose mind is dim,
> Before the Ineffable appear,
> And on my naked spirit bear
>   The uncreated beam?
>
> There is a way for man to rise
>   To that sublime abode;
> An offering and a sacrifice,
> A Holy Spirit's energies,
>   An Advocate with God.
>
> These, these prepare us for the sight
>   Of Majesty above;
> The sons of ignorance and night
> May dwell in that Eternal Light
>   Through the Eternal Love!

Then comes the reading of the Word — always from the Bible itself, *never* from a "selection" at the back of a hymnbook! Then, a second hymn (congregation standing, of course, which is *far* better for singing!). Let it be another favorite (this one usually sung to the tune, *Trentham*).

> Come and rejoice with me!
> For once my heart was poor,
> And I have found a treasury
> Of love, a boundless store.
>
> Come and rejoice with me!
> I, once so sick at heart,
> Have met with One who knows my case,
> And knows the healing art.
>
> Come and rejoice with me!
> For I was wearied sore,
> And I have found a mighty arm
> Which holds me evermore.
>
> Come and rejoice with me!
> My feet so wide did roam,
> And One has sought me from afar,
> And beareth me safe home.
>
> Come and rejoice with me!
> For I have found a Friend
> Who knows my heart's most secret depths,
> Yet loves me without end.
>
> I knew not of His love;
> And He had loved so long,
> With love so faithful and so deep,
> So tender and so strong.
>
> And now I know it all,
> Have heard and known His voice,
> And hear it still from day to day;
> Can I enough rejoice?

Then comes a brief talk to the children (a feature in many British churches) followed by the notices, the receiving of the offering, and the rendering of an anthem by the choir; then the gathering of all hearts and minds together for the longer pastoral and intercessory prayer (in some senses the focal center of the service). And now the congregation rises for a further hymn, just before the message. Perhaps it is one of Charles Wesley's (please linger over those rapturous verses 3 and 4!):

> Thou hidden Source of calm repose,
>   Thou all-sufficient Love Divine,
> My help and refuge from my foes,
>   Secure I am if Thou art mine;
> And lo, from sin and grief and shame
> I hide me, Jesus, in Thy Name.

> Thy mighty Name salvation is,
>   And lifts my happy soul above;
> Comforts it brings, and power and peace,
>   And joy and everlasting love:
> To me, with Thy dear Name, are given
> Pardon, and holiness, and heaven!
>
> Jesus, my All-in-All Thou art,
>   My rest in toil, my ease in pain,
> The medicine of my broken heart,
>   In war my peace, in loss my gain;
> My smile beneath the tyrant's frown;
> In shame, my glory and my crown.
>
> In want, my plentiful supply,
>   In weakness my almighty power,
> In bonds, my perfect liberty,
>   My light in Satan's darkest hour;
> My help and stay whene'er I call;
> My life in death, my heaven, my *all!*

Or maybe it is C. E. Mudie's best-loved hymn which with silken bands lifts us up heavenwards to Him who is the "altogether lovely":

> I lift my heart to Thee, Saviour divine,
> For Thou art all to me, and I am Thine:
> Is there on earth a closer bond than this,
> That my Beloved's mine, and I am His?
>
> Thine am I by all ties, but chiefly Thine
> That through Thy sacrifice Thou, Lord, art mine:
> By Thine own cords of love so sweetly wound
> Around me, I to Thee am closely bound.
>
> To Thee, Thou bleeding Lamb, I all things owe,
> All that I have and am, and all I know:
> Why should I keep one precious thing from Thee,
> When Thou hast giv'n Thine own dear Self for me?
>
> How can I, Lord, withhold life's brightest hour
> From Thee, or gathered gold, or any power?
> All that I have is now no longer mine,
> And I am not mine own, Lord, I am Thine.
>
> I pray Thee, Saviour, keep me in Thy love,
> Until death's holy sleep shall me remove
> To that fair realm where, sin and sorrow o'er,
> Thou and Thine own are one for evermore.

To all present, what preparation are such hymns for the message which now follows — usually the opening up and pertinent application of some Bible passage. (How often did I see rapt adoration and tears of intense communion as those dear people prayerfully sang such hymns!). Let the closing hymn clinch or climax the message in just the appropriate way. Maybe it is:

> O Thou who camest from above,
>   The pure, celestial fire to impart,
> Kindle a flame of sacred love
>   On the mean altar of my heart.
>
> There let it for Thy glory burn
>   With inextinguishable blaze,
> And, trembling to its source return,
>   In humble prayer and fervent praise.
>
> Jesus, confirm my heart's desire
>   To think and speak and work for Thee;
> Still let me guard the holy fire,
>   And still stir up Thy gift in me.
>
> Ready for all Thy perfect will,
>   My acts of faith and love repeat,
> Till death Thine endless mercies seal,
>   And makes the sacrifice complete.

Or perhaps it is that heartsearching hymn of longing, from another page of the book, which begins,

> O Jesus Christ, grow Thou in me,
>   Let all things else recede,
> My heart be daily nearer Thee,
>   From sin be daily freed.

How many such well-written, delightful hymns there are which put an exquisite capstone on a reverent Sunday morning service!

Perhaps so simple a form of service would not fully satisfy those who have been brought up in the Church of England and love its liturgical form of worship, but the contrast which I am striking here does not concern *that;* it is the contrast between the kind of *hymns* in other English-speaking countries and those which are commonly used among the *evangelical* bodies of America. I certainly do not wish to make invidious comparisons, but how different are the hymns just quoted from the usual coterie in many evangelical churches over here! I am not criticizing the latter kind for what they *are*. Nay, they have their useful place, and some of them are exceptionally likeable. What I am meaning is that they are not the worship-inspiring, heart-subduing, mind-elevating hymns of rich or expansive spiritual truth such as belong to *believers* in services of worship. For instance, "Sing them over again to me, wonderful words of life"; or "Be not dismayed what'er betide"; or "Count your many blessings." I forbear mentioning more, because, as I have said, they have their own place in a certain type of meeting or effort and have undoubtedly been used in many a heart.

Such hymns have a distinct value and power in evangelistic campaigns and in the more popular type of Christian gatherings; but when they become the staple stock from which our Sabbath-day hymns are continually selected, the sanctuary worship is incalculably impoverished. Beloved brethren, please hear me: in most American evangelical churches there is urgent need for changing to a maturer, more substantial kind of hymn, blending well-expressed doctrine, real poetry, and heart-deep spirituality. Never can I thank God enough that both my wife and I were brought up from childhood through youth to the accompaniment of such hymns, played in our Sabbath services by a Spirit-filled genius of an organist who infused his own rich devotional life into the hymns through his four-manual organ. It was an education in communion with God such as comes only that way.

Oh, the unique importance of the hymnbook! So much is it on our minds (forgive this further self-reference) that for some time now, as a result of our recent travels and observations, Mrs. Baxter and I have been working on a new hymnbook, containing between nine hundred and a thousand hymns, in seventeen sections, combining what we consider the best-quality hymns and most singable tunes of both British and American types. Our hope is that in at least some places it may answer a need. Incidentally, this reference to it is not a subtle way of advertising it (though, with a finer subtlety, we hope it may serve that wholesome purpose!).

On my earlier visits to the U.S.A. I used to think how advantageous it was that over here all the people who come to church are supplied with *music* editions of the hymnbook. (In Britain we supply and use *words-only* editions, except, of course, that all our choirs have music books). However, I have been obliged to revise my thinking on that score. Without any prejudices, I believe that in general the words-only book is preferable.

For one thing, over here, the supplying of *music* copies to all the congregation involves much bigger expense. Another thing is that the hymns take much more space, make a bulkier whole, and therefore result in books containing considerably *fewer* hymns. Furthermore, the printing of the words inside the music staves means that only four verses can be inserted comfortably — for which reason many precious old hymns have been unsympathetically truncated. Again and again I ache as I see well-tried British favorites, now in dismembered form, plaintively looking out at me through American musical prison bars. Surely such curtailment of hymns, merely to fit stave capacity, is a form of treating the raiment as more important than the body!

Nor is even that all. There is a proven advantage in having the words only before our eyes when, in the sanctuary, we are singing great truths with the *heart* even more than with the voice. The wording, the truth, the poetry, the upreach all capture the mind far more easily thus than when (as between music staves) the very syllables of the words have to be split up to fit the turns of the tune. Also, how many persons there are, even in America, who do not read music, and therefore never need it! And how many others there are who do not sing the parts, but only the melody or soprano, and therefore have no need for the music if they know the tune! And (forgive my naughtiness) I would stake much on the opinion that in general the congregational singing of British, Australian and South African congregations, with words-only hymn-books, is decidedly heartier than is usual over here. I love America far too well to make that observation with any bias. And (dare I?) would it not be much better, in not a few churches, if *all* the people had words-only books rather than only *some* have music books because of shortage due to the heavy cost of music editions?

Others, I know, may well have other ideas on such aspects; but my observations are submitted with warm esteem and with serious longing to provoke improvement at a sadly deficient point in an important part of public worship.

I gladly agree that on Sunday mornings the first one or two hymns in our U.S.A. evangelical churches are often of the more dignified kind, but they are continual repetitions of the same few which we have now come to expect wherever we are, almost as certainly as the dawn of Sunday itself — "Holy, Holy, Holy, Lord God Almighty"; "O worship the King, all-glorious above"; "A Mighty Fortress Is Our God"; "When morning gilds the skies"; and two or three others. These are certainly among the unsurpassed, but why the exclusion of many others equally superb? And why, nearly always, in three out of four just cited are verses left unprinted over here, thus depleting the original full message of the hymn?

I am not surprised if some exasperated brother now flings at me, "Physician, heal thyself! What about the broken-down church attendance in Britain these days?" I have already touched on that earlier in this series. It has mainly to do with the deadly havoc of modernism before and especially *between* two world wars which ravaged and dislocated things in Britain far more than the most sympathetic American can easily realize. It certainly has nothing to do with our rich inheritance of great hymns — which are now proving their unfailing worth more than ever in a time of dark testing.

A richer quality and variety of hymnody could wonderfully transform public worship in not a few places and prove a wonderful new ally of the pulpit. Even those dour members of the congregation who profess obstinacy against learning new hymns are usually soon educated into love for them when the richness of the words and the values of the tunes are gratefully *commented on* from the pulpit. If the minister and praise leader become kindled into new eagerness, the congregation will ere long fall an appreciative prey; and the sanctuary worship will have found new wings!

SUNDAY EVENINGS

He that hath looked death in the face as oft as I have done, I will not thank him [i.e., not be surprised] if he value his time. I wonder at those ministers who have time to spare — who can hunt, or shoot, or use the like recreations two or three hours, yea, whole days together — that can sit an hour together in vain discourse, and spend whole days in complimental visits, and journeys to such ends. Good Lord! what do these men think on! — when so many souls around them cry for help, and death gives us no respite, and they know not how short a time their people and they may be together.

Richard Baxter

SUNDAY EVENINGS

All of you will be one with me, I presume, as I now express deep regret over the large breakdown of the Sunday evening service in America. I am a convinced believer that the Christian observance of Sunday is one of the most vital bastions in the preservation of our Christian faith. My own conviction is that we simply cannot afford to let the Sunday evening service drop out. Evangelicals should put everything they know into rescuing it. As I try to peer into what may lie ahead, I seem to sense that if Sunday *evening* is lost to the churches, we may find ere long that Sunday *morning* is in jeopardy too.

However, I will indulge no hypothetical pessimism. I am far more concerned to promote practical recuperation. Albeit, I do here register my conviction that a withered or forsaken Sunday evening service is a major tactical reverse, especially for the evangelical churches. For one thing, it seriously undermines *pastoral Bible teaching* of the flock. I first began to realize this in the early part of my present long itinerary. One Sunday morning, as we approached a large, handsome church where we were starting a few days of Bible teaching, we were puzzled to find (as it seemed) almost as many persons *leaving* the building as coming to it. "They are people who have been to Sunday school, but are not staying to church," we were told. That was something peculiarly new to us. Still, the big, fine church was practically full, and the audience was responsive. In the evening, alas, we had a mere handful, by comparison, which circumstance occasioned the following little interlocution between the pastor and myself.

I asked him, "Do you use Sunday mornings mainly for the teaching of the members, and Sunday evenings mainly for evangelistic emphasis? (That is still the usual pattern among evangelicals over in Britain. It certainly was so throughout my own twenty-five years in the pastorate). He replied, "No, I have to try for conversions and new members on a Sunday morning, because most of the people who come then are not with us again at night." So I enquired, "Are the fewer who come at night, then, the keener or more spiritually minded ones?" He answered, "I suppose that would be pretty near the truth."

My mind went back to my Edinburgh ministry, where I used to feel that on Sunday morning I had the church, the membership as a body, solidly before me, so that I could open my heart to them as my own people on all the deeper truths of the Word or on the pressing issues of the day. I asked, "When, then, do you have your dear folk *as a church* before you, so that you can counsel or challenge or open your heart to them *as such?*" The answer was somewhat elusive. There *were* times in between Sundays, he explained, when the church members were called together, but that was usually for "business purposes."

Next I asked, "When do you give your deeper teachings from the Word to the members and those who are already born-again believers?" The reply surprised me: "Well, you see, the teaching is now mostly done in the Sunday school by the teachers; then usually I follow it up in the Sunday morning service by evangelistically 'drawing in the net,' so to speak."

To my own mind such a *modus operandi* seems all wrong. That minister is a degreed man of solid pulpit gift. With a touch of sincere playfulness I asked, "Have all your Sunday school teachers done Greek and Hebrew? Have they all had seminary training in biblical and systematic theology? in church history? in exegesis or hermeneutics?" The reply was too obvious to need wording. As he well knew, he had virtually handed over the highest function of his pulpit — handed it over to others who did not have either his own special call or his own special training.

Brethren, this strange capitulation of the pulpit is *far* too common today. I am all for the Sunday school (being myself a grateful product of it) but its usurpation of that central and supreme place which belongs to the pulpit is wrong, and must eventually bring spiritual leanness to a local church. I can *prove* that such does happen. "That which we have seen and heard declare we unto you." I mention no particular denomination or geographical area, but in that body and in those areas where such overloaded emphasis is put upon the Sunday school (or, as they prefer to name it, "the Christian Education Department") we have observed the following traits. (1) Considerable numbers go regularly to Sunday school on Sunday mornings but attend the church service only intermittently. (2) Many say they get more help from the Sunday school than from the church service, the pulpit ministry having now become thin, elementary, solely evangelistic. (3) On Sunday mornings, as already mentioned, people are coming out when they should be going in. (4) There is a fairly ready knowledge of Bible *contents* going with a very poor apprehension of Bible *truths*. (5) There is a busy-looking display of Christianity, eager, active, but morally anemic and spiritually superficial. (6) There is an immature doting on numbers, statistics, and amounts of money-offerings, instead of a longing for the powerful moving of God's Spirit among leaders and members. (7) There is a pitifully dwindled Sunday evening service. (8) The mid-week so-called "Prayer Meeting" is poorly attended in proportion to the membership and is anything *but* a prayer meeting in the true, Pentecostal meaning of the word.

My heart weeps with a heavy sorrow as I think of the breakdown in Britain. The continual thought of it gives painful edge to my concern as I ponder trends over here. Please do not turn on me with "Dost thou teach *us*" (John 9:34). I am urging upon you a giant effort to resuscitate the Sunday evening service and to attempt a restored *teaching* ministry on Sunday mornings; or, if the older morning and evening pattern has now become *unalterably* reversed, to build up a powerful teaching ministry for the membership and visiting believers on Sunday *evenings*.

Of course, I shall be asked, "*How* is the Sunday evening service to be revived?" Well, there is no magician's wand which can suddenly work the miracle, but I would respectfully submit some considerations which arise out of our widespread ministry among the evangelical churches.

Here is the first. To be candid, in many places the evening service no longer deserves to be called a "service." Some of the new style Sunday evening ensembles are not services at all in the time-honored sense of the word. They are a rasping irritation to those who mean serious business with God. They are pangs of grief to the prayerful-minded. They are as spiritually vapid as they are smart in showmanship. Instead of hearts being gently induced to new worship amid the shades of evening and lifted Godward on wings of dear old hymns which truly blend worshipers in congregational praise, those who attend have to sit (with scarcely a stand) while a "service" is *put on* for them; a program of items more like a sacred *concert* — with solos, trios, quartettes, violin or trumpet contributions, and sometimes a full orchestral selection.

With my own eyes I have seen it: instead of the pastor's entering the pulpit and bowing in silent prayer before daring to commence the service, a "song leader" breezes prayerlessly to the front, and says, "Come on, folks! Let's lift the roof off with hymn number fifty!" or "Hands up, everybody who's happy to be here," or some other unbecoming flippancy. Often five or six "hymns"(?) are sung, one after another, but (oh, the craziness of it!) only two or three verses out of each, and not one right through. Is common sense dropping away as well as reverence? Such behavior is pathetic inanity — and that comment is not one bit too strong. I deplore it, and so do thousands of others who now say so by staying away.

No one appreciates a glad Sunday evening service more than I if with brightness there is godly decorum, but that which I am here denouncing is a travesty. The pastor meanwhile sits by like an immobile paralytic, and some of the congregation (notably the older ones who wistfully remember better days), as I have perceived, limply tolerate it until at last the pastor (now the mere shadow of the former Protestant prophet) gives his meek or fervid word. There is no time any more for an adequately developed exposition. It must be a "simple gospel" sermonette, elementary, anecdotal, with a plaintive appeal at the end, based on a doctrinal vacuum. No, brethren, I am not exaggerating — and many of you know it. I have seen it, and heard it, and loathed it, and wept over it.

I can well appreciate how, soon after the brave, early evangelical split-away from the main modernism-infested denominations over half a century ago, those men of conviction and initiative and drive, besides building new churches, publishing new magazines, initiating new enterprises, and invading the public via the radio wanted to go "all out" for a popular Sunday evening service; but I am sure they never envisaged the present-day degradation of it.

The big question now emerging is: Has this experiment of the bright and breezy, free and easy "singspiration" type of Sunday evening menu succeeded? The answer is a capital "NO." There *are* exceptions, thank God, not a few, to the more general Sunday evening breakdown, but they are churches where a far less frilly form of procedure has been preserved; which reminds me also to add that not all song leaders are of the claptrap type I mentioned a moment ago. I am not "tarring them all with the same brush." Some of them are among the finest Christian workers I have met.

What then about *rescuing* the Sunday evening service? Well, before I criticize the ways in which it is distorted in many places, let me mention one or two present-day factors outside the Sunday evening service itself which militate against it.

The first of these is an *overloaded Sunday.* Even younger fellows and girls have told me that they are wearied by the time the evening service comes, because of all the other Sunday fixtures which they are expected to attend as loyal church youth. First there is the early morning Sunday school, then morning church service, then an afternoon or early evening youth group, then a hymn sing around a refreshment break; then (with a new emphasis) all must attend "Training Union" or some other group which is designed to fill a present keenly felt lack in making well-informed members of the denomination. *Then* comes the evening service, and in not a few places that again is followed by an after-church singsong or get-together accompanied by punch and cookies. No wonder that by this time our indoor hothouse plants are paling and wilting, and even the young sopranos drag flat on the top notes! The "day of rest" ends with yawns such as only come after such a chain of indoor sessions.

Such a crowded Sunday tends to defeat its own purpose. Its victims are not the laggardly stay-at-homes nor the pleasure galavants, but our church loyalists who dutifully comply, often to the point of undisguised lassitude. Furthermore, such movements as "training unions" are another shifting of the church's teaching ministry away from the pulpit, which in the long run will likely prove a bane rather than a blessing. *The true center of the church's teaching ministry is the pulpit.* From apostolic times it was designedly so. The church's auxiliary groups or movements are meant to be complements, not substitutes.

If the American minister had not been cajoled into becoming a general factotum — preacher, pastor, visitor, social hobnobber, administrator, moneyraiser, and other things too, until he has scarcely time either for studying the Word or for regular waiting in prayer, he could supply *all* that teaching ministry which has now been shunted away from his pulpit and committed to sideline auxiliaries. He could do it far *better* than they, if my own experience in visiting some of those auxiliaries is any guide. However, I will restrict myself to the one point which I am here making, namely, that an overcrowded Sunday detracts from the evening service.

Tied up with this overloaded Sunday is the problem of our modern *automobile* tyranny. In many homes, if mom and dad are not going to the evening service, the two or three juniors are kept in domestic dry dock as well. Even where the children are old enough for driving licenses and the family has two cars, the problem often exists in modified form. It is difficult to be motoring to and from the sanctuary more than two or three times per Sunday.

Others who require transport are dependent on those who drive and have cars. Fewer in-between meetings on Sundays would help toward a better attendance at the evening service — if there is a service worth coming for. It might even help toward inducing *family* attendance on Sunday evenings again.

The main requirement, however, is a radical change in the Sunday evening service itself. Until that is effected, any hope of recapturing attendance is a forlorn hope. For myself, I would not waste my time on the paltriness served up on Sunday evenings in many evangelical churches. It cannot be inveighed against too strongly. Let me seize "by the scruff of the neck" some of the wrongs which need ejecting.

The first is *aping the world*. I was in a service not so long ago where one of the soloists was a converted night club singer. She was a prize hit, now, in the sanctuary. Bless her heart! how could I help but feel a peculiar uprush of praise to God as I saw her singing there with such evident love for Christ beaming from her face. But, oh, the cosmetic lips, brows, cheeks, and eyelashes! the crooning, dreamy, swingy, slurring, rolling love-song type of singing! Some of us inwardly writhed.

It is wonderful that night club artists get converted. Let us exercise utmost kindness, sympathy, understanding, helpfulness, realizing what an extreme contrast there is between their former bizarre goings on and the fellowship of the Lord's house. Yet we dare not let them transfer their type of artistry to us. It is *not* suitable to Christian worship and should not be allowed in it. They must somehow be educated *out of* that throaty, drawly, cooing way. It is utterly distasteful. The trouble is that our own young people are slopping into it, so that even in church one sometimes hears that brazen, female top-note blare which tortures us through radio and television and even through some religious recordings. Brethren, however many sensitive corns we may have to tread on, that kind of solo, duet, trio, quartette must be kept out of the sanctuary *for our Lord's sake*. The vocal ministries of the church must strike an utter opposite to it. Several persons, in different places, have told me they stay away because of it, which suggests that probably many others do too.

Another obnoxious feature in many Sunday evening services is the behavior of the *song leader*. For the life of me, I cannot see why the pastor himself cannot lead the service right through, letting the song leader's part be complementary. But if the song leader *must* handle all the earlier part, let him do it "with reverence and godly fear"! Why this idea of a bunch of hymns, one after another, for the first ten or fifteen minutes? There can be no dwelling on the *message* of any one hymn in such a medley. What makes it worse is the strange craze for a bit of this hymn, a bit of that, and a bit of another. What do song leaders think hymn writers wrote hymns *for?* And why, since more than ample time is assigned for hymn singing, must the pace be that of race horses? and why the gallop from one verse to another without a sensible, between-verses, momentary halt for a breath? And why the fad for rousers instead of the more devotional type through which the "still small voice" from heaven can whisper to the heart? And why always the same *few* hymns, such as "Jesus May Come Today," and "Wonderful Grace of Jesus," and "Down at the Cross," and "I Serve a Living Saviour"? And why have them sung in a way which (when accompanied by jerky organ and piano playing) sometimes makes them sound like hurdy-gurdies? All these things are offshoots from a misguided notion as to what is required in a Sunday evening service. The idea is to make it "popular," to give it sparkle, to whip up a fervid enthusiasm, a sort of hilarious "We're having a good time whether we are or not." Such artificiality is of the flesh, not of the Spirit.

There is yet more to add concerning this aspect of the matter. Why must everything be *conducted?* Cannot congregations of grown people sing properly unless there is a song leader perpetually waving his arms in front of them? Seldom have I seen behavior more juvenile, needless, ridiculous, than the time-beating in some Sunday evening services. Only days ago I was the evening preacher at a small church where the pastor thus handed over the service: "Good evening friends. We shall begin by singing hymn number sixty-two. Our brother [the song leader] will lead us in it" — as though the minister himself were incapable of reading the first verse out, and the worshipers were mere boys and girls who must be coaxed or guided in order to sing properly. The song leader thereupon got up and, after imparting the profound information that we could only sing loudly enough by opening our mouths widely enough, he "led" us. He was one of those who grip the book with one hand and beat with the other. Our one hope of singing seriously was to keep our eyes away from him. His was the sword-swinger style, and he waved his invisible weapon in one unvarying savagery, coming down at two places in each verse with assassinating swiftness upon an invisible head which must have been hovering near him.

I recall, also, another church where the choir had to be elaborately conducted as they simply sang the dear old hymn, "What a Friend We Have in Jesus." Even then it was limp compared with the spontaneous singing of it by a *congregation* — for which it was meant. Brethren, I cannot help asking how long some of you are going to keep "playing at it" instead of doing the real thing. Some of the contributions which your choirs sing to the obtrusive time-beating of a song leader are simple hymns which my wife and I used to sing long ago when we were in the infants' department of our Sunday school! In other countries church choirs sing all but unusually difficult anthems with no leadership but that of the organ; and congregations sing the good old hymns just as lustily or smoothly without incessant signaling from pulpit or platform. The congregational singing in a church does not *need* to be led in the way required by a mammoth evangelistic campaign. But if there simply *has* to be the usual song leader, let his part be done with modesty and restraint. Let there be an avoidance of those "hymns" which have little merit apart from a springy tune, and let the praise leader rather call attention to the *words*, so that the congregation may not sin by singing hypocritically.

And now for a burst of shrapnel! Should not the pastor himself prayerfully select the hymns and guide the service in suchwise as to prepare for his message? Should not the pastor (and assistant or song leader) always wear a neat *suit* on Sunday evenings instead of different jacket and trousers? and should there not be well-polished black shoes?° Should there not be earnest prayer with the choir beforehand, and the choir members come into the sanctuary reverently, not hurriedly and chattering? Should not the "service" follow a progressive pattern instead of a fill-time sing-song and platform items? Should there not be a proper *pastoral* prayer? Should there not be a reading from the Word of God? Why will the pastor (or song leader) persist in calling on "Brother So-and So" in the audience to open with prayer, when some of the dear brethren cannot frame any but a few staccato sentences in public, and (as often as not) cannot be heard by more than the nearest few? And why, when the "ushers" are called forward before the offering is taken, does the pastor (or song leader) call on one of *them* to pray the offertory prayer — with his back to the

---

° It occurs to me that in some parts of the U.S.A. this could evoke mild surprise. It reflects my British upbringing, of course; but it also recalls a time in the U.S.A., not long ago, when careful dress was rightly deemed necessary for pulpit ministry.

audience, often with stumbling syllables, sometimes in a mere whisper, and usually inaudible even to the second row of pews or seats? Everything in a public service should be *heard by all*. Brethren, all such bad behaviors as I have mentioned give raggedness to the "service" and diminish reverence. Is it being quite forgotten nowadays that a Sunday evening service is for two purposes mainly: (1) devout evening *worship*, and (2) carefully prepared biblical *witness?*

Again, is it not better to preserve the archaic "Thou" and "Thee" in publicly addressing the triune deity than to use the recently popular "You"? The former *does* tend to reverence if only by the distinction which it makes between our speech to others and our address to God. I will not press this unduly, but the slipshod fault with too many evangelical men today is the atrocious mixing of both, i.e., "O God, we draw nigh to *'You,'* and thank *'Thee'* again that *'Your'* presence is still with *'Thy'* people" — of which impropriety there is a slovenly abundance.

And, further, at the end of a service, is it always necessary to hammer away at an appeal? How uncomfortable, how ashamed have I felt sometimes on behalf of our divine Master when I have heard Him cheapened by a gruelling "appeal"! There has been a determination *somehow* to get an outward response — as though the Holy Spirit could not possibly do His work apart from it. It has eventually driveled down to this: "Well, even if you just want to be prayed for, lift up your hand." Can we wonder that thoughtful people are nauseated! After a thoughtful, expository message, given in the unction of the Spirit, such spurious beggings and bargainings are a monstrosity! The proper thing is a silent waiting in prayer — yes, with a loving invitation or an opportunity of outward confession if such seems to be the Holy Spirit's leading; but none of your cheap-Jack pressuring, *please!*

Brethren, should not the Sunday evening service end with *the benediction?* Why does a minister of our warmhearted Lord Jesus terminate a season of Christian worship and fellowship with the colorless announcement, "You are dismissed" — as though he were releasing a Boy Scout troop? Or why will he call on some husky whisperer in the audience to "lead us in a closing prayer"? Out of my own experience I can wearily testify that more than one Sunday evening service has thus ended like the last sigh of a flat tire. Why, on the plea of informality, must we forsake the true dignity and supreme appropriateness of the great apostolic benediction? — and why does not the minister himself reverently utter it?

MAY THE GRACE OF OUR LORD JESUS CHRIST AND THE LOVE OF GOD, AND THE FELLOWSHIP OF THE HOLY SPIRIT BE WITH YOU ALL. AMEN.

Brethren, as Hebrews 6:1 puts it, "Of the things which we have spoken this is the sum": If the Sunday evening service is to be rescued from public neglect, it must be rescued from inward abuse. In many places, so I maintain, it needs wholesome reconstruction; and with that as my conviction I respectfully submit the following positive suggestions.

Let the service have the kind of *form* and *progress* which makes it indeed a sacred *service*. It will be no less joyful for that, but it will be far more effective. Let it begin with *one* good congregational hymn of praise and then a brief opening prayer by the pastor (all the congregation then together saying the Lord's Prayer). Then let there be a briefer hymn (during which latecomers can be seated). After that there should be a Scripture reading, maybe with brief explanatory or applicatory comments here and there (which can be a really enriching part of the service: see some of C. H. Spurgeon's printed Scripture readings with interspersed comments). Then let there be the musical contribution by choir, solo, or quartette. Others points I leave open, except that prior to the sermon there should be a truly pastoral prayer, and then the congregation should *stand* to sing a suitable preparatory hymn just before the message.

Brethren, that matter of an adequate Scripture reading and a truly pastoral prayer is vital for both morning and evening services. C. H. Spurgeon, in one of his lectures to ministerial students, says that he would sooner forego giving the sermon than omit leading the congregation in the prayer! I recall how, about a year after my settling at Edinburgh, reports began floating to me that many people who flocked to our services were coming not so much for my sermons as for my pulpit prayers. To my shame I confess that at the time I was so concerned about *preaching* effectively that I did not quite appreciate the comments about the pulpit prayers as much as I now do in retrospect, though I always did grasp the importance of praying the congregation through to *God* as a prelude to preaching the Word of God through to *them*.

I am sometimes asked if I *prepared* my pulpit prayers. My answer is: Yes, but never verbally. I generally left the wording to be the spontaneous product of the moment, but I foreplanned items of thanksgiving, intercession, and other matters of congregational concern. Sometimes I incorporated short, printed prayers or "collects" of others, praying them just as ardently as if they had originated in my own heart; and I *know* that they were an uplifting outlet of devotion for my people. Why should we not feel liberty to bring *all* such enrichments into the worship of the sanctuary? Some who fulminate against it as "formalism" or "ritualism" or "quenching the Spirit" are poor advertisements for complete spontaneity. They never need boast that their prayers are not in any way prepared beforehand; we can all tell it! When shall we learn that haphazard public praying by a minister, week after week, is a *sin?* Is it not a sacred *obligation* to prepare for leading a whole congregation of souls in their united address to God?

During the earlier years of my ministry, the greatest preacher in London — at least in the sense of pulpit oratory, textual exposition, and popular magnetism — was Dinsdale T. Young. He was an unusually big man physically, with large dome-shaped head and a prepossessing, prophet-like appearance. He had the most wonderful preaching voice I have ever heard — a kind of musical thunder. Without any difficulty he could be heard by all the several thousands people who packed in to hear him Sunday by Sunday at Westminster Methodist Central Hall. Even in London's large Royal Albert Hall (seating 10,000) he could be heard without a platform microphone. I was always sorry for his co-speaker (most of all on one occasion when I myself was due to follow him!). He never used a single note, whether preaching or lecturing, not even in his address to the British Methodist Conference when he was its president! He had the choicest facility of extemporaneous phraseology which I have ever known. *Yet he prepared his pulpit prayers beforehand* (he told me so); not the wording, but the main upreaches and the order of mention. He made it known that *always* before going to his Westminster services he meditatively read through one of Joseph Parker's printed prayers (which are fairly long). In Spurgeon's printed pulpit prayers we detect the same evidence of an advance mental preparation. The wording is that of the moment, right from the heart, and there are asides which indicate unfettered freedom to turn to the right hand or to the left; yet there is a pre-envisaged pathway of thought.

Do I need to add that in advocating such preparation for public prayer I am far removed from suggesting any mere *verbal eloquence* in it? There is a brilliance of speech which may be alluring in a sermon but is pathetic and repugnant in a pulpit prayer. I think of that showy divine who commenced a public prayer, "O Thou who paintest the petals of the polyanthus," and of another who remarked heavenward, "Doubtless, omniscient Lord, Thou didst see in yesterday's newspapers . . ."! Such florid decorations and presuming familiarities in public prayer are not only silly, they are disgusting. True eloquence in prayer is that which is of the Spirit. As soon as we hear it we know it. And *that* kind of pulpit praying does something in a service which nothing else can. I never shall forget some of the pulpit prayers I heard in my younger years — prayers which not only made the presence of God seem to "fill the house," but did something to my concept of God which no sermon ever did.

That brings me to the last two matters which I want to mention in connection with the Sunday evening service. They are the song leader and the sermon. Doubtless, my remarks about the *song leader* will erect many gallows for me (or perhaps some would prefer to have me skinned alive!). Well, as the old saying has it, "I may as well be hung for a sheep as for a lamb," so here goes. I would not say one word of it if I were not sure that I speak with sincere esteem and brotherly love. What pleasant fellowship have I had from time to time, these past years, with gifted song leaders! and what fine help some of them have rendered! I do not forget this; so let all such on whose territory my words may impinge know that I speak with true appreciation of them *personally*.

It seems to have been in D. L. Moody's younger days that the song leader definitely emerged as a recognized cohort of the preacher. Moody must have his Sankey. Torrey must have his Alexander. Since then it has been so in all large-scale evangelism; and most of us, I imagine, would give it our unqualified endorsement. What a superb compliment to Moody was Ira D. Sankey! What a masterly adjunct to Torrey was Charles M. Alexander! Both my wife and I were converted to Christ in one of the evangelistic campaigns conducted by the Brothers Wood, founders of the National Young Life Campaign in Britain. Mr. Frederick Wood was the preacher, and his brother, Mr. Arthur S. Wood, was the song leader. A more lucid gospel preacher than Mr. Frederick Wood one could never hear; and what an artist at preparing those large gatherings for the message was his brother Arthur! It was while traveling around with them as their pianist for a year or so that I first saw how very important to an evangelist is the right kind of song leader.

Nowadays, however, in America, the song leader is not only the recognized co-worker of the itinerant evangelist; he has become an accepted institution in the local *church*. Let me be clear as well as kind: I am *not* saying that I could wish it were otherwise; nevertheless I maintain that we err to great disadvantage when we make the song leader in the public services of a local church the parallel of the song leader in an evangelistic campaign. Indeed, I hold that even his title should not be "Song leader," but "Choirmaster." In other English-speaking countries where church administration is simpler (I do not say better) than in America, the *organist* is usually the choirmaster. If in America there must needs be a minister of music *besides* an organist, then, so I cordially maintain, his ministrations should not invade or arrogate any part of a sanctuary service which rightly belongs to the pastor.

As I write these lines I am just back from a Sunday evening service in which the minister did nothing but pray a short introductory prayer and then hand over the service to a "song leader," who led everything until the time came for my message to be given. There was no Scripture reading. Not one of the several hymns were we allowed to sing right through. Not one comment was made about the *words* of the hymns through which the song leader abbreviatedly hurried us. There was superfluous hand waving all the while. He added nothing spiritually but subtracted a whole territory which should have been progressive *worship* led by the pastor. When I got up to speak the people looked tired rather than "tuned in" to hear "what the Spirit saith to the churches."

Conversation which I have had with ministers of music who are on the paid staff of local churches has convinced me that more than a few of them would welcome release from overparticipation on Sunday evenings, and that they would prefer a worthier sort of hymn and a truer form of worship instead of the present lax and lighter species. The fact is, when we hand over the singing of a church to a minister of music or paid song leader the whole of it becomes basically changed — though this may not be realized at first. The song leader knows well enough that he is expected to "manage" the singing of choir and congregation efficiently, to give finesse to the choral renditions, and to "get the congregation to sing." Naturally, therefore, he tends to choose hymns for their singable quality, their tune appeal, or their stirring effect, rather than for the pure value of the words. The changeover is subtle but real. For a time the congregational singing registers stimulation; then there comes a sameness. Later the effect becomes the opposite of what it was at first; the rousers no longer rouse, and the catchy tunes are like pretty dinnerware without anything to eat.

Only recently, in the deep South, I sat with a Baptist minister in his pulpit, or, rather, on his platform while the early hymn singing was conducted by his song leader. Observing that the pastor had no hymnbook, I offered him one, but he whimsically whispered, "I never sing the hymns; I just sit this part out." A glance at the audience showed me that despite an energetic song leader others in the service were likeminded with the pastor; they had not even opened their hymn books. But, even sadder, that service represents more or less generally a point which has now been reached in the history of the free-and-easy type of Sunday evening service. Originally, it was meant to make the evening service popular, but it has now reached a juncture where it is depopulating it.

Unfortunately, many of our younger people, including even some of the young ministers now coming out of seminaries, cannot remember the older kind of service; but there are still very many scattered through all the evangelical churches who long for the old-time Sunday evening worship when the pastor stood to announce the opening hymn, then led the people in an unhurried prayer, read from the Word, and unburdened his soul through some thoroughgoing exposition of Scripture truth.

One thing I would reemphasize: I am *not* questioning either the true place or the high value of the praise leader or minister of music in the operation of the local church. What I *am* insisting is that in the public services of the sanctuary he should not be the parallel of the song leader in itinerant evangelism. The emergence of the song leader or music director as an accepted figure in the local church coincided with the new emphasis on a "popular" Sunday evening gathering. The specialist song leader seemed just the ally a minister was needing. He would whip up the singing and enliven the whole congregational praise. But to turn the precious ally into a field marshall was a mistaken handover. Gifted song leaders do their conscientious best in many places, but, be it remembered, their training and speciality are different from that of the pastor. No song leader can choose hymns in just the way that a message-burdened pastor prayerfully chooses them with a view to his "Thus saith Jehovah."

Thank God for every gifted, consecrated minister of sacred praise in the churches, and for every true improvement in the choral ministries of today; but so far as your "popular" Sunday evening is concerned, the observable results, in general, are crying with loud voice today, *GIVE THE PULPIT BACK TO THE PASTOR!*

Finally, let me speak about the *sermon*. There are many ways of inveigling the people into our church premises, and I pay ungrudging tribute to the inventiveness of the American mind in that respect. But the only thing which keeps normally thoughtful people coming is *truth*. There is a place for entertainment, for educative lecture, for banquet and party, for social intercourse, for group discussions, and for what men think; but, so far as the Christian Church is concerned, what human beings want is *truth* — truth which is *vital*, truth which is authentically the Word of God, truth which really saves the *soul*. They are not always saying this in so many words, but they inwardly think it, feel it, and in critical moments of frankness they confess it. Indeed, the Church has no vital relevance unless it has divine truth. Men may run away from the truth today, but in sudden trouble run *after* it tomorrow. They may hate it now, but love it then. They may scorn it with derision today, but plead for it in desperation tomorrow and prize it with exultation forever after. Whatever may be the changeful outward attitude at any given moment, men and women need saving truth; deep down they know it, and most of them secretly believe that the Church has it. Therein lies the real magnet of the Christian Church; and therein lies the transcendent significance of the *sermon*.

Brethren, it is time to start really preaching again on Sunday evenings. Basically, what people need and really want is not merely a pleasant little hymn-sing topped off by a complementary "pep talk." Less and less are they bothering to come for that, as you know. If *you* were not a minister, would *you* come out on a Sunday evening just for that? Then why should we wonder overmuch at the present dropping off on Sunday evenings? I maintain that despite television and other Sunday distractions a real *prophet of God* in a Christian pulpit will never lack an audience. I believe that vital truth preached in the invisible envelopment of the Holy Spirit can fill our Sunday evening services again.

I do not, I dare not, say such words lightly. I know how far the drift has gone and how difficult are the problems in some communities. The easiest churches today, so far as building up numbers is concerned, are those in growing suburbs. The hardest (with very few exceptions) are those in downtown or city-center locations. There are some sets of circumstances in which it is well-nigh impossible to collect more than a handful of people together, even if there could be a Spurgeon or a Whitefield or a flashing-eyed Finney in the pulpit. My remarks, therefore, must be taken as applying to the present situation only *generally* (and I believe that they fairly *do* apply generally). The true answer to the big Sunday evening fall-away is *prophets in the pulpit.*

If I risk a few parting suggestions here, will you please decide not to prosecute me for trespassing into a domain which is peculiarly yours and not mine? I would recommend some of you to have a quiet chat with two or three of your most understanding officeholders (elders or deacons, or your closest leaders by whatever designation) confiding to them your concern for the sanctuary services, particularly a reshaping of the Sunday evening format. Tell them your deep longing to get more time for prayer, for Bible study, for unhurried pulpit preparation — predominantly with a view to the revitalizing of that Sunday evening service. I have a premonition you will win them. If you do, then forthwith transmit your concern *through* them to all the other brethren in office, and then through them to the membership. Seek their prayerful cooperation in refashioning, reemphasizing, rebuilding the Sunday evening service. Keep pressing on them the urgency of attending on Sunday evenings. Keep nudging them to bring friends and neighbors, both unconverted and believers, on Sunday evenings, the more so if other local churches are then closed. Keep reminding them by frank word or diplomatic hint or announcement of pulpit subjects that you concentrate your extra-best ministry on Sunday evenings. Somehow make them feel they are missing something if they stay away. Get your more striking themes into the newspapers and over the radio, if you can. Get it through to the public, somehow, that you hold a reverent worship-type, Bible-teaching service on Sunday evenings.

But all this, of course, heads up in the ultimate importance of the *message.* Away with the paltry! Away with those few alliterative bones which have no flesh on them! Away with snooping round in books of other men's sermons to find your material! That is not how true prophets come by their heartshaking messages from God! Get down to the one Book which is the Christian minister's authoritative "original." Give that Book its chance to preach *through* you. Let *it* do the preaching. Start reading it consecutively every day. No, I do not mean *study* it (do that as well, according to available time). I mean just *read* it in large enough consecutive quantities day after day. Do not read it looking for sermons, or they will never come! Just read it and read it and read it for sheer interest's sake and for spiritual benefit — and so many sermons will come to you when you are not looking for them that you will not have enough pads on which to jot them quickly down or enough Sundays to cope with them!

When the meteoric young Spurgeon became the pulpit cynosure of Victorian London, one of the common remarks was, "He preaches on the big themes." Brother preacher, expatiate on *the big themes!* Let that be your Sunday evening motto. Small congregations usually grow bigger most quickly when a minister ably handles the big truths of our Christian creed. Do not be a clever sermonizer in snippets. Let your pulpit spill over with copious truths. Do not always be reaching round for *topics;* open up big *texts.* Topical preaching is much harder than textual, yet it is not nearly so spiritually educative to your hearers. Of course, preaching on *biblical* "topics" (as distinct from popular topics of the day) is all the more informing to the hearer and at the same time enriching to the preacher himself.

For instance, why not a fourfold Sunday evening series on *The Bible Doctrine of Life After Death?* Why not six Sunday evening studies on *Things to Come,* i.e., the "age to come," the "wrath to come," the "Judgment to come" (maybe that series should be more than six!). Why not a glorious series on the *Person and Work of the Holy Spirit?* and another series on *The Being and Attributes of God?* and another series on *Sanctification According to the New Testament?* I would not suggest successive series all the time, but used periodically they have a unique holding power.

Your people and many others will start coming on Sunday evenings for carefully prepared ministry on themes like those. They will start dreading to miss. When as a young man of thirty-two I launched out upon my ministry in Edinburgh, Scotland, I feared that such an one as I, with my very limited abilities, would scarcely hold an Edinburgh congregation week after week. (Edinburgh is the Athens of the British Isles. It has a psychology and superiority-complex all its own). I shall never forget how relieved and grateful to God I was, after being there eighteen months or so, when different members of my congregation — even younger ones — would say to me, "Pastor, I can scarcely wait from one service to the next for the opening up of the Word. As soon as Sunday evening is over I am longing for the Thursday evening Bible lecture, and, after that, for the next Sunday morning." How I thanked God that I had a Bible of such endless variety and interest to preach!

One further counsel: I am not just playing with words when I recommend: On Sunday evenings *be evangelistic without trying to be.* There is more in that than some brethren may suspect.

In the first years of my own ministry, my Sunday evening preaching became a sore problem to me because I wanted it always to be soul-winning. I found a sameness hanging around my Sunday evening sermons. Moreover, there was reason to infer that some of my people were equally conscious of it. Those who were my Sunday evening "regulars" began to know just the kind of text their pastor would take, just how he would handle it, and just how he would apply it. That is fatal to any preacher's retention of interest. But what could I do? I tried to argue: those who know the gospel so well will have to put up with a bit of sameness for the sake of my winning souls on Sunday evenings.

Then, as I cogitated and prayed over it, suddenly this obtuse brain of mine stumbled upon a discovery which changed my whole concept of Sunday evening, and banished my sameness forever! I had been confusing *mission* evangelism with *pastoral* evangelism. Mission evangelism must always more or less conform to a standard pattern, whereas pastoral evangelism may have a never-exhausted variety of aspects. Let me be more specific. When an evangelist comes to a church or a town for an evangelistic mission, he comes for that one purpose concentratedly. His texts and subjects will be directly and obviously evangelistic. He is purposely self-limited, and we all expect that to be so. His message (whatever his text or opening approach) may be summed up as: (1) What is salvation? (2) Why do we need it? (3) How do we receive it?

In contrast to that, *pastoral* evangelism, other than being compressed into a short visit and set form, spreads itself expansively over months and years, links itself to an endless variety of exposition, and gets over to the hearer from all kinds of unsuspected angles of application. I gave up looking for evangelistic texts to use on Sunday evenings. I started letting the Bible itself suggest what I should preach. *Any* biblical text or subject rich in truth, interest, information, edification now became my precious cargo for Sunday evenings, and I found that *every* such subject had its evangelistic bearing. My Sunday evening problem was gone and has never returned. Many of our most delightful conversions occurred in response to seemingly *un*evangelistic sermons! and believers were getting fed from the Word at the same time.

Well, I have "said my say." All I have said has welled up and overflowed to you from brotherly esteem and sincere conviction. God bless you and make you, ever more truly, "ABLE MINISTERS OF THE NEW COVENANT."

NEWFANGLED PERILS

Alas! It is the common danger and calamity of the Church to have unregenerate pastors, and to have so many become preachers before they are Christians. . . . and so to worship an unknown God, and to preach an unknown Christ. They do but walk in a vain show. . . . while they busy their wits and tongues about abundance of names and notions, and are strangers to God.

Richard Baxter

NEWFANGLED PERILS

It is with some apprehensiveness that I here mention certain developments today in church services, Bible conferences, and evangelistic campaigns; developments which I believe are wrong, and in some instances even of satanic instigation. I realize, rather unnervingly, that in speaking out I "run the gauntlet," and that some may call for my immediate martyrdom; but in Paul's words, "necessity is laid upon me," so I must take the risk if I would live comfortably with my conscience.

I am convinced that to the degree in which we pander to certain new trends now to be mentioned, evangelical witness in America will suffer, and spiritual deterioration will result. Perhaps it will be diplomatic if I refer to some of the milder innovations first, and to the more serious later.

Indeed, before anything else, let me express devoutest thankfulness for a simply incalculable contribution which America has made to modern Christendom — one which is all too often overlooked. It is America's mighty initiative in mass evangelism. The American is distinctively the go-getter. Let the rest of us acknowledge without jealousy that the American is "way out front" in business "drive" and "push," in improvising, adapting, and big-scale planning in international commerce, and most of all in *"promoting."* This expresses itself not only in industry, but in sports, politics, religion. Who sent Moody and Sankey around the world preaching and singing the gospel? America. Who sent Torrey and Alexander around the world preaching and singing the gospel? America. Who sent Chapman and Alexander around the world preaching and singing the gospel? America. Who sends Billy Graham and Beverly Shea around the world preaching and singing the gospel? America.

Recently, my dear wife and I have gone through some thousands of hymns, in the process of making a new compilation. Where have nearly all our well-known evangelistic hymns come from? America. We wept tears of grateful reminiscence as we peered back to our youthful years in Britain and realized that nearly all those gospel hymns over there which sang us to the foot of the Cross, in our teens, were from America. By comparison, not many of the deeper hymns have come from this side of the Atlantic; but never should the mighty contribution be forgotten which American Christianity has made in the evangelistic, witness-bearing, and practical exhortation type of hymn. Those hymns have been a wonderful part of the exemplary American lead in matching gospel outreach to the challenge of our twentieth-century urbanized society.

It is with this thankfulness in my heart that I now touch on a subtle yet unmistakable difference between public Christian gatherings in the U.S.A. and those in other countries such as Britain, Australia, and South Africa. It is not easy to express it with fine exactness; it is *felt*, rather than verbally definable. Again and again in those other lands we have seen whole crowds bowed before God through the singing of a rich-quality, penetrating hymn in a way we have never yet seen here. We have seen audiences indescribably moved and broken in adoring worship at our Lord's feet through a heart-searching solo, whereas over here the most marked response has been genial appreciation of the rendition.

Speaking generally, in the U.S.A. the *choral* singing in churches and campaigns is distinctly ahead of that in the average overseas counterpart, at least in variety and modernity; but the *congregational* singing over here is disappointingly poorer. This latter difference is not just imaginary; it is subtle but real; and there is a *reason* for it, though (as remarked) it is not easily put into words.

Perhaps the nearest we can get to it is to say that over here ministers and song leaders are trained experts at putting a service *on*, but they do not seem to have developed the art of *drawing out* from a congregation *spontaneous worship*. What with the singing and leading being entirely in the hands of a song leader, and a program providing choral piece, solo, quartet, instrumental item, etc., it is rather like serving a *menu;* and so-called "services" tend to become more like sacred concerts. Remember, it is the style in our *evangelical* churches to which I here refer.

In our continual travels we notice more and more the omitting of congregational participation. In many places, on Sunday mornings, there are now only *two* congregational hymns, and even then the leader sometimes deletes a verse or so. Oh, there can be *so* much Christian fellowship in a rich-quality hymn fervently sung! From my own twenty-five years of pastoral ministry, I know what such hymns can mean. A "service" should really *be* a service, a uniting in reverently led but congregationally *spontaneous* worship. Many are the hungry-hearted church members who have told me how sick at heart they are with the type of "service" which is now put *on* — by choir, soloist, trio, etc., all cutting down time for pastoral exposition of God's Word, for sanctuary prayer, and for the drawing out of hearts in quiet worship!

And now there are other incoming fashions, some of which, in my judgment, are undesirable superfluities. More often in Bible conferences, but also now creeping into our churches, is the new additament that the soloist or quartet leader or other contributor must start *explaining* (before rendering the item) how he or she or they come to be rendering a particular item, or else make some prior comment, such as telling how it has blessed them. While that may be fitting where a whole musical *program* is being given by a musical artist or artists, it is (with rare exceptions) out of place in our sanctuary services or in the usual kind of gatherings for the opening up of the written Word. The solo or other item should itself be the message; for of course Christian solo hymns, duets, etc., are so written that they *are* the intended message in themselves, needing *no* verbal preamble.

Let no one think that I am here "airing my own view" only. If those dear brethren who must always *say* something before they *sing* something could hear some of the many observations about it, they might raise their eyebrows. As one would expect, the comments are Christianly kind by truly appreciative hearers, but they are nonetheless definite, and they arise from an innate sensitivity as to what is most desirable in such services.

So far as my own experience goes, not once has the good-natured preamble effectively added to the message in song. Sometimes it has been a peripatetic waste of time, and one could sense that the audience was saying, "Please, do get to your message in song." Sometimes, through inexperience in public speaking, it has been more or less unintelligible; and sometimes, alas, it has been a thinly camouflaged self-advertisement. Such preliminary comments should be eliminated. In general, they are timewasters. All too often they call attention to the singer rather than the Savior.

By now, the engines of wrath will have been set rolling against me; but as I am still alive, there is yet more on which I would fain "deliver my soul." Through a variety of factors the tendency now (even though unintendingly) is to divert attention from our Lord Jesus to the preacher or singer or other contributor. This is done by glamorizing advertisements which overpresent the preacher, or by the kind of solos which are sung, or by the *way* in which they are sung.

During the past sixty years there has been a strange dearth in the writing of new *congregational* hymns. But with increasing specialization in sanctuary *music*, along with our numerically multiplying "ministers of music," there has developed a very spate of *choral* pieces; of solos, duets, quartets, and other published items for platform use. Less and less now, do we hear the simpler kind of gospel solo or spiritual message sung. More and more the solo is of an artistic type with a fairly elaborate and often delightful instrumental accompaniment. Understandably, in such compositions the movement reaches a high climax which gives the soloist ample scope to show off his or her vocal powers and trained finesse. It is all so attractive, so well done, so talented, and sometimes so brilliant that one simply cannot help admiring it; the natural impulse is to clap or applaud. Yet therein lies the sad fault. When one is left applauding the singer instead of adoring the Savior, the solo has been a brilliant *failure*. It has entertained the natural rather than searched hearts, challenged the spirit, or inspired the soul Godward.

There is so much of that now! It is so aesthetically beguiling, so highly enjoyable, so hard to criticize, yet so subtly divertive! How careful we preachers and other public servants of our Lord need to be! How determined must be our passion to turn people's gaze *away* from ourselves to that dear and glorious Savior who in all things must have the preeminence!

That, however, brings me to a more disagreeable aspect in present trends. To no small degree there now intrudes itself into our evangelical services a pitiful *apeing of the "world."* Not only do solos and other musical contributions depart from the simpler hymn to the more classy composition; they slop down into "pop" style and become a sickening mimic of the inane stuff thrown at us by the modern stage or night club. I am one of thousands who detest it, especially in the house of God and amid the convocations of Christians; and in their name I appeal to all our ministers of music and song leaders to help repel the evil invasion.

"Mod" music (?) with its vamp and beat and thud and slurs, its screeching cacophonies and sensuous suggestiveness, its primitive incoherence, its whining and cooing and frantic yelling — let it be far from our evangelical sanctuaries. It is a form of pseudomusical insanity. The Christian church was never meant to take its musical style from the Beatles or other such rock 'n roll oddities of this crazy age. That sort of music (?) has nothing to do with the tabernacles of the Most High. To try and harness *that*, or anything like it, to the great doctrines of our holy Christian faith is an insult to the Godhead.

There are those who try to get "pop" styles in edgewise by telling us that our young folk want it. One thing which comforts me is that in the churches and conferences where *I* am privileged to minister, it is the young people themselves who tell me they *resent* the "pop" style. Only a year and a half or so ago, during crowded meetings in Sydney, Australia, after every gathering the platform was stormed by young men and women asking questions about the Christian faith, and bombarding me with their ideas as to what they should be getting from the Church and its ministers. There were university students and graduates, fine athletes, airplane pilots, some of them great, lanky fellows, along with gifted modernly alive young women. It was *they* who kept telling me that they did not want pandering to and did not want this sloppy new music. "We want to know the *Bible*." "Give us something that hits us, hurts us — something that *costs*." "We're tired of all these strum-strum groups with their jerky 'pop' numbers. We've had enough of it on the stage, and we abhor it in the Church."

I have found pretty much the same in the U.S.A.; but because of a vociferous minority song leaders are misled into thinking that more of our young people want 'pop' style than is actually so. To ministers of music I would say: Brethren, amid changing times and peculiar problems and much clamor for novelties, keep an open ear not only to the voices of earth, but to the voice of the Holy Spirit. For the sake of our holy Master, resolve that *whatever* changes may be permitted, there shall never be any compromise with the inferior or worldly or unworthy. Remember how high and sacred is your ministry. We are looking to you song leaders and music makers to lead our churches in the right direction. God give you grace and wisdom and firm purpose to do it.

The fact is, we are at a critical juncture so far as church worship, music, methods, and patterns are concerned. There is a craze for the new and an infatuation with the unorthodox. A craze is never logical. An infatuation is never reasoning. Both are perilous. Not only to hippies, but to thousands of our college and university youth under the influence of new philosophy and psychology, anything handed down from yesterday is disqualified. To be accepted it must rebel against the old and well proven. Everywhere, already, we see the damage and wreckage due to this. Concurrently, all kinds of new and sometimes risky experiments are being advocated in our evangelical churches. We are told that unless we unshackle ourselves from yesterday and change everything to fit the "now" concepts, we shall lose the people and become voices on desert air. But the more excitable this impatience with the "good old" may be, so the more is this a time for level-headedness, or we are likely to be stampeded into foolish and costly aberrations.

Make no mistake: I am no die-hard champion of the old-fashioned; I am all for keeping abreast of the times. If changes are needed, let us have them, so long as they are changes from poor to good, or from good to better. But some of the changes advocated today are *downgrade*. I believe the time has come when, instead of copying the world, we should deliberately strike the note of *contrast*. Many a time I have been in those new-type, streamlined "services," with their tick-of-the-clock timing, tunes with jiggy lilt, guitar or banjo groups, tiptop talent, culminating sermonette, and it has all added up to a spiritual vacuum.

How I have longed (as do thousands of others) for the quiet, steady, restful worship service in which one has time to breathe, to think unhurriedly, and to *worship*, instead of being regaled with a pulpit-and-platform performance! The challenge to all of us evangelical ministers and song leaders is to rescue our sanctuary services from all "mod" and "pop" infiltration and to train our people to love the better-quality hymns. If they see that we ourselves treasure them, they will be affected by our example. Our motto should ever be: Nothing but the purest and highest for the Lord's house, in hymns and music and form of service. As for solos and other such contributions, we should carefully guard our Sabbath services and all other Christian gatherings from the showy, Hollywood finalé sort. All solos and kindred musical ministries should conform to the following eight-point standard.

1. Self-effacing, not, as so often, self-obtruding.
2. Should point to the Savior, never to the singer.
3. Should inspire Godward worship, not applause by the human.
4. Should evoke deeply serious response, never amusement.
5. Clear Scriptural message, never repetative vagaries.
6. Worthy melody and harmony, never incoherent or ranty.
7. True singing with pure tone; never raucous or shouting.
8. Should appeal to highest in us, never to the lower.

"POP" MUSIC: WHY NOT?

Now and then I am met by the head-on challenge: "*Why* are you against 'pop' music coming into the churches? Why should it not be used in Christian gatherings?"

First, I am against it because of its kinship with *"rock 'n roll."* Few of us who are older, or whose evangelical convictions insulate us from the mad doings of ungodly society, realize the sinister meaning of rock 'n roll. To begin mildly, rock 'n roll is not real music at all. Music, especially *good* music, blends four characteristics: (1) beauty of theme and design, (2) purity of melody or richness of harmony, (3) coherence and development, (4) variety, or balance between tension and release.

Judged by those four canons, rock 'n roll is not strictly music. It may surprise some to learn that it is not even meant to be. Rather, it is a medium of *thought* through *sound*. It has to be a certain *kind* of sound to convey a certain kind of urge, and the urge which is meant to be communicated by rock 'n roll is *animalistic*. Therefore in rock 'n roll we have the following four contrasts with true music.

1. Instead of beauty in design, insistent *repetition of phrase* — a same group of notes over and over again.

2. Instead of pure melody or rich harmony, *repetition of chord* — the same from beginning to end.

3. Instead of coherence and progress, a determined *repetition of beat* — a driving, thud, thud, thud which never gives up.

4. Instead of alternating stimulus and relaxation, intense *repetition of sound and tempo* with ever-increasing force, loudness, often to the point of sheer din.

The two fundamental trademarks of rock 'n roll are repetition and the insistent beat. Without those two it is *not* really rock 'n roll, for rock 'n roll essentially *is* that gradually overpowering repetition and interminable beat. Rock 'n roll is a *vocabulary of sound*, and it is used to say something vulgar, sensual, evil. Let me open this up a little.

All musical sound is created by infinitesimally minute aerial vibrations. These strike upon the auricular nerve of the human body, and, through sympathetic vibration there they enter via the nervous system into the brain, thus registering in our consciousness, where the mind either approves or disapproves. Thereby, music has effects upon both body and mind.

The effects of sound upon the *body* are realized more scientifically today. All of us know how a military band playing a martial strain can strangely stimulate us both physically and emotionally; but there is more to it than that. Because sounds are dynamogenic, their stimuli of pitch and intensity can increase muscular energy. It may surprise some to learn that a listener's eyesight may improve as much as twenty-five per cent through certain musical and rhythmic sound.* What is more, through audio-analgesia (the dulling of pain through sound instead of an anesthetic) operations have been painlessly performed. Dentists, instead of using Novocain, can feed music or "white sound" through earphones in increasing degree to the patient, until the volume of it nerve-jams the system beyond feeling pain.

Even more jolting is the fact that among potted plants all growing in the same soil and under similar conditions, all those (and *only* those) which were exposed to rock 'n roll "music" *died* within a month!** If it does that to plants, what is it doing to our teenagers? That will become clearer as we think of the effects which music has upon human *minds*.

For more such data let me recommend a powerful pamphlet, *The Big Beat,* by a musical expert, Mr. Frank Garlock, chairman of the Music Theory Department at the Bob Jones University. Nothing could be more timely, especially among those who may doubt the baneful effects of rock 'n roll.

Perhaps many of us who are older have wondered why young people under the influence of rock 'n roll will shout, scream, run emotionally berserk, become irresponsible, wild, sexually excited, obscene, and at times even sadistic. But it is a response which is calculatedly induced. Indeed, unless an audience "gives" itself and gets "turned on" in that way, our rock 'n roll artists feel that their blatant apparatus has failed.

Rock 'n roll is the use of new knowledge to achieve a specific effect. Since we now know more scientifically how musical sound enters through the human ear into the nervous system and registers in the brain, thus affecting mind, will, and emotions, why not make music (?) of a kind scientifically *adapted* to bring about certain definite results? That is what is behind rock 'n roll; and if anything was ever a weapon of Satan to demoralize youth, the rock 'n roll technique is.

See how it works. There is a swingy tune or catchy phrase, with a beguiling rhythm, and the subtle but dogged thud, thud, thud of that beat underneath them, which goes knock, knock, knock at your first response-susceptibilities. If through sympathetic vibra-

* *Music and Your Emotions,* by Leonard Gilman and Frances Paperte.
** See *Columbus Dispatch Magazine,* July 26, 1970.

tion you let it in, then stage two begins to come into play: it is the technique of *repetition*. As everyone knows, in hypnosis the captivating factor is *repetition,* getting a person to repeat something over and over and over until the mind yields to it. When the swing, the catch phrase, the rhythm, the beat of rock 'n roll have "got" you, then the repeat, repeat, repeat so hammers it into your consciousness that you cannot shake it off; it gets its fingers firmly round you and pulls you further in. Then stage three begins to operate — that is, the use of sound *intensity,* sound graduated to a final din and loudness which is often nothing less than overpowering to those who have fallen prey to stages one and two.

Sound is measured by decibels. At a certain decibel pressure it affects one's respiration and digestion, because the body's automatic system which controls respiration and digestion is sensitively susceptible to the effects of sound. At 140 decibels a person loses control of the nervous system. Thus, at intensified decibel measure, sound can gatecrash the normal resistances of body and brain. Through combined repetition and this intensified sound there occurs hypnogenesis. When we reflect what is being rock 'n rolled into the minds of our more or less hypnotized youngsters we may well shudder.

Intensified sound can reach a point where it disorders and overpowers the mind. Hitler knew something about that in the early days of the Second World War, when he had the Nazi airplanes fitted with noise-and-screamer devices. Because one body can cause another body to vibrate in sympathy with it, if the two have the same frequency, it happens in the case of teenagers already "tuned in" to rock 'n roll that a point is reached where, through louder, louder, louder sound pressure, there is a complete "takeover" of the nervous reflexes, the brain, the mind, the will. The last feeble resistance of reason collapses, and irrationality ensues. Thus, by the manipulation mechanics of sound, the purveyors of rock 'n roll actually invade and demoralize other minds with the evil that is in their own.

Rock 'n roll is itself designedly sensual, anarchic, defiant of all decency and restraint. My own first contact with it was back in 1950, during time spent in the Belgian Congo. Once or twice we went where white people were seldom seen. A pigmy chief brought out his people to greet us. They performed a "dance" in our honor. It was rock 'n roll, though of course that name for it had not yet been coined. There was the same insistent repetition, thudding beat, pelvic jerking, and suggestive movement. We became aware that under its strange influence they were working up to a pitch of wild excitedness. The chief himself must have sensed it, for he suddenly stood up between his two wives and commanded immediate cessation.

Rock 'n roll comes to us from the jungle, the savage, the cannibal, in glamorized, twentieth-century orchestration, and it has similar effects, especially upon the volatile minds of young people.

Let me here give some quotations (by gracious permission) from Mr. Frank Garlock's pamphlet.

> I have personally watched teenagers (and have heard many testimonies from teens themselves to substantiate the phenomenon) and have seen them at the first few sounds from a rock 'n roll tune hallucinate, go into ecstatic gyrations, get a faraway stare in their eyes, and act as if someone had just given them a dose of LSD. Frank Zappa, the leader of the Mothers of Invention, who *Time* magazine says is so bizarre that he even shocks pop musicians, has said that a teenager can get the same effect from music that he can get from dope. And Timothy Leary, who was jailed for his unlawful drug activities and then became a fugitive from the law, not only contends that rock 'n roll is designed to "blow your mind" through a reconditioning experience, but with his followers has produced a film and a record which are intended to give the viewer or listener a drug experience if he has already had one.
>
> It would be impossible to make a complete list, but here are a few of the "associates" of rock: drug addicts, revolutionaries, rioters, Satan worshipers, dropouts, draft dodgers, homosexuals and other sex deviates, rebels, juvenile criminals, Black Panthers and White Panthers, motorcycle gangs, blasphemers, suicides, heathenism, voodoism, phallixism, Communism in the United States (Russia outlawed rock music around 1960), paganism, lesbianism, immorality, demonology, promiscuity, free love, free sex, disobedience (civil and uncivil), sodomy, venereal disease; discotheques, brothels, orgies of all kinds, night clubs, dives, strip joints, filthy musicals such as "Hair" and "Uncle Meat"; and on and on the list could go almost indefinitely.

A group of boys involved in stealing told Mr. Garlock that in order to get "high" and lose their fear before a robbery they would sit in their car for about an hour, with a radio rock 'n roll station as loud as the set could give it. That was enough to nerve-jam them against their qualms!

Take the following from a very secular magazine. "The Rolling Stones played there . . . and what happened was that a man was killed there, knifed and beaten to death within twenty feet of Mick Jagger as he was singing 'Under My Thumb' . . . At the stage site things became increasingly chaotic. People tried to climb onto the stage. A hysterical, topless girl . . . tried to get onstage and the (Hell's) Angels pulled her down. . . . Every time the bands played a violent song there was trouble."

What about the progenitors of rock 'n roll? Take the Beatles. Mr. Garlock quotes their press officer. "They're rude, they're profane, they're vulgar. . . . They're so completely anti-Christ they shock even me, which isn't an easy thing." Take the group known as the Jefferson Airplane, of which Gracie Slick is female performer. Marty Balin, their lead singer says, "The stage is our bed, and the audience is our broad (i.e., woman). We're not entertaining, we're making love." The *Detroit News* of July 7, 1967, writes up a performance of theirs: "Backstage . . . after the show the Airplane put on another performance – this time it was less than mediocre . . . Friendship and love? No; vulgarity and crudeness. (Gracie insisted on posing for the camera with a poster depicting the American flag marred with an obscene slogan). In addition to free love and free sex, members of the Airplane advocated the use of marijuana to open the mind. If Gracie's backstage performance is any indication of her vision and perception, her mind should be opened – *cleaned and fumigated.*" This, reflect, is a purely secular comment. By its very beat and sound, says *Time* magazine (October 31, 1969) rock 'n roll has always celebrated sexuality.

Here is one further culling from Mr. Frank Garlock's telling pamphlet. He quotes rock 'n roll idol, Frank Zappa.

> The big beat matches the great rhythms of the human body . . . I knew further that they [the teens] would carry this with them for the rest of their lives. Responding like dogs, some of the kids began to go for the throat. Open rebellion. . . . To deny rock music its place in society was to deny sexuality. . . . I'm sure the kids never really believed all the Beatles wanted to do was hold your hand. . . . Hendrix's music is very interesting. The sound of his music is extremely symbolic: orgasmic grunts, tortured squeals, lascivious moans, electric disasters . . . are delivered to the audience at an extremely high decibel level. In a live performance environment, it is impossible to listen to what the Hendrix group does . . . it eats you alive.

Well, that is what beguiles, bewitches, seizes, and fouls our young people. It is satanic. It contradicts everything Christian.

To open our churches and Christian gatherings to it is to admit frogs from the abyss.

It will be argued, however, that "pop" music is different and should not be so decidedly classed with rock 'n roll. Even though the bizarre vulgarities of rock 'n roll should be firmly interdicted, surely the pleasant catchiness of mere "pop" is innocuous. Rock 'n roll, *no;* but "pop," why not?

Well, first, "pop" music is condemned by its family connections. Be-bop, honky-tonk, ragtime, dixieland, "blackface" minstrelsy, rockabilly, soul rock, jazz rock, "pop" rock, rock 'n roll, are all close relatives. You cannot separate "pop" from its kith and kin. You excuse it as a "milder form"; but the very excusal is an admission that it *is* a milder form of that which is satanically evil. At the very least, to countenance "pop"-style music in our churches is to let in the "thin edge of the wedge," a wedge as morally and spiritually ruinous as it is demoniacally deceptive.

There are those who argue that in music itself there is nothing inherently either sacred or secular, either morally good or morally bad. But they are wrong. There is music which by its very nature elevates the mind; and there is other music which has the opposite effect. There is music which by its very kind and quality is suited to sacred uses; and there is that which is just as *un*suited. There is a kind of music which by its very structure is a most effective means of transmitting gospel truths and expressing Christian themes; and there is a kind of music which simply does not "belong" to such ministry. I maintain that "pop" music is of the latter sort. Its distinguishing peculiarities are alien to the lofty concepts of our Christian faith.

There are those who argue a place for rock 'n roll, or at least "pop" music, in the churches on the ground that "the end justifies the means." But where moral and eternal issues are involved, *evil* "means" are *never* justifiable. What is more, in this instance, even if we *allow* the "means," the true "end" is not achieved. If you examine those rock 'n roll songs which are supposed to preach something which is somehow something like the gospel, what do you find? The vital truths which *save* are just not in them. A real witness to Christ as Lord and Savior is just not there. Instead there is a sentimental, emotional, puffy mimic. As one example, take "Tell It Like It Is" by Ralph Carmichael and Kurt Kaiser, published by the Broadman Press. Mr. Frank Garlock says of it:

> The first thing that a person must realize before he can even see his need of salvation is that he is a sinner. Does "Tell

It Like It Is" tell him he is a sinner? The next thing a person must do in order to be saved is to repent of his sin. Does "Tell It Like It Is" even hint at or mention repentance? The third thing a person must do is trust in Christ's sacrifice on the Cross as taking the sinner's place. Does "Tell It Like It Is" tell the sinner about the cross of Christ and His sacrifice? Fourth, it is the blood of Christ that cleanses a person from his sin. Is the fact of the blood told in "Tell It Like It Is"? And last, Jesus said that a person must be saved, born again, if he is to see and enter the kingdom of God. Where is this mentioned in "Tell It Like It Is"? To anyone who knows the Word of God, it is obvious that this musical does *NOT* tell it like it is. It tells it like it isn't! It shows a lack of reverence for God and a lack of understanding of man and his sin; and it denies the absolute truth of God and makes truth relative. I have not used this particular music because it is any worse or better than any of the others, but only to give an example of the kind of music that is being written and performed today.

Both words and style of this new music fashion slant *away* from the written Word of God. Our divine Lord becomes a soft-hearted friend rather than the one and only *Savior* who saves sinners from sin by His atoning death and mighty resurrection; and the "message" of the song, instead of expressing urgent need for individual regeneration, slushes into a merely social gospel. Tested pragmatically, our usual "pop" products are pathetically ineffective. Pop style, lilty, swingy airs or strummings simply do not fit the rich, deep, urgent, serious truths of the Bible and the gospel.

My prayer is that at this point, especially, I may speak with sympathy and without prejudice; for there are groups of Christian young folk going around today, sincerely trying to use pop-style compositions effectively in evangelistic and other Christian gatherings. It is good that such young people are so keen to serve our dear Lord in what they regard as a "mod" way of getting the gospel message through to *other* young people. I have warm appreciation as I think of them.

Such appreciation, however, does not exonerate the "pop" items themselves from the charge that they are *inferior in their nature,* as well as undesirable in certain other ways.

Let me make one thing very clear here. I am not against guitars, lutes, mandolins, trombones, accordions, or any other musical instrument *per se.* I have no doubt that most of them could be handled as befits the house of the Lord and Christian assemblies. It is plain that long ago in Israel's worship of Jehovah various instruments, stringed and otherwise, were used. Many of the poetical compositions which now appear in our "Book of the Psalms" were intended to be metrically chanted and musically accompanied odes. No, we are not against hitherto unfamiliar instruments coming into Christian worship and evangelism, if there can be a truly dignified and practically advantageous use of them. It is the *way* in which they are used and the style of *contribution* they embellish which is mainly in question.

It is not so long that even organs and pianos were considered doubtful or even "worldly" penetrations into our sanctuary services. To this day, some of the stricter Christian bodies will not allow *any* musical instrument. What a mighty evangelistic and spiritual impact Moody and Sankey made in Britain, and particularly in Scotland, just before the nineteenth century gave place to the twentieth! I have often wondered what their feelings were on that Sunday afternoon when they went to hold a meeting in the Lady Glenorchie Church, Leith Street, Edinburgh, and found Sankey's precious organ sitting rejected in the gutter at the edge of the sidewalk, having been dumped there by the indignant church leaders, who said, "We're no havin' any such 'kist [chest] o' whistles' in *our* kirk!" Yet how mightily God used that organ! and how repentant, later, were those misled zealots who had earlier denounced it!

To this day some of the "Wee Free" churches in Scotland prefer the precentor and his tuning fork to the organist. Certain other groups, even in the U.S.A. (so I am told) still hold to *a cappella* without any kind of instrumental accompaniment.

Few would differ from me, however, when I say that the pipe organ has proved itself a wonderfully helpful and uplifting accessory to our sanctuary worship, and that the piano has been a remarkably useful instrument in public evangelism. What Sankey's harmonium meant in the Moody "visitation," and Robert Harkness's piano in Torrey's global gospel tour, who can ever measure? Well, it *may* just be that certain other instruments are now to have a worthy vogue. After all, there is a difference of only four strings between David's "instrument of ten strings" and our modern guitar!

Certainly, there are *some* present-day instruments which by their intendedly squawkish, bleating, impudent sounds are at once disqualified; but there are those others which *may* serve a useful purpose. So we come back to this: it is the way they are *used*, the style of words and music, which is the main issue. My own summation is that the swingy, joggy *style* of "pop" music is unacceptably out of keeping with Christian worship and evangelism (especially when using the beat or jerky syncopation), and that the "message" put over is *inferior*. At least, all my own experience of it says so.

In one of our meetings not long since, a nice group of youths with guitar or ukulele and two or three other instruments (having electric connections) gave two selections. The first was the continually repeated idea: "I'm never goin' a leave Jesus, cos Jesus is never goin' a leave me." The second had a different motif but was in the same repetitive "pop" style, accompanied by a slight, rhythmic knee-flexing. Both items were thoroughly well-meant, and the adult audience tolerantly appreciated them as a pleasing group of modern young folk devoting themselves to the service of our Lord: but what was the spiritual or evangelistic *value* to the meeting? Nil. Just before I got up to speak, a lady with a sympathetic contralto voice sang that almost forgotten gospel favorite: "If you could see Christ standing here tonight." There was no Hollywood top-note climax or any other attempt at "effect"; but its influence in that meeting who can forget? If I may say so without seeming unkind, the very contrast between its direct, coherent message and the juvenile repetitiveness of the preceding "pop" pair accentuated the irresistible way in which it sang Christ into our thoughts.

Let me recall one other meeting where we had a group of young people with lute, muzzled trumpet, accordion, tambourine, and a violoncello to thrum the beat. It was a pleasing ensemble of exuberant young personalities; but their renditions were the usual lilty reiterations of two or three elementary strophes rhythmically punctuated by the monotonous beat. As for evangelistic penetration or spiritual uplift there was none, though the audience was too kind not to show a natural appreciation. The one other musical contribution that evening was a duet by a brother and sister.

> There was One who was willing
>   to die in my stead,
> That a soul all unworthy might live;
> And the path to the Cross He was
>   willing to tread
> All the sins of my life to forgive.
>
> *They are nailed to the Cross,*
> *They are nailed to the Cross,*
> *Oh, what grief He was willing to bear*
> *With what anguish and loss*
> *Jesus went to the Cross!*
> *But He carried my sins with Him there!*

There may be no literary merit in that hymn, but it is a clear-thinking, direct, progressive message. Never will my wife or myself and others forget the impact of that duet. It bowed all hearts before our Savior.

Until our banjo, guitar, accordion groups free themselves from "pop"-style lilt and beat and jingle; until they get to something musically, mentally, spiritually mature, they should be *discountenanced* — which we say with only sincere appreciation of their good motive.

Anything savoring of the theatrical, of entertainment, or merely pleasant artistry should be excluded from our gatherings for Christian worship or fellowship or evangelism. There is a place for it in *other* gatherings of a purely social nature, but *only* there.

One argument put forth in favor of "pop"-style items in our Christian services is that never before has youth been so musically minded; never before have so many played various musical instruments or so enjoyed hearing them. If the banjo or the guitar is now the *"thing"* (as they say) should we ban it? If younger folk will *not* be interested in our traditional modes of worship, but *will* listen to the gospel via the guitar and "pop" style, must we deny them the gospel in their own idiom? Such pleading misses the real point. First: if youth today is more musically minded, should it not be turned to the *best* music? Second: in city after city we find that it is many of the young people themselves who do *not* want "pop"-style groups. Third: *are* the "pop"-type groups really getting the gospel over to young people in their own "idiom"? Here and there, perhaps, yes; but in the many, *no*, for it is such a thinned out menu as to have little saving force at all unless accompanied by some clear preaching of the true New Testament message. Fourth (as already said) the issue is not so much the instruments as the quality, style, coherence, and worth of what is put over.

In a parting effort to show that our comments are not narrowly bigoted, let me say that in my own judgment at least, there *may* be some place even for traditional jazz, Dixie, rhythm, blues, and folk style when used by groups going right out for evangelism among the many godless youth of our day to whose badly perverted susceptibilities such pseudomusic styles appeal. I know of at least one group which has had wonderful response to its variegated "pop" repertoire, with many conversions to Christ. But in that group the music has always been only the means of capturing the hearers' attention to a clear-worded *preached* evangelistic message. It has been an evangelistic team with *its own evangelist,* going outside the churches to operate among hippies and others on their own ground.

What is more, after a sympathetic but careful reading of their comparatively cautious musical tactics and their unswerving evangelistic purpose, I am convinced that their real drawing power among our teenagers has been their *novelty,* i.e., their being a sextet of young "mods," all "out-and-out" champions of our Lord Jesus; for no matter *what* kind of music they use, the young folk are curious and eager to hear this versatile ensemble of musical virtuosos with their banjo, guitar, mandolin, piano-accordion, cello, and vocal talent.

Sincerely do I pray God powerfully to use such groups among the outside crowd unreached by our more usual church activities. Indeed, such groups *are* the church reaching out under the urge of the Holy Spirit. Yet at the same time I find myself equally praying that our churches themselves may be saved from *any* kind of musical compromise in their sanctuary worship, fellowship meetings, and public evangelism. Least of all let there be *any* imitating of the crazy, depraved freak music of this "present evil age," gone mad amid the din and chaos of its vulgar humanism.

PREACHERS AND SEX

Furthermore, while we are here thinking about modern perils to the Church, is it not overdue that some of us should inveigh against the new overproneness to talk sex from pulpit and platform?

Let me here utter a protest against those preachers nowadays who seem to think that in order to appear modernly psychological or bravely attractive they must always bring *sex* into their public speaking. I, for one, am nauseated by it, and I believe that a long-suffering majority of others feel the same way. The jolting over-frankness with which some ministers and conference speakers talk about marital relationships and sex experience is disgusting.

They tell me that one has to be boldly frank in order to deal with the sex problems of the day. I deny this. Much that goes by the name of frankness is veneered vulgarity. Sometimes the speaker can scarcely disguise his own sickly relish and morbid pleasure in the subject. Far fewer of us are deceived than such speakers think; and when they punctuate their overintimate comments with jocular sex anecdotes or remarks which evoke a few inane giggles from folk in the congregation who will laugh at anything spicy, we despise them.

Let us get a few things straight. If for some acute reason sex matters simply must be publicly spoken of in some Christian service or conference, it should be done without descriptive detail, with very carefully restrained phrase, and with becoming reticence. That which belongs to private counseling is *not* for public parade. I have known persons for whom these public expatiations on sex matters have created problems which they never had before. Instead of solving problems the speaker has inflamed them.

In these days, when there are so many books written on sex and marriage, including wise and useful publications by Christian ministers, doctors, and psychologists, what *need* is there for this pulpit and platform lingering with face-reddening intimacy over the sex-quarrels, sex-disappointments, sex-fulfillments, or sex-estrangements, and so on, of married couples and others? To me it is like a conducted tour of drains and sewers, and the preacher seems to love being down there.

One of the most angering things of all is that the sexual matters descriptively dilated upon could be referred to *far* more effectively with respectful restraint. People know well enough what we mean, and how we are trying to help, without a lot of smutty elaborating. Twice recently I have walked out of a public service, in silent protest against the rudely frank sex talk of the preacher. I hope many others will do the same, until these preachers who talk with such shameless cheek on sex matters learn what many of us think about them. I myself am a minister; and my own experience is that if I ever have to touch on sex matters, the more carefully picked and reticent my words are, the more effectively do they influence the minds of my hearers in the right direction.

Today, we live in a sex-mad society. We should avoid anything in our Christian services and fellowships which *adds* to the general sex-emphasis. We should do everything we can to restore a sense of *sacredness* to the subject of marital relationship. Things which were divinely meant to be private and sacred and referred to only with reverent respect are discussed with blatant freeness, until nearly all the decency and dignity of life is being martyred. Such trends do not engender social purity and happiness; they bring uncleanness and misery.

Our churches and Christian meetings should strike a deliberate contrast. Instead of lingering on fleshly, ugly, animalistic aspects of nuptial and sexual relationships, we should keep turning the minds of our people to the higher and purer and holier aspects of love and wedlock and family life. It is in the light of those *higher levels* of thinking and of Scripture teaching that *most* matrimonial problems find true solution.

Perhaps someone still objects: "Oh, but the Church should face up to the sex problems of the day." My reply is threefold. (1) They should *not* be "faced up to" in the brazen way which is common today. (2) They should *never* be thus "faced up to" in mixed meetings, with males and females, married and single, parents and children, older and younger, all together. (3) Any such *public* "facing up" should be *avoided* in favor of private counseling.

Finally, all such public "facing up" in the objectionable way which I have here denounced is utterly *unscriptural*. Listen again to Ephesians 5:3. It says, "But fornication, and all uncleanness, or covetousness, let it not be once named among you, as becometh saints." In other words, there are some things which, in Christian gatherings, instead of being "faced up to," should be faced *away from*.

It is time we put away this dirty-puddle-stirring from Christian platforms. All who may happen to know me and my own ministry will know that I am no habitual declaimer or critic of others. Nay, my tendency has always been to err on the side of silent toleration — perhaps blameworthily so at times. But this irreverent and unblushing "free speech" about bodily relationships, on the plea that it is being helpfully realistic, is a make-believe of sickly minds. It belongs to the garbage dump not the Christian desk. It is time some ministers had something more elevating to talk about.

Not long since, I was Bible teacher at a large denominational conference representing hundreds of churches. Among the speakers was an outstanding Christian psychologist for whom I have high regard. The printed conference folder announced that he would speak on sex and Christians. That was enough! We other preachers did not have a chance when *our* sessions ran at the same time as *his*. As I saw with what feverish curiosity the delegates flocked to hear what he had to say, I marveled at the strange relish which they showed for the subject and at their gullible idea that a professional psychologist is much more exciting than a Bible expositor. I also saw how easy it is to get a crowd these days, if you spice the announcement with sex.

That was not all, however. I was able to get into just one of his sessions — it was his first, I think. There was the same ultramodern, almost offhand frankness about his dealing with the sex subject. To old-fashioned me it was revolting. It felt like being undressed in public. I blushed and inwardly writhed inasmuch as there were ladies on each side of me. Was it worth the torture? The gist of what he was saying was nothing wiser than the counsels our mothers gave us. *They* simply called it godly common sense. That is just what the Christian psychologist was giving us, but in sophisticated psychological parlance, and with lurid, overfrank reference to private sex affairs. At a convenient moment I slipped out for some fresh air.

Even that is not all. Others must have felt as I did, for as the week progressed I noticed that his hearers grew fewer, and they were back with the Bible teacher! How long are we going to be before we learn (and I make no reference here to my unworthy self) that despite all our modern psychology and psychiatry can tell us, the truest and safest of all advisers is a true Bible-teacher filled with the Holy Spirit? What we are needing today is not more minister-psychologists, but more ministers steeped in the inspired Word and filled with the Holy Spirit. Or course, psychology and the Word of God and the infilling of the Holy Spirit *can* go together. But *unless* those three all go together, the truest and wisest of all counselors is the man of the Bible, filled with the Holy Spirit and with "the wisdom which is from above." Some of the most ridiculous and dangerous advice I have ever heard has been given by non-Christian psychologists to people whom I myself have met and known, and with the most deadly results in moral degradation. However, into that I will not go here. My one purpose is to strike hard at those preachers who keep turning up at conferences talking sex with a bland glibness or jolting familiarity utterly unbecoming to a Christian minister and detestable to many of their hearers.

ANOTHER PERIL TODAY

All our work must be done spiritually, as by men possessed of the Holy Spirit. There is in some men's preaching a spiritual strain, which spiritual hearers can discern and relish; whereas in other men's this sacred tincture is so lacking that even when they speak of spiritual things their manner is as if they were speaking of common matters. Our proofs and illustrations of divine truth, also, must be spiritual, being drawn from the Holy Scriptures rather than from the clever writings of men.

Richard Baxter

ANOTHER PERIL TODAY

IS THE LOCAL CHURCH EFFETE?

There is another present-day peril, too, against which all of us evangelicals should be throwing our weight. It is the disparaging of the Church as an institution, and, more particularly, the suggested discarding of our *local* "churches." Many of us are too prone to leave unchallenged the easy affirmation that the Church is no more than a traditionist, culture-bound institution of western civilization. Not only among non-Christian thinkers but among ministers, chiefly liberalist groups, this mistaken idea concerning the Church and the churches has gained a footing. The spiritually blind, of course, never did and never can grasp the true nature and purpose of the Church — either the Church invisible and mystical or the Church visible and organized.

With the Church in its essentially *spiritual* aspect, as the mystical body and bride and temple of the eternal Son, we are not here concerned so much. *That* Church, the collective totality of all truly born-again Christian believers, is timeless and supradenominational. But that Church has its visible and temporal counterpart in the so-called "*organized* Church"; and it is that which has latterly become a butt of new skepticism.

Strangely enough, the "*local* church" concept is under criticism from two opposite types: (1) the liberalists, especially the younger; (2) spiritually keen evangelicals who are estranged by the average poor performance of the local church today.

Recently in New York State we were apprized that a considerable number of younger ministers, notably those of a large Protestant denomination, were in favor of scrapping Sunday altogether as a special day of worship, and meeting during the weekdays, say on a Thursday evening. Along with that, so we gleaned, is the idea of group meetings in homes, rather than some larger gathering for a set "service" in a church building. In a way, I am not oversurprised that such an idea should eventually insinuate itself into the thinking of liberalist brethren. Such is the steadily dwindling attendance in many of their sanctuaries, and such the spiritual vapidity, they may have cause enough to sense failure in their customary forms of Christian assemblage. It is something which they themselves have brought on. Already most of their sanctuary doors are closed on Sunday evenings.

But if ever their new ideas of Sabbath and sanctuary *prevail*, an inconceivably crippling blow will have been struck against Christian faith and effort in the land. The honoring of Sunday as our "Christian Sabbath" is of utter momentousness *strategically*. Until lately it has not only been a "day of rest and gladness" for America's millions, but the vital pause for marshaling our forces, for re-equipping our soldiers in the holy war, for healing the wounded, for training our young cadets, for winning new recruits, for enunciating saving truth and spreading Christian principles throughout the nation. To let go all that and stagger activities in bits and pieces through small weekday groups, not only spread-eagles and complicates operations; it so disperses them as to *dissipate* them.

To say that the relinquishing of special Sunday observance and the return to house-to-house fellowships gets back to Christian forms as they were at the *beginning* of our Christian era is a pretty lame idea. Those Christians of the first days only met *as* they did, and *when* they did, and *where* they did, because they did not yet have the privileges and conveniences for Christian witness and fellowship which *we* now have. Many of those early heroes suffered martyrdom that such emancipations and provisions might become ours. Shall we now throw away what they bled to purchase?

What is more, this idea of disbanding the "local church" in favor of small house groups is decidedly against the New Testament *norm;* for in the Acts and the Epistles the vital cell in the propagation and preservation of the Christian faith is the local *ecclesia*.

To operate cottage meetings *along with* the local church may well be an ancillary activity of great effectiveness, but to revert to them as an *alternative* to the local church is out of line with the main New Testament emphasis.

Already our Christian Sabbath is a Statue of Liberty badly disfigured by secular vandalism. More and more, nowadays, Sunday is desecrated by commercial, political, and sports invasions. Increasingly, now, stores are open on Sundays, which means that more and more employees are tied up in them, as also in the Sunday political and sports events, so that they cannot get to church, even if they would. We are feeling the effects of this everywhere.

Instead of our supinely surrendering Sunday to its carnal immolators, should there not be a mighty effort to rescue it for the preserving of that glorious Christian faith to which America owes more than to any other uplifting and liberating influence? Is it not time that Christian ministers attempted some cooperative stand — and congregations in nationwide concertedness *boycotted* stores and businesses which open on the Lord's Day? Such a boycott would be a thoroughly upright and truly *democratic* device of public action in such an issue.

In these days we are seeing such shocking compromises in some of our well-known denominations that one wonders what next. With easy-ozy pandering to divorce, the marrying of couples in the nude, the wedlocking of homosexuals, the clerical smile on the illicit use of drugs, what have we come to? Yes, thank God, those are the extremes; but what of the denominational leadership which winks at them and allows in some of its leading pulpits men who, while ostensibly representing Christ, openly deny His deity, the atoning content of His death, and the factuality of His bodily resurrection? Is it to be wondered at that along with such betrayals and weakenings the "local church" is struggling against heavy weather, and that the very concept of it is being questioned?

But now let me swing over to what perhaps may be called a *right wing* skepticism toward the "local church." It is found among thoroughly conservative and spiritually-minded evangelicals. In their case the skepticism arises from disappointment with the *poor performance* of the present-day local church, not from shaky theology. Even now I have before me a well-written monograph on this subject, written by a gifted, scholarly evangelical for whom I have high regard. Out of esteem I leave him anonymous. Much of which he complains is so obviously true that one is easily carried along into agreeing that the only solutions are those which he suggests. His criticisms are as follows.

1. We have divided the Church both by denominational and nondenominational distinctives.

2. We have taken evangelism away from the marketplace and kept it inside the local church, where it does not rightly belong.

3. We have taken local church worship away from the body of believers and made it something put on by minister and choir.

4. We have substituted entertainment elements for the Holy Spirit's working: rhythm and tunes geared to senses rather than spirit.

5. We have centered the Church's life in large material structures and lost the idea of compact neighborhood centers for worship and witness.
6. We have so crowded Sunday with services, Sunday school, groups, etc., as to have almost destroyed it as a family day and a day of rest.
7. We have removed collective worship from member participation and made it (contrary to Scripture) a function of professional clergy.
8. We have turned public worship into a prestructured formality which excludes the free moving of the Holy Spirit among us.
9. We have allowed churches to become so large that individuals who make up the membership cannot effectively minister to each other.
10. Memberships consist of many who drive considerable distance, passing other equally evangelical churches (too much the "church of my *choice*").
11. Our local churches function for only the large service in which minister and choir operate: a fault of our "largeness syndrome" which cripples a true spiritual functioning.

Well, there they are: eleven fingers of blame. They may well remind us, of course, that it has always been much easier to find fault with tried and proved methods than to replace them with better. Does the author of those eleven very pertinent criticisms have something better than the local church to offer? In the ensuing part of his treatise he certainly makes some cogent suggestions, but they all refer to desirable practices which need resurrecting *inside* our local churches, or operating *along* with them, not using *instead* of them.

In these days when impatient impulse too often overrides reasoned reflection there is a craze for drastic change. Does American democracy have faults? Then finish it off (they say) and let's have Communism. Yet despite lingering failings, that democracy of free men is infinitely preferable to the totalitarian slave-state. Also, there is not one persisting wrong which cannot yet be put right (as so many others have been) *inside* the framework of that democratic system which has given America the highest economic living standards in the world. The mania for change today is as dangerous as it is unreasonable. If a few things go wrong with the engine or other parts of a car, do we say, "Scrap it; we'll never have an automobile again"? If, as we grow older, certain physical ailments develop, do we say, "The human body is a failure; commit suicide"? Similarly, because there are certain defects in our local churches today, are we to abandon the local church as a basic *idea*? Not at all; for beyond doubt the local church is an institution having New Testament origin, sanction, and example; and however much times may change, the local church is meant to be a continuing *modus operandi* throughout the present dispensation.

Glance back over those eleven criticisms and then at what is offered ostensibly as a *substitute* for the local church. The first criticism is that we have divided the Church by "denominational and nondenominational distinctives." Nay, the deepest divider in modern Christendom is *not* denominational; it is theological — between those to whom the Bible is the truly and fully inspired Word of God and those to whom it is less. That first criticism, therefore, belongs to the Church *total*, not to the church local. As for the nondenominational "distinctives" (which I presume to mean ethnic and social segregatings) in many places *they* have already been overcome, and in others are *being* overcome, and in all others *can* be, just as easily within the framework of the local church as by jilting it. In fact, it is often easier inside a local church than in private homes.

Take the second criticism: We have taken evangelism away from the marketplace where it belongs, and "introduced it into the church, where it does not belong." But if there is a breakdown of evangelism in the marketplace, that is a fault of Christian *individuals*, not an argument against the local church as a basic idea. Also, why strike such an antithesis between evangelism in the marketplace and evangelism in the local church? Why make them alternatives when they should be complementives? I cannot understand how anyone can say that evangelism "does not belong" in the local church. Admittedly, a primary purpose of the local church is to provide fellowship for Christian believers, but one of the most vital expressions of such fellowship is concerted activity in evangelism, using the local church premises as a strategic center for it. Throughout the A.D. centuries, of all means by which sinners have been converted to Christ the local church has been far and away the greatest. Millions upon millions have been evangelized in and by the local church. One of the healthiest stimulants to local Christian fellowship is to see the evident moving of the Holy Spirit, effecting supernatural conversion through such corporate activity of a local group. Is there anything, in fact, upon which the Holy Spirit has ever more clearly set His seal? Are we now to throw all that away?

The esteemed author whom we are quoting says: "One can search the New Testament to find the body of believers gathered together for evangelism. Worship and evangelism are incompatible; for non-believers cannot worship God. The unregenerate cannot join in praise, prayer or edification. The worship service is not designed to evangelize believers, but to build them up in the Word. . . . *They* are to carry the Gospel to the unsaved, not bring the unsaved into the fellowship and worship of believers."

But how wrongly overrigid is that separation of worship from evangelism! Was not Spurgeon nearer the truth when he said that one of the highest forms of worship is to preach and gratefully to hear the gospel, with heartfelt praise to God for it? And how contrary to Scripture it is to say that none but the regenerate can worship, praise, pray! I, for one, prayed — sometimes very earnestly — long before I was converted. What about all the Israelites of the old covenant dispensation? They were all taught to worship Jehovah sincerely, but were they all "born again" in the New Testament sense — even those of the "godly remnant"? What about the Italian Gentile in Acts 10? Before ever he was converted to our Lord Jesus Christ he "feared God with all his house" and "prayed to God continually." Moreover, his worship and praying were accepted of God (Acts 10:34, 35), yet he still needed to be evangelized and regenerated, which was why God brought Peter to him. As for our author's remark that in the New Testament we never find believers gathered together for evangelism, is it not plain from 1 Corinthians 14:23-25 that unbelievers *did* come in (presumably brought or invited) and that they became converted thereby? And even apart from that, one might just as reasonably argue that we should not use hymnbooks in our services because we never find believers doing so in the New Testament, or that we should not run Sunday schools, or bring our babes to be dedicated to God in the Christian assembly, because there is no New Testament precedent.

This strange idea that evangelism does not belong in the local church overlooks the fact that Christian believers, as members of a local church, can unitedly *decide* that as a *part* of their local fellowship certain of their gatherings shall be *designedly* evangelistic for the purpose of bringing the unsaved under the sound of saving truth. Such evangelism is a vital *ingredient* of healthful group fellowship, not something to be sundered from it, leaving fellowship inlooking instead of outgoing. Were not *most* of us converted because the local church was evangelistic *as well as* being a center of fellowship and build-up for believers? To tear away evangelism is to fossilize the local church. In fact, I *know* of certain local churches which have acted on this idea that evangelism is an activity outside local church fellowship, and they have all gradually atrophied.

As for criticisms 3 to 11 (please glance back) there is much in them with which most of us would fully agree. They are needed and timely; but they are all matters which can and should be put right *inside* the local church; for not one of them, nor all of them together, can be seriously regarded as a reason why we should *discard* the local church. Indeed, I would eagerly augment numbers 3 and 7 (which are much the same) and number 9 (about overlarge churches). Numbers 3 and 7 complain that we have taken Sunday worship away from the body of believers and made it something which the minister and musicians perform on our behalf; that we have made the ministry the function of a professional clergy, whereas the New Testament tells us that the divine Spirit endows and equips lay people for ministry. That indeed is one of the things which need correcting inside the usual local church today; and on other pages of these studies I have made comment.

On the other hand, surely our quoted writer has confused the issue by making it appear as though the *Sunday* services in the sanctuary represent the *entire* "ministry" of the local church. Obviously, if the *Sunday* gatherings are to be specially of a *public* sort, for *all* the members, and for all others who can be made interested, there simply must be some suitable outward form which best achieves the purpose of Bible teaching, spiritual instruction, and evangelistic exposition. *Those* services of any local church are *not meant* to be like smaller gatherings for fellowship and testimony in which *anyone* can get up and speak. The pastor is meant to be, and *should* be, an expert in teaching the written Word of God; and those Sunday services, therefore, *should* be mainly under his guidance as he himself is led of God.

The small fellowship group for mutual interchange of testimony, experience, and insights can never be a satisfactory substitute for the specialized teaching of the Word by the specifically trained and consecrated pastor — not unless the small group itself has some really competent leader-teacher. The fault today is not in the *kind* of Sunday service (than which no better has yet been devised and which never needs to become stereotyped). No, the fault is in the very poor *quality* (generally speaking) of the pulpit teaching and praying and the superficial sort of hymns which are sung nowadays. Services and preachings which once were rich, powerful, alive, prophetic, challenging, edifying, have given place now to the bitty, mediocre, puffy.

It is in *addition* to rich-quality Sunday services that the local church today should be providing group fellowships, study circles, or other such closer contacts for different age-levels, and giving opportunity for other ministries besides that of pastor and praise leader. *That* is where too many local churches default and shrivel. We certainly are needing to resuscitate the *fellowship* emphasis in our churches. As we have noted on an earlier page, in some instances churches seem too large, causing individuals to feel lonesomely unnoticed in a forest of anonymity. But in far more cases the trouble is that we have become so sophisticated or so proper that we are politely closed to each other. The answer to that does not lie in impugning or metamorphosing the Sunday sanctuary services, but in providing fellowship *as well*. Perhaps, therefore, we are needing to rediscover the importance of the small Christian group, after the early Wesleyan pattern, *inside* the church and *apart* from the sanctuary "services." In many of our churches, if there were half as much "fellowship of the Spirit" as there is spicy gossip, what foretastes of heaven they would be!

Amid the flux and pathos all around us there are hearts hungry for genuine Christian fellowship, to solace or strengthen them in their exacting daily encounter with the strain of modern life. Let us adapt from John Wesley again. Wesley magnified the "preaching office," but he also put large stress on group sharing — which was a resurrecting of the New Testament *koinonia,* and a rearticulation of James 5:16, "Confess your faults one to another, and pray for one another, that ye may be healed." Today, generally speaking, is there not a vacuum where *koinonia* should be? Do we not pay dearly for this in both numerical and spiritual paucity? It leaves our churches too chill to draw many of the most needy.

Some of us still need convincing that there is indeed the *need* for mutual sharing, even including confession — from which latter we self-protectively recoil. We selfishly ignore that there are honest hearts which at times *poignantly* need to confess and confer with some really trustable Christian adviser. Many of us who are willing enough to listen are not humble enough to be frank in a way which could impart our victory-secret to another brother or sister. That which keeps such sharing sacred and safe is its saturation in *prayer*, hence, James 5:16 adds, "And *pray* one for another, that ye may be healed. The effectual fervent prayer of a righteous man availeth much." Under mature guidance such group interchange among born-again believers has twice as many benefits and only half as many risks as dubious doubters suppose. However, I forego further comment on such group confession if only to urge again the reviving of this reciprocal group *fellowship*. Ideally a Christian church is not just a congregation, it is a "communion of saints"; but in most churches is that conspicuous? Ideally we are "members one of another" (Rom. 12:5); but actually, being all on one *roll* is far from being all "of one accord" (Phil. 2:2). Thousands who need what only group fellowship can give are kept at arm's length by a polite but tightly buttoned reserve. True group sharing *never* means improper exposure of details. Even Oxford Group insisted that "detailed sharing should be with one person only." What we need is a general thaw; a new melting together in the warm sympathies of our Lord Jesus and maybe a "revised version" of the Wesley "class meeting."

Yes, if revival glow is to return, we must somehow change our churches into contagious *fellowships* again. But how? Well, obviously unless we have something rich to *share*, our insiders will remain mute; and unless we have something magnetic to *give*, the outsiders will remain absent. Our *expression* of Christ is poor because our *experience* of Him is thin. We sing classic old hymns about the refining fire and sanctifying power of the Holy Spirit, but do we inwardly *know* such renewal into holiness? Has not that very word "holiness" now become merely a theological term, a foreigner to modern parlance, and distant from the mishmash of modern life? Do we eradiate the "spiritual glow" or is there pallor? The big need, if there is to be permeative fellowship *inside* and persuasive influence *outside,* is a richer experience of Christ.

But now, reverting to the author whose animadversions we have reviewed, what are his proposed *substitutes* for the local church? It may seem surprising, yet on second thought it is what we might have expected: in reality he has *no* substitute to offer. All he can do is to recommend correctives. The fact is, there is *no* equally effective substitute for the local church. Our quoted author says we must recover the sense of being "an alien institution in a foreign land." Whatever may be his precise meaning, that is no argument against the local church as such. He rightly avers that the church will be self-defeating so long as it remains "a self-serving institution"; but neither is that an argument against the local church idea in itself. He adds that it is difficult for "the world" to see anything but the church's "continuing irrelevance in the secular struggle for meaning"; its "middle-class mentality and culture conformity, its cultic isolation from the world's hurts and needs, its paranoiac preoccupation with its own divisions and distinctives, its tradition-bound inability to innovate and change." But is not that an astigmatic overstatement? Even though it may be true of many a more formal type of church, it is *not* a true picture of our evangelical churches in the aggregate; nor, in any case, is it an argument against the local church *per se*.

Our well-meaning critic certainly demotes the *preacher*. He says, "The key to the Church's advance in our day is no longer preaching! This again (i.e., 'preaching') is symptomatic of the one-directional nature of our worship services. Young people are being raised on multi-media presentations, dialogue and feedback techniques, interaction over any and every subject, and a strong distaste for authority — including ministers! Preaching can no longer be as prominent as in the past when the minister was the most highly educated, informed person in the community, and when the only way to be taught the Word was through his preaching. Today it is a different world, with information available on all subjects, with opportunity to hear prominent experts on any subject over T.V. and in public forums."

Perhaps that should be my last quotation, lest some should think our critic simply has "a bee in his bonnet." In truth, however, he is too educated and sincere for that; though I think perhaps that in the above quotation he indulges the luxury of overplaying present-day differentials. Over against what he says, my own conviction is that if ever there was a time when real preaching was both needed and *wanted*, it is now. I mean, of course, efficient, instructive, earnest preaching and teaching of the Word with a sense of prophetic vocation on the part of the man in the pulpit. To say that *it* is now effete, ineffective, unnecessary, or unwanted is egregiously wrong. It certainly contradicts all my own experience. I am now elderly, but as I continually move around the churches all over the U.S.A. and occasionally in other countries, I find that so long as I eagerly and carefully expound the great truths of the Bible and relate them to twentieth-century need, there is not even a "generation gap"! Especially do I find so on college campuses. Also, in nearly all our meetings, the younger folk seem to be the most openly responsive.

To decry "preaching" as being now "symptomatic of the one-directional nature of our worship service" is semantic phrasing with no real substance. In the Lord's Day worship of the sanctuary, specialized preaching of the Word was never more pertinent; and today education makes far better hearers than illiteracy used to do. Moreover, the education which our young people are getting in these days, while it often gives them specialized forms of knowledge with which no Christian minister could compete, does *not* teach them the truths of God's written Word. My own contacts show me that many of the most ignorant people today, biblically and spiritually, are the best-educated.

As for well-educated persons who are also born-again Christian believers, *they* are the ones who most of all desire, appreciate, and benefit from an educated, Spirit-filled preaching ministry in the pulpit. During my twenty years in Edinburgh, Scotland, I always knew that in my audiences there was a sprinkling of academic, intellectual, and specialistic topnotchers. I knew, humbly enough, how utterly outclassed by them I was in their particular fields. But why be embarrassed when I was expounding to them nothing less than the infallibly inspired Word of God? That, and nothing less, was *my* special domain; and I determined that they should *never* outmatch me in expert hermeneutics and exegesis of that supreme Book! The fact was, I never needed to crumple up with a stultifying inferiority complex, so long as I kept myself to being a careful expositor of the Word; for it was those topnotchers of education and intellect who always seemed to be the humblest and most grateful recipients of the message.

If I rightly read my New Testament, the public and pastoral preaching and teaching of the Word is a divine ordinance; and I believe, therefore, that any man should think twice before he suggests relegating such ministry to an inferior place. There will always be a prime need for it. None of those small fellowship-and-discussion groups which are now so much advocated are a real substitute for such pulpit ministry. As complements of it, yes; but as replacements of it, *no*. We have been to some of them, and the waste of time through lack of prepared teaching, through inchoate exchange of so-called "insights," and through peripatetic circumlocutions which tend to accompany all but the best-guided discussions has been disappointing, to say the least. Let there be no mistake: there is *no* substitute for a Spirit-endued Bible specialist who knows how to preach the Word; no substitute for a man called of God Himself to the ministry of that Word; no substitute for a Christian minister who knows that "by the ordination of the pierced Hand" he has been appointed to the prophetic office of the Christian pulpit.

Nor is there any substitute for the local Christian church. Nay, the Lord's day, the Lord's house, and the sacred calling of the pastor-preacher, instead of being lightly regarded, need defending, preserving, and prizing more than ever. They are more vitally relevant today than at any time hitherto; and they should therefore be all the more conscientiously upheld by all who have Zion's well-being at heart.

PREACH THE WORD!

I shrank not from declaring unto you *the whole counsel of God.* Take heed unto yourselves, and to all the flock in which the Holy Spirit hath made you overseers, to feed the church of the Lord which He purchased with His own blood. . . ." (Acts 20:27, 28).

Had the bishops and teachers of the Church but thoroughly learned this short exhortation though to the neglect of many a volume which hath taken up their time and helped them to a greater applause in the world, how happier had it been for the Church, and for themselves!

Richard Baxter

PREACH THE WORD!

I think it was the famous Spurgeon who apostrophized, "Defend the Bible? One might as well defend a lion!" To me, Spurgeon ranks greatest among gospel preachers, though I am not sure of fully agreeing with his remark. Even a lion might welcome defense from some kinds of foes. However, if I mistake not, Spurgeon's meaning was that the best way to defend the Bible is to declare it, to turn it loose; and that is one hundred percent true. There is a place for "religious evidences" and "Christian apologetics." The Butlers and Paleys and Machens have always been useful to lay low the Tom Paines and Bob Ingersolls and modernists. Yet still the best way to *prove* the Bible is to *preach* it. The most telling demonstration that it is "the word of God, living and active" (Heb. 4:12, AVS) is the way it works when expounded by a preacher under the power of the Holy Spirit.

Brethren, if our Bible is the Word of God in the exclusive and transcendent sense, then the first need of the world is to hear it, and the first duty of the Christian Church is to *preach* it. That is the urgent matter which claims our attention here. Is the Protestant pulpit really teaching the Bible to the people nowadays? I am playing no role of peevish faultfinder, but after years of widely traveled *hearing,* my reluctant verdict is that in proportion to the aggregate of Protestant pulpits real Bible teaching is woefully rare. "Canons to the right of us, bishops to the left of us, parsons all round us, volley and thunder," says C. T. Studd, parodying "The Charge of the Light Brigade," but how much of it all is dynamic communication of "Thus saith Jehovah"?

Legion may be my faults as a preacher, but few can excel me as an appreciative hearer. I am always predisposed in favor of the preacher. No listener has readier ears than mine. Yet despite my hungry hunting for exposition of the Word by men of spiritual insight, in nine cases out of ten I have come away with scarce a crumb, sometimes pained that the preacher vaporized away the rich force of the Word, and often wondering why people keep coming to church week after week for such paltry fare or verbal vacuity. The apostolic motto was, "We preach Christ"; but only a few Sundays ago in a beautiful Presbyterian church with superb furnishings and ornate service we heard the Savior's name only twice — once in a hymn and once in the benediction. When we were at the leading Methodist church in the same area, His dear name was not spoken even once until the benediction! Of course, it may have been coincidence, but was it? The Presbyterian minister, a fluent speaker, danced round his text like a spear-brandishing Zulu, until he oratorically danced away from it, leaving us wondering what had become of it. The Methodist, a "social gospel" type, simply used his text as a peg on which to hang his hat and coat — by which he hid the peg most successfully.

Oh, the sin of our modern Protestant pulpit! "Woe unto the foolish prophets that follow their own spirit, and have seen nothing!" "Woe be to the shepherds of Israel that do feed themselves! should not the shepherds feed the flocks?" (Ezek. 13:3; 34:2). Oh, the opportunity that is being missed today while multitudes in America still have a mind to inquire in the house of Jehovah! A missionary on furlough from an overseas battlefront groaned to me, "Out there we are desperately set on shaking the devil's kingdom; over here they seem content to be just shaking hands." There are exceptions, of course, not a few, for which we thank God, but the overall "famine of hearing the words of the Lord" (Amos 8:11) is grievous in the land.

Among the larger Protestant bodies how *can* there be Bible teaching with telling authority where the Book itself has lost its old-time command? In many places the attitude is: We must remain anchored to the Bible as our historic mooring, but we scholarly moderns know better than many of its teachings. Among the thoroughly evangelical bodies there is enthusiastic loyalty to the *authority* of the Bible, but considerable failure to teach the *deeper truths* of the Bible. There is more pounding of the pulpit than expounding of the truth! Again let me gratefully agree that there are relieving exceptions; nevertheless what I am saying is mournfully true in general. This is all the more heartrending because if ever there was an hour which cried out for more Bible it is now.

So, in the main, let me here address my *evangelical* brethren. We are needing Bible experts in our evangelical pulpits, and every one of us should covet to be of that order. Our first requirement is not for outstanding pulpit gift — though the more of that the better; the call is for Bible *experts*, by which I mean men who have both mastered the Bible and have been mastered *by* it and have developed a masterly proficiency in opening up its truths to others. I do not mean "expert" or "masterly" in a mere professional sense, but a spiritual grasp and insight communicated from the pulpit with that freshness and originality which belong to a Spirit-endued man of God.

Reading the Bible

At the risk of seeming strangely elementary, I urge the habit of *reading* the Bible, that is, of reading it copiously and continually. I am not referring here to our studying it, but to an habitual reading of it. What this can mean to a preacher words can hardly exaggerate. There is a wide difference between reading the Bible and studying it. Many who realize the importance of studying it do not equally appreciate the value of reading it.

There have been few more prolific Bible teachers than Dr. Harry Ironside, former pastor of the Moody Memorial Church, Chicago. When he died, at the age of 73, he was reading his Bible right through for the seventy-third time. He once told me that early in his Christian life he had resolved to read the Bible right through once for every year of his life. He gradually caught up with the years already gone, and thereafter kept his Bible reading equal with his years.

Dr. G. Campbell Morgan, prince among Bible expositors, said that early in his ministry there was one period when for two full years he read nothing but his daily mailbag and the four Gospels. Day after day, without break, for two years, he read Matthew, Mark, Luke, John, over and over again . . . with transforming effect on his ministry. Quite apart from concentrated study of the Bible, there are big values in reading it. Let me mention a few.

First, to read right through the Bible again and again gives one a vivid sense of *the presence of God in history,* which is very important to the preacher. I know of nothing else which does this so vividly and lastingly. Bible history and prophecy span the human drama from its first dawn to its last sunset, and relate God to it all.

Second, this repeated consecutive reading of the Bible begets a profound awareness of *the divine sovereignty.* According to the Bible, God is before all, above all, beneath all, within all, around all, beyond all; and though man is free within wide permit all is overruled to the ultimate accomplishment of divine purpose. Frequent rereading of the Bible right through vivifies this and fosters a settled confidence within us. That also is a big factor in shaping the kind of message a man preaches.

Third, this repeated reading of the Bible as a whole gives us a *comprehensive grasp of divine revelation*. This is of utmost value in giving us a rounded view of truth. We see each particular aspect and component in relation to the whole. It saves us from lopsided emphases; from exaggerating any one doctrine at the expense of others. It is important exegetically; for when we are interpreting any part in particular, all the other Scriptures rally to our assistance. Many a preacher who has "gone off at a tangent," or "ridden a hobby," or offered "strange fire" on the Lord's altar would never have done so if he had seen his beguiling novelty against the background of Scripture as a whole.

There are other values of reading the Bible right through again and again — such as the sheer interest of its many parts, the kaleidoscopic picture which it gives of Bible unity amid diversity, and the way it exhibits progress of doctrine through the successive books; but these we must leave for the time being. I only mention here one further consideration, namely, that this continued, consecutive reading right through the Bible is of all practices the most *prolific in sermon suggestion*. Often I feel sorry for those brethren who, without any abashment, tell me they buy books of other preachers' sermons to use, more or less, *as their own!* Such procedure is expository suicide: it destroys sanctified originality, genuine artistry, and all sense of a direct prophetic "burden" from God. Do some brethren need reminding that palming off another man's composition as one's own is plagiarism? Do some need warning that the preaching of other men's sermons as one's own is a dishonesty which slowly but surely kills conscientious communication of the divine Word? But why the need for such snooping around when the whole Bible keeps saying, "Read *me;* read me *continually,* and I will give you 'twelve baskets full' for every twelve months of preaching!"

Maybe even you, my well-educated ministerial brethren, will allow me to risk three words of advice on this "reading the Word." My first word may seem rather strange; but it is reverent. *Beware of Leviticus!* A Christian woman said to me, "Three times I have started to read through the Bible, and each time I have broken down at Leviticus." Her discouragement came from failure to distinguish between reading and studying. I pointed out to her that some books of the Bible were never meant just for reading; they must be studied. Leviticus is one. It mainly consists of ceremonial and hygenic regulations. In a continual *reading through* the Bible, we should never let parts like Leviticus detain us. We need not tax the memory with details. We should pass through quickly, noting the main ideas but no more. Such parts require a return visit for separate study!

Again: we should read enough at a time to get into the throb and flow of it, to get caught up and carried on by it, just as we do with a fine novel. Also, along with reading enough at a time, the reading should be daily, or as continual as circumstances allow. Long interruptions diminish both the enjoyment and the spiritual impact.

Finally, we should not be afraid of reading the Bible for the pleasure of it. To read it thus helps rather than hinders the spiritual good. Use a large-size Bible, with reference column and good margin. Make side notes of all special thoughts which occur at different points as you travel through. For my own part, I would recommend the American Standard Version or the English Revised Version, especially in the poetical and prophetical parts of the Old Testament, and the doctrinal parts of the New. Brethren, the whole of the goodly land lies before us. The preacher who travels it continually, right from Dan even to Beer-sheba, will find every part fertile with spiritual suggestion and rich with produce for the pulpit.

Mind you, as I have said before, if you read it only *looking for sermons* they will be tantalizingly elusive. You can no more command the Bible to yield sermons than you can command a cloud to drop rain or a rosebud to open its petals. If you always read the Bible for sermons somewhat in the way that a hunter stalks a deer, you will scarcely ever glimpse the fleet-footed prey, though the terrain abounds with them! You must be *its* prey! When you are not looking for sermons, but are reading the Bible for your own edification or relaxation, sermons will leap out from their hiding places and pounce upon you like glorious panthers which you simply cannot shake off. That is my own experience, and the experience of many others. Have you not had experience of it yourself? Just this morning my own daily reading has brought me to First Corinthians, and, altogether without consulting any commentary or even turning up the Greek, but simply in enjoying the American Standard Version and its marginal notes, I have been captivated by so many new sermon gleams (especially in the references to the Holy Spirit's ministry) that I could wish myself back in the settled pastorate again!

Night after night young D. L. Moody used to sit reading his Bible, scarcely knowing in those youthful days how to "study" it. Night after night, for hours, he would read it and eventually drop off to sleep still reading it. Think again what it did for *him!* I lay it down as a first proposition, that continuous Bible *reading* is one of the best aids to high-grade Bible preaching.

Studying the Bible

Especially in the case of Christian ministers, however, Bible reading must be accompanied by Bible *study*. To say so may sound trite enough, yet the unhappy fact is that most pastors nowadays find Bible study a problem, i.e., some *method* adjustable to the small amount of time which present-day pastoral absorptions (alas) leave for it. I can never be too grateful that in my late teens my sister gave me R. A. Torrey's little book *How to Study the Bible for Greatest Profit*. It is thoroughly Torrey-like, not a wasted word, right to the point, *multum in parvo*. It was that little book which set me off on my first Bible-study excursions. It taught me the best means of travel up and down the goodly land — with *Strong's Exhaustive Concordance* as my main baggage! Long before I knew a word of Greek or Hebrew, Torrey and Strong had shown me my way around and taught me how to dig for treasure. Later, that father in Bible erudition, Dr. A. T. Pierson, taught me how to use a telescope on mountain ranges, and a microscope on significant incidentals.

Brethren, there can be no rich pulpit ministry, no nutritious feeding of the flock, no consistently powerful preaching without regular Bible *study*. Would some of you, perchance, be willing to let R. A. Torrey start you off again? though of course you need no Torrey if you have devised workable procedures of your own. The crucial necessity is to get down to Bible study and keep at it. Your people must somehow be made to understand and respect the fact that you will allow nothing to rob you of that study. The supreme factor in the fellowship and witness of a local Christian church is *not* the visitation of the members, but the *pulpit*. Any degree of failure there, at the center, inevitably registers itself in spiritual deprivation right around the circumference. It needs to be shouted loudly again today until it echoes through our evangelical churches: The *pulpit* (i.e., the Book and its prophet) is the organic center of the local church! Going with that is the need for a new insistence that the minister shall really study the Book so as to be proficient in expounding its "breadths and lengths and depths and heights."

May I tear another leaf out of my own diary for you? During the Second World War, when most ministers in Britain had to do several other persons' work besides their own, too often Saturday evenings would find me (through no fault of my own) unprepared for the Sunday services. Yet it was during those days, so my people said, that I gave them my richest ministry. This was the reason: I had decided that although most reading must be cut out, my mornings should be inviolately fenced round for consecutive Bible study. I asked our members to leave me uninterrupted, as far as possible, until noon each day. As a result, when those Saturday evenings caught me without specific preparation for the Lord's day, my problem always melted away in gratifying solution as I let my mind wander back over the pathway of my Bible study during the mornings of the preceding week. I would find myself exclaiming, "Yes, that's the Word for tomorrow!" As I stood before the congregation, my messages maybe did not have the homiletical finesse or studied eloquence of which Scottish audiences are still commendably fond, but there was *teaching*, the product of keen study, and the solid comfort of the Word. Usually the subject matter had already so fascinated my own mind that I felt like a successful prospector who had made a big "find" and was now sharing it with his relatives! Among other things, this helped to keep the ministry *fresh* amid taxing days. I bear witness, from experience and observation, that for consistent freshness and strength in the pulpit nothing can take the place of pertinacious Bible *study*.

Furthermore, a wedlock of consecutive Bible *reading* with painstaking Bible *study* is an effective preservative against faulty exegesis. Some years ago, at a large convention "for the deepening of the spiritual life," I heard two addresses, both in the same meeting, which created a gloom the like of which I never saw elsewhere at a holiness convention. The first speaker's subject was *Hairbreadth Salvation,* based on 1 Peter 4:18, "If the righteous scarcely be saved, where shall the ungodly and the sinner appear?" The second preacher's theme was *Hell,* and his text was Luke 16: 23, "In hell he lift up his eyes, being in torments." I could not help musing what strange topics for a convention ostensibly bearing witness to "full salvation" and the "victorious life." Well, if the choice of topics was strange, the handling of them was more so. The first speaker urged that the words, "If the righteous scarcely be saved," meant that though our salvation had cost God the infinite price of Calvary, we Christian believers were saved only "by the skin of our teeth"; therefore none dare presume. The second speaker somehow managed by heteromorphous hermeneutics, to make "hell" a warning to us believers; and his description of its "torments" was no little harrowing. By the time those two energetic pummelers had finished there was glum bewilderment. What now about the life "more abundant" and the "assurance of salvation"? I never before saw the crowd break up in such silent depression. They might have been the heavy-hearted men of Israel after hearing Goliath shout across the valley, "Choose you a man, and let him fight me"!

Both those preachers had given us bungled exegesis — the kind from which a continual reading and planned study of the Bible saves us. Who are the "righteous" in 1 Peter 4:18? Both Petrine epistles make a threefold distinction: (1) the righteous, (2) the unrighteous, (3) the Christian believer. The Bible uniformly marks that same cleavage between the righteous and the unrighteous (the sincere godly versus the ungodly wicked) quite apart from Christian believers. For instance, when Psalm 1:6 says, "The Lord knoweth the way of the *righteous:* but the way of the ungodly shall perish," it is obviously *not* making a distinction between Christian believers and unbelievers, since it was written long before our Christian era. Simply and clearly the distinction is between upright, godly people of that Old Testament age and others who were *un*godly. Among the Jews to this day there are still the upright and godly (though blind to our Lord Jesus as their Messiah) and there are still the Jewish *un*godly. It is a distinction which we ourselves see every day around us among those who make no Christian profession. There are the upright and there are the evildoing. Is God going to deal indiscriminate punishment both to the upright and the evil? — both to the godly and the ungodly among those who have never been brought into union with our Lord Jesus? No, for in the words of Malachi 3:18, the Lord "discerns between the righteous and the wicked, between him that serveth God and him that serveth him not" (see also Acts 10:35; Rom. 2:6, 7).

That is the distinction which Peter has in mind when he says (writing to a Jewish clientele) in 1 Peter 4:18, "If the righteous scarcely be saved, where shall the ungodly and the sinner appear?" Even Lot is classed as "that righteous man" (2 Peter 2:8) because although he had compromised for selfish ends he abhorred the sensuality of Sodom. So, when Peter writes, "And if the righteous scarcely be saved" (i.e., from coming wrath) he is no more suggesting that the justified, Spirit-born Christian is saved "by the skin of his teeth" than that birds swim or fishes fly! We Christian believers have a perfect *imputed* righteousness in Christ. Both

PUBLIC WORSHIP: PREACH THE WORD! 245

Peter's epistles are about an *abounding* salvation (1 Peter 1:3) with a *"richly bestowed"* entrance (2 Peter 1:11) into the "everlasting kingdom" of our Lord!

As for the second speaker's cannonade on hell, he seemed oblivious that in the twenty-two occurrences of the word "hell" in our King James Version, eleven times the Greek is *Gehenna*, and ten times *Hades*.* In his text (Luke 16:23) "hell" is not the final doom *(Gehenna)* but the place of intermediate detention *(Hades)* between the death of the body and the final judgment of our race at the Great White Throne. No born-again Christian believer ever goes to *Hades* when the body is discarded (2 Cor. 5:8), nor will any of the Lord's saved ones ever go to *Gehenna*, the doom of the finally impenitent. "They shall *never perish*, neither shall any man pluck them out of my hand" (John 10:28).

Brethren, how important indeed it is, that we know the whole Bible familiarly by repeated rereadings and careful accompanying study! At the moment I emphasize *study*. Will it take you by surprise if I remind you that a minister's "study" is meant for *study?* That unexcelled word artist of the Congregational pulpit, J. H. Jowett, said, "When the study is a lounge, the pulpit is an impertinence." To that I would add, with cunning sympathy for my American brethren, when the study is replaced by an "office" the prophet easily slumps into being an administrator.

Preaching the Bible

That brings me to this matter of *preaching* the Bible, which is the gravity center of the Christian pastorate. Brethren, most of us who are in the ministry because of eager response to Christ and with a sense of "ordination by the pierced Hand," *love* to preach the written Word. To us the Bible is the most wonderful book in the world. We say of it, as David said of Goliath's sword, "There is none like it." And how often have we exclaimed with another of the godly ancients, "I rejoice at thy word as one that findeth great spoil"! For that very reason, though, if any of you should be like me, you will often need to guard against becoming so engrossed in the *subject* that you lose sight of the *object*. One of the precautions which has often saved me from preaching merely the interesting or informing at the expense of the vital has been

---

* In the English Revised Version and the American Standard Version, and some others, wherever the Greek word is *hades* it is so transliterated for us, which is much better.

to ask myself while shaping up a discourse, "What is my main *purpose* in this sermon? and what is my real *motive?*"

There is a clear-cut difference between the essay, the poem, the drama, and the *sermon*. The essay has to do distinctively with the intellect, the poem with the imagination, the drama with the emotions. But the sermon is the expounding of God's Word, which (whatever it may have to do with intellect, imagination, emotions) calls for an activity of the hearer's *will* and a conforming of the *life*. Apropos of that, the pulpit is not a desk for the delivering of lectures, nor a platform for the making of speeches, nor a stage for the exhibition of gifts. The pulpit is meant for the *sermon,* which, in the time-honored Christian sense, is a message from God, derived from His written Word, under His guidance, through meditation, prayer, study, and illumination by the Holy Spirit. It may be formulated into methodical structure, a cumulative argument, even an alliterative device; it may express itself through skillful explication, illustration, application (being all the more effective through able hermeneutics and homiletics!); it may flower into impressive eloquence and even employ legitimate rhetoric; but that which makes it truly a "sermon" is its being a *message from God,* all other features and qualities being only accessories to its persuasive transmission. Brother pastor, are all *your* pulpit deliverances truly "sermons," prophetic "burdens," God-given messages?

Only that kind of preaching is real *Bible* preaching — and what need there is today for a revival of it! How much there is of ministerial "scraping through" with mediocrity or inferiority due to prayerless hurry! What dearth of theological preaching! What risky escapades of clumsy exposition through lack of time for study! One can dolefully appreciate the remark of a thoughtful listener one Sunday morning after hearing a study-starved pastor's perilous handling of a fine point: "I greatly wondered whether he would manage to *save God!*" Expert exposition in public requires ample concentration in private. Big preaching comes only by big preparing. Great sermons are never by-products of bits and scraps. Powerful Bible ministry demands *time*. Hurry is the devil's cleverest assassin of good preaching!

Did I say good preaching? Yes; and why not? Oh, for a new generation of great preachers! Along with the spiritual profit of Scripture exposition, why should there not be the aesthetic pleasure of sermonic art? Think of the magnificent poetry, elegance, and rhetorical touches with which some of the Old Testament prophets present their messages! Why should not truth always be presented in her most becoming attire? I warmly recommend you younger men to study some of the bygone pulpit masters: Spurgeon for evangelical passion and textual skill clothed in flowing robes of purest Anglo-Saxon wording; W. L. Watkinson of Manchester for masterly homiletical patterns; Alexander MacLaren, maybe, for choice verbal exactitude; and certainly J. H. Jowett for educative word artistry. Yes, why not more Bible exposition in the form of *great preaching?*

A short time ago I preached one Sunday morning in a large New York church. My text was Hebrews 7:25, and the sermon was a straightforward gospel exposition. Yet after the service the pastor surprised me by saying, "We don't hear many sermons like that nowadays round here; such careful build-up and measured speech. This being 'on the air,' having the 'mike' always in front of you, and knowing you must finish to a split second gets you into the way of hurling out your thoughts at breakneck rate." I felt sorry for him: he was worried about it despite the contacts which his radio outreach gave him. Brethren, the microphone, in not a few places, is a gravestone marking the burial of good, old-fashioned preaching.

I am not overlooking the strategic values of radio ministry, but if I myself were back in the settled pastorate I would avoid having my Sunday services on radio, except in certain special circumstances. For one thing, being on the radio restricts one's subject matter, and one's way of handling it. You must not mention the Roman Catholics, the Jews, the Jehovah's Witnesses, the Christian Scientists. You must not attack the brewers, the tobacco industry, or other vested taboos. Even the prayers, since they are on radio, must not touch on certain concerns, even though every evangelical congregation should be crying mightily to heaven about them. On how many issues the pulpit has to remain dumb to the local membership when services are on radio! What shrinkage of Bible instruction this inflicts!

You may ardently counter what I am saying by reminding me of the effective evangelistic contacts which Sunday radio makes with people who do not come to church and of its comfort to shut-ins and others who are prevented from attending sanctuary worship. Yet all such grateful considerations do not alter the fact that what I complain of is true. Of course, I am referring only to broadcasting of *Sunday* services. Furthermore, there is a way by which churches *can* be on radio without affecting the pastor's ministry to his own flock. Those churches which regularly invade the air on Sunday mornings should allow their pastor ample time off to build up a repertoire of taped messages suitable in theme and length for Sunday broadcasting. Then, in each Sunday's service, when sermon time comes, the *taped* message could come into play for the radio hearers, with closing hymn and benediction, also taped, while in the sanctuary itself the pastor delivers the message he has prepared specially for his own people. Extra work? Yes, for a while; but it would unfetter the pastor's pulpit ministry to his own flock.

However, I have deviated a little. My mention of radio ministry slipped in only on account of its effect upon preaching. My plea is for a reemphasis on great Bible preaching, which leads me now to add that a true preaching of the Bible is a declaring not merely of its contents, but of its *truths*. Can I make myself clear enough on this point, I wonder? There is such a thing as preaching out of the Bible, on this or that incident, on this or that statement, without preaching its truths in the way which builds up our people in Bible *doctrine*. The sixty-six books of Holy Writ are not just a collection held together by printer's binding. There is an underlying cohesion which unifies them into *one book*, an organic unity of progressive divine revelation. Therefore its unfolding records and teachings develop and harmonize into consistent *doctrines*. In the main, it is those doctrines which we need to expound and apply.

Let me tell you a sadly singular thing about one of the most brilliant pulpiteers I ever knew — a Scot. He was academically distinguished, but supremely he was a preacher. He had the face, the domination, the voice, the versatility, indeed all the gifts of the born preacher. Talk about an eye for sermons! He could see them anywhere. He could take any text (sometimes he alighted on the quite unusual) and with one touch of "the homilist's silver hammer" (as Alexander Maclaren calls it) the text would break apart in some elegantly symmetrical pattern. A few selections from the pigeonholes of his spacious vocabulary and he would frame euphoniously worded divisions. He was a voracious reader in wide fields and had an industrious filing system from which he could generally draw superb illustrations for his products.

How often I envied him (in the right way, I hope!). He was always in demand for special occasions. Yet somehow he was a preacher without being a teacher. There was no doctrinal coordination binding all his perorations into one constructive whole. His people never grew in the great theology of the Bible. He maintained a fashionable crowd during all his years at a large church which I knew fairly well. His sermonic level was unintermittently superior. As with a string of expensive costume jewelry, each new sermon was a jewel with its own flash and sparkle. Yet here is the melancholy singularity: his people became tired of it. When he resigned there was much polite regret but little sense of deep bereavement. As one of them remarked, "His sermons were gems, but what we needed was *food*." Another reflected, "We have had sugary confectionery, but never the 'strong meat' of the Word." I know of no young people there who ever volunteered for overseas missionary work or even for the home ministry. Many new members were received, but I never heard of conversions.

Brethren, do you get what I mean? There is preaching which is not teaching. There is discourse which is not doctrine. One may be ably sermonic without being truly prophetic. Bible texts are not just texts, they are truths. Bible record is not just record, it is revelation. Bible contents are not just contents, they are communications. All the incidental parts of the Bible are contributories to great, developing, divine disclosures which all weave into one complete doctrinal whole. When Paul writes, "Christ died," he simply states a fact; but as soon as he adds "for our sins," he utters a stupendous *truth* arising from it. When John writes, "God is," he pens a fact, the foundation fact of the universe, but as soon as he makes it "God is *love*," he declares a sublime *truth*, the sublimest even about God. Brethren, it is the *truths* of the Word which we are to preach. Let us not absorb time preaching anything less. You younger men, habituate yourselves to expounding those *truths*. If you want a princely example which you may emulate, I recommend Spurgeon, in his many volumes of printed sermons. I do not forget John Wesley's printed sermons, or those of more recent men, each outstanding in his own way. But in popular textual exposition to the general public, Spurgeon is your man *par excellence*. Did you ever hear Hudson Pope's catchy little limerick on Spurgeon?

> There was an old Baptist named Spurgy,
> Who strongly disliked a liturgy;
>   But his sermons are fine,
>   And I use them as mine(!)
> As also do most of the clergy!

Brethren, I fervently wish it might be so with "most of the clergy," despite the sermon abduction involved! In my young days we used to sing, "Dare to be a Daniel," but my song to you younger preachers today is, "Strive to be a Spurgeon." Let our people have a new generation of preachers who excel in preaching the doctrinal *truths* of the Word.

Teaching the Bible

Have you never heard it said of a minister, "He's a preacher rather than a teacher"? or of another, "He's a teacher rather than a preacher"? There *is* a difference between preaching, in the more general sense, and teaching, in the more particular sense. That difference I willingly acknowledge here, and in fact call fresh attention to it; yet at the same time I do not think too keen a cleavage should be made between them. As I have often said, all preaching should be teaching, and all teaching should be preaching, by which I mean that all our *preaching* should impart biblical substance, while all our more specialized *teaching* of Bible areas or topics, by analysis, synthesis, etc., should be punctuated by admonition, challenge, encouragement, consolation, and other such practical urges with a view to edification.

Many preachers need to aim at being *teachers*. There is a thoroughgoing teaching of the Bible to which our Sunday services do not lend themselves. On Sundays the preacher has just enough time for a concentrated message, but not for any expansive Bible treatment. Yet our people need that latter kind of instruction. What are we to do? Most churches in America hold their midweek gathering on a Wednesday. It is usually called the midweek "Prayer Meeting," though I doubt whether in many places it really merits that name any longer. My own feeling is that it should either be given over entirely to *prayer* (for no church ever thrives spiritually for long without fervent fellowship in supplication and intercession), or else turned into a "Bible school" — with the prayer meeting on another night. If not, then keep the prayer meeting on the Wednesday and build up a "Bible school" on some other evening. Do I hear that present-day circumstances preclude most of the members from coming *two* nights each week? Then (if that is really so) the Wednesday night gathering should be for a full hour-and-a-half, with the first half devoted *wholly* to prayer, and the second (after a distinct break) to the "Bible school."

Make your Bible school well known. In Edinburgh, until the Second World War came and squandered us, hundreds came to our Thursday Bible school from all over the city, of whom many were not our own members, which fact I mention frankly to you, my evangelical brethren, as a reminder that there are probably many people in *your* area who are longing to know of some such "Bible school" where they can get scheduled, educative Bible teaching such as their own churches are not giving them. Flee any thought of "sheep stealing," and do not hesitate to share your green pastures with *any* of the Lord's hungry sheep! If their own churches are not feeding them, then there is no law in heaven or earth against your giving them the Word if they come to you.

But now, a comment or two about the *nature* of Bible teaching. It is strange, the misconceptions which float around. Let me whisper some words of advice suggested by a recent *faux pas* on the part of an eminent American preacher. Out of esteem I leave him anonymous, though to divulge his name would do him no harm now, as he has since passed to the everlasting fulfillments in the Beyond. He told me that he was determined to give his people exhaustive Bible *teaching* and that on Sunday mornings he was now taking them through the Epistle to the Romans. Seven Sunday mornings had now gone, and he was still in the first verse of chapter one! He was sure that his favored people were blessedly amazed at what "exhaustive" Bible teaching could bring to them out of one verse. Slyly I wondered whether he should have called it "exhaustive" or *exhausting* Bible study! I suspected he might be copying the Puritan Jewell on Job; but I held my peace. Soon afterward I was with one of his elders, who sighed, "Do you know, I've come round to thinking after all that the Church *will* go through the 'great tribulation.' *Our* church is in it already! For seven Sundays, now, our preacher has been in one verse. It's getting on our nerves. I never knew he could be so dry. Every Sunday morning it's just as though he tramps us weary miles only to find we're still where we started!" Now what a mistaken idea of popular Bible teaching that preacher had! What he was really doing was giving them a verbal *commentary,* a verse-by-verse annotation! and that is *not* pulpit Bible teaching. There certainly is a place for "word studies," and there are bookfuls of them; but neither are they what we mean by popular Bible teaching.

In the main, Bible *teaching,* as distinguished from the more usual form of "preaching," is the handling of larger *areas,* longer *series,* and wider *topics* in the Bible than are feasible in the normal sermonic cast of our Sunday ministry. It has values unsurpassed in developing strong churches, well-furnished believers, and godly character. Also, there is something mentally satisfying and permanently informing as well as spiritually enriching in having some book or area or subject of Scripture panoramically opened up so that all the parts are seen and interpreted in relation to the whole. (From a minister's viewpoint, of all exegesis mechanics this is the safest. Apart from it, etymology can easily beguile us into a "bypath meadow" of error).

There is *book* teaching. The epistle to the Hebrews and its arguments can remain more or less a "garden sealed" to many humbler members of our congregations until its major movements are vividly demonstrated:

1. *Jesus:*   The New and "Better" Deliverer (1 - 7)
2. *Calvary:* The New and "Better" Covenant (8 - 10:18)
3. *Faith:*   The New and "Better" Principle (10:19 - 13)

The book of Genesis may be read many a time without its central significance being seen until the four tremendous events in part one (1 - 11) and the four pivotal persons in part two (12 - 50) are seen in unified pattern exhibiting *the sovereignty of God* in physical creation and divine election. Ecclesiastes often remains puzzling until it is seen as a quest reviewed *in retrospect:*

1. The Quest by Personal Experiment   (1 - 2)
2. The Quest by General Observation   (3 - 5)
3. The Quest by Practical Morality   (6 - 8)
4. The Quest Reviewed and Concluded (9 - 12)

The book of Exodus leaps into new clearness of meaning as we see the exodus (1 - 18) displaying the divine *power;* and the law (19 - 24) expressing the divine *holiness;* and the tabernacle (25 - 40) revealing the divine *wisdom.*

Paul's Galatian polemic gains new force of argument and present-day relevance when its consecutive logic is shown cleaving its way through those three progressions:

1. The Authenticity of the Gospel (1 - 2)
   Genuine in its origin (1)
   Genuine in its nature (2)

2. The Superiority of the Gospel (3 - 4)
   In the new relation it effects (3)
   In the privileges it releases   (4)

3. The True Liberty of the Gospel
   Love-service ends law-bondage (5:1 - 15)
   The Spirit ends flesh-bondage (5:16 - 6:10)

Then there is *theme* teaching; a traveling link-by-link along various *chains* of truth extending through the Bible. What mounting interest people show, and what accumulating wealth of Scripture knowledge they acquire, as they are taken, week after week, through the successive teachings of the Bible on the *attributes of God,* or on the person and work of *the Holy Spirit,* or on the developing revelation of the *Lamb,* or on *godly separation* – these being but samples of the many!

And, of course, there is *synthetic* teaching: the collating and integrating of all the references to any one subject, so that from the many contributory parts there emerges one doctrinal whole. For sheer interest this kind of teaching is uneclipsed, and at the same time it promotes firm-grounded, well-balanced Christian convictions. What gripping, rewarding series can be pursued on such subjects as (already mentioned) the Bible doctrine of *life beyond the grave,* or (much needing restudy today) the *fatherhood of God,* or (another present-day challenge) Christian *sanctification,* or the New Testament doctrine of *the Church* – not to mention others!

There are teaching series on special subjects, such as the *tabernacle;* or (as uplifting as it is fascinating) Hebrew *poetry,* with its completive and contrastive, and constructive parallels; or again the Old Testament *theophanies,* culminating in the incarnation of our Lord; or Old Testament *typology;* or the presence and marvel of architectural *structure* in the Bible; or again our Lord's *parables;* or the instructive interrelation of the four Gospels.

There is also *biographical* teaching, such as a week-by-week pilgrimage with Abraham, or a reconsideration of that lovely scholar-saint, Samuel, or again character studies in David or the apostle Peter; or (closely allied to this kind of teaching) the missionary journeys of Paul.

But I must desist, for my only purpose here is to illustrate what we mean by Bible *teaching* as distinct from the usual Sunday kind of preaching. Of course, *some* of the subjects in the foregoing categories might be suitable for Sunday morning or evening series; but no Sunday series should be as long as those of a Bible school syllabus. Spurgeon would *never* commit himself to a Sunday series. Perhaps he was slightly wrong but largely wise, since each Sunday brought many tourists or other visitors to the tabernacle. A prolix Sunday-by-Sunday series is fatal. F. B. Meyer tells of an Anglican clergyman in a southern county of England who bravely but naïvely hit on a long Sunday morning series through the minor prophets. It was not long before his rustic congregation found the minor prophets a major problem. One morning the fond old cleric began: "This morning, brethren, we come to the prophet Amos. Ah, yes, the prophet Amos. Now what shall we do with Amos?" A farmer called out from near the door, "He can have my place, yer riv'rance; I'm going home"!

We should aim at wise variety; and in that setting a periodic Sunday series can be a powerful strategy. Sanctified common sense will guide any man as to what best fits local need and circumstance.

Here let me light a red lamp of caution. No matter whichever method of preaching or teaching appeals, beware of "running it to seed." Years ago a great pianist came to Manchester, England, for a week of Beethoven recitals. To me, Beethoven is practically *ne plus ultra* in the realm of music, yet by Thursday some of us would have given anything for the relieving contrast of a few riotous or melancholy flourishes from Chopin, or even a dash of Tchaikovsky!

Let me tell you about two great preachers, each in his own way a Beethoven of public Bible teaching. Each of them so labored one unvarying method that he eventually wore away his congregation, and each, in his mid-sixties, suffered a period of weary recoil from the pulpit. The first of them was the book-by-book preacher. On Sunday mornings he would be going through the Acts; on Sunday evenings, through Ezekiel; and in the midweek meeting, through First Corinthians. Year in, year out, he kept at it; and how well he could do it! Yet his people grew tired of always knowing just what to expect, just where he would resume, and where he would likely break off. They longed for a *sermon,* for the surprise of a fresh and complete discourse such as makes an audience feel, "This is a man of prayer to whom God has given a message specially for this present hour."

As for the other preacher, he was the *analytical* Bible exponent. Whether it was a book, a paragraph, a text, or a topic, it must be analytically vivisectioned, and the analyzed parts be given a scholarly-sounding description. It was masterly, ingenious, and occasionally a bit comical (since not everything is meant to be analyzed!). Eventually the everlasting clank of his analytical hammer became wearisome and echoed round emptying pews. Yet he was a pulpit paragon. The last time I heard him, years ago, was at the annual meeting of a large Methodist mission. Of the three outstanding speakers he was the ablest — and dullest. We each had a printed "Report" of the year's mission work. This he meticulously analyzed as though it were a passage of the New Testament! We could not actually see his chains, but he stood there the fettered slave of his own ironcast method.

Such pulpit genius in such needless shackles may well be heeded. Our Bible is a book of such varied content that it calls for a variety of method in the preaching and teaching of it. Surely, if we listen with our "ear to the Book" as the Indian scout used to listen with his ear to the ground, the Bible itself will suggest ever-fresh forms of communicating its endless treasures to our people. If there is one complaint which the Bible preacher and teacher need *never* incur, it is the complaint of sameness or dullness!

Brethren, if ever there was a time when men and nations needed to hear the Bible it is now. If ever there was an hour when you and I needed to preach the Bible, it is now. Let us read it again and again. Let us know it through and through. Let us learn it, live it, prize it, prove it, preach it, teach it, with prayerful zeal and perseverance. It is not merely I who say it to you, but the Holy Spirit through Paul: "Meditate upon these things; give thyself wholly to them; that thy profiting may appear to all. Take heed unto thyself, and unto the doctrine; continue in them: for in doing this thou shalt both save thyself, and them that hear thee" (1 Tim. 4:15, 16).